Ethics:
An Introduction to Theories and Problems

the text of this book is printed
on 100% recycled paper

ABOUT THE AUTHOR

William S. Sahakian did his graduate work at Harvard University and at Boston University, receiving his Ph.D. degree from the latter in 1951. He is Professor of Philosophy and Psychology and Chairman of the Department of Philosophy at Suffolk University. Among his published works are *Ideas of the Great Philosophers, Systems of Ethics and Value Theory, History of Philosophy, Realms of Philosophy, Psychology of Personality, History of Psychology, Psychopathology Today, Psychology of Learning,* and *Social Psychology: Experimentation, Theory, Research.* He has served as consultant to research organizations and educational publishers and has contributed to a number of scholarly journals. Dr. Sahakian has been a member of numerous academic associations, including the New York Academy of Science, the American Philosophical Association, the American Association for the Advancement of Science, the American Psychological Association, the American Ontoanalytic Association, the Association for Realistic Philosophy, the Massachusetts Psychological Association, and the American Association of University Professors.

COLLEGE OUTLINE SERIES

ETHICS:

An Introduction to Theories and Problems

WILLIAM S. SAHAKIAN
Professor of Philosophy
Suffolk University

BARNES & NOBLE BOOKS
A DIVISION OF HARPER & ROW, PUBLISHERS
New York, Evanston, San Francisco, London

To My Daughter
Paula Leslie Sahakian

whose delightful companionship has
always been a treasured joy

 For information address Harper & Row, Publishers, Inc., 10 East 53d Street, New York, N.Y. 10022. Published simultaneously in Canada by Fitzhenry & Whiteside Limited, Toronto.

First BARNES & NOBLE BOOKS edition published 1974.

LIBRARY OF CONGRESS CATALOG CARD NUMBER: 72–11244

STANDARD BOOK NUMBER: 06–460139–0

Preface

It has been many years since a publication on ethics from a systematic, historical, and problems approach has appeared. Most books in print today are content to deal with a few major ethical issues, or to offer sporadic treatment of great ethical systems (more from a sampling approach rather than assembling the major systems throughout the history of ethical theory). One of the purposes of this book is to fill that void.

Another objective of this work is to provide the reader with a systematic approach to the issues confronting the student in a course on ethics today, providing him with the fundamental ideas necessary for an adequate comprehension of the field, together with the requisite terminology.

The first chapter, an introductory one, is more than an overview furnishing the reader with a perspective of the field and its major issues; it explains a number of essential technical terms and will be useful either as a preview of succeeding topics or as a review of concepts already familiar to the student. However, the order of the chapters need not be followed strictly. The book is so organized that the reader is not dependent on antecedent chapters before being able to appreciate following ones. With the possible exception of the final chapter on metaethics, he may, if he prefers, move fully among the various chapters without being severely impeded.

Beacon Hill,
Boston, Massachusetts

WILLIAM S. SAHAKIAN

Contents

Ethics:
An Introduction to Theories and Problems

Violence annihilates itself
and leaves gentleness alone in the field.

Toynbee

I

What Is Ethics All About?

Philosophers conduct comprehensive investigations into the nature of reality. Their findings provide a systematic, rational view of the universe and constitute the subject matter of philosophy as a field of study. Its subdivisions and chief concerns are: *metaphysics* (the basic nature of reality); *logic* (processes and laws of thinking); *epistemology* (ways in which knowledge is acquired); *aesthetics* (the meaning and experience of beauty); and *ethics* (the formation of moral value judgments). Ethics is the branch of philosophy which explores and analyzes moral judgments, choices, and standards.

Moral Value Judgments. Philosophers disagree about the precise scope of ethics. They differ widely as to the meanings of common terms used in this discipline, such as 'good', 'right', and 'duty'. Some believe ethics should provide a set of principles to guide human behavior; others assert that ethics should analyze the statements men make when they express moral beliefs. Despite such differences among philosophers, the central motif of ethics is generally accepted to be the study of moral value judgments and the basis for those judgments.

The distinction between ethics and other systematic disciplines (as, for example, psychology, biology, and theology) should be noted. A. C. Ewing has pointed up this distinction in the following comment:

> If "good" were made the fundamental ethical term and defined simply as "what human beings desired" Ethics would become just a branch of psychology, since it is the latter science which studies events and dispositions in mental life such as are covered by the word desire. If it were definable as "what is in accord with the process of natural evolution," Ethics would be just a part of biology; if as "what is conducive to a stable society," part of sociology. . . . Others would start by defining good as "what God wills.". . . If it were, Ethics would be part of Theology.[1]

Obviously, man's moral value judgments and the basis for his choice of moral beliefs and standards require more comprehensive analysis

1. A. C. Ewing, *Ethics* (London: English Universities Press, 1953), pp. 11–12.

than is obtainable from the pertinent data of other disciplines. It is the function of ethics to provide that analysis.

A practical distinction may be drawn between science and philosophy. While he is acting in his professional capacity, the scientist does not find it necessary to pass value judgments on his work. He may even disclaim responsibility for the misuse of his findings and devices (as in the destruction wrought by war missiles and explosives to which he has contributed) and perhaps refuse to evaluate morally the applications made by governments or other employers. But philosophers do evaluate and pass moral judgments on the work of scientists and its applications, since philosophers make it their business to evaluate all aspects of human character, conduct, and experience. Nor is the scientist entirely absolved of moral responsibility. Possibly not as a scientist, but surely as a thinking person and in this sense a philosopher, he will make value judgments concerning his own work and its consequences. He cannot escape from his philosophy—his view of the universe and human relationships—and the inner conflicts which may ensue should he strive to ignore the end results of his activities.

Moral, Amoral (Nonmoral, Unmoral), and Immoral. The term *moral,* as used in philosophical literature, has two meanings. (1) It refers to the capacity of a human being to make value judgments, that is, judgments concerning what is right and good. In this first meaning, *moral* is the correlative of *amoral, nonmoral,* and *unmoral,* for the latter three terms denote persons unable to judge what is right and good. An insane person may be adjudged amoral, not to be held responsible for his acts. (The three terms are also used in reference to infrahuman animals lacking altogether the ability to discriminate morally or to execute moral decisions.) (2) The term *moral* may denote a person whose behavior is consistent with ethical standards. In this second meaning, *moral* is the antonym of *immoral;* the moral person does what is right and good, whereas the immoral person does what is wrong and evil.

The Right and the Good. Traditionally, philosophers defined ethics as the study of the right and the good. Until recent times this definition was satisfactory because it covered the two main approaches to the field of ethics. The vast majority of philosophers were concerned primarily either with the right act or with the supreme good (*summum bonum*) as the fundamental consideration. Philosophers choosing right action as the basic factor asserted that doing the right thing will necessarily produce what is good. On the other hand, those according primacy to the supreme good argued that once the *summum bonum* has been identified, right action is automatically recognized and performed, since right action is known to produce the greatest good. In other words, for the first group, the good is determined by right action, whereas, for the second group, right action is determined by what is good.

The traditional definition of ethics as the study of the right and the good fails to take into consideration a new approach contributed by philosophers, known as the *analytic,* or *linguistic,* school. They regard the main task of ethics to be the logical analysis of the terms and statements used in the expression of ethical theories and beliefs. These philosophers are exponents of views known as *metaethics* or *non-descriptivist* doctrines. Taking their views into account, we can revise the definition of ethics to read: Ethics is the study of the right and the good together with the logical analysis of ethical terms, theories, and beliefs.

Normative Ethics and Metaethics. Normative ethics sets forth moral norms as a guide for life. It investigates moral theories and attempts to establish moral principles on a rationally justifiable foundation. Some adherents of normative ethics believe that there are objective moral truths which reveal one's obligations and responsibilities, indicating what one "ought" to do or refrain from doing. Other philosophers believe, on the contrary, that an ethical principle or norm represents only what one desires or espouses as worth doing; thus, the ethical naturalist, Schlick, would say that "I ought to do something" means only "Someone wants me to do it," and the ethical subjectivist, Bertrand Russell, would say "ought" is the universalization of personal desires so that "Thou shalt not lie" means only that it is my desire that I and everyone else will not lie. But extreme adherents of metaethics oppose all normative views on the ground that normative ethics interferes with a person's freedom to make his own moral choices. They accuse normative philosophers of posing as seers endowed with special insight into moral truths and attempting to enjoin people regarding correct moral conduct.

Metaethical philosophers are interested primarily in the analysis of moral concepts or in the logical analysis of moral language. This interest is reflected by the titles of some of their well-known works, such as: *Reason in Ethics* by Toulmin, *The Language of Morals* by Hare, *Ethics and Language* by Stevenson, and three that include more than ethics, namely, *Philosophical Analysis* by Urmson; *Logic and Language,* edited by Flew; and *Language, Truth, and Logic* by Ayer.

These philosophers do not attempt to construct a systematic ethical theory for use in daily living; they endeavor to analyze moral concepts or the logic involved in moral concepts. This point of view is exemplified in Toulmin's book by the jacket copy, which informs us that the purpose of his work is to answer such questions as: "How can we decide which ethical arguments are to be accepted, and which denied? What kinds of reasons for moral decisions constitute *good* reasons? And anyway, how far—if at all—can we rely on the use of *reason* in coming to moral decisions?"[2] Similar copy in Nowell-Smith's *Ethics* (a significant contribution to the analytic movement in metaethics) states that the book does not address itself to such questions as: "What ought I to do?" "To what moral code ought I to adhere?" "Why should I adhere to any moral code at all?" Rather, the book purports "to make clear the complicated connections between such words as 'good', 'right', 'ought,' 'choose', 'duty', 'desire', and 'pleasure'. The author has applied to moral language some of the recent discoveries made in logic; but the concepts discussed are the traditional concepts of ethics."[3]

Some persons believe that progress in normative ethics is contingent upon metaethics, because normative ethics depends upon logical analysis of moral language for a coherent base on which to build. Actually, such analysis is not an entirely new approach in philosophy, for it dates at least as far back as Socrates, but throughout the history of philosophy it has been considered ancillary to the search for truth, beauty, and the good. Nevertheless, some adherents of metaethics assume that analysis of language is the prime and even sole task of philosophy. Focusing their attention on this approach, philosophers of the linguistic school refrain from offering moral judgments, though they are constantly investigating the meanings and functions of words and sentences expressing moral values. Thus, they discuss the same ideas as the traditional philosophers of the normative schools, such as the naturalists, hedonists, utilitarians, and intuitionists, but base their conclusions upon linguistic criteria.

Philosophers adhering to normative ethics do offer moral value judgments and are therefore interested primarily in questions such as: What is right? What is good? What is worthwhile in life? Is life worth living? What ought I to do? The point of view and concerns of these philosophers are reflected in the titles of some of their best-known works, as, for example, *Realms of Value* by Perry, *The Right and the Good* by Ross, *Moral Obligation* by Prichard, *Value and Obligation* by Sesonske, *Valuation* by Urban, *The Problem of Choice* by Roberts, and *Human Conduct* by Hospers.

Garner and Rosen have well stated the main difference between normative ethics and metaethics in the following succinct comment:

> A study of normative ethics, which begins with a consideration of such theories as hedonism and utilitarianism, inevitably leads to other problems and questions. It is possible to ask whether

2. Stephen Edelston Toulmin, *An Examination of the Place of Reason in Ethics* (Cambridge: Cambridge University Press, 1960).
3. P. H. Nowell-Smith, *Ethics* (Baltimore: Penguin, 1954), jacket.

> pleasure, for example, is good, and it is possible to argue that an action is wrong because it causes suffering—these are normative questions and arguments. But it is also possible to ask what 'good' or 'right' means, and this differs from asking what is good or bad, right or wrong, in that these are meta-ethical questions, questions *about* the normative judgments we are making.[4]

The term *metaethics* was coined by Ayer, who used it in 1949 in an article entitled "On the Analysis of Moral Judgements."[5] He meant it to convey the idea that all moral theories, as theories, including intuitionism, naturalism, emotivism, and the rest, are neutral in respect to actual conduct, for they neither seek to reform nor purport to be the "champion of virtue." He explained that an ethical theory "is not a set of suggestions as to what moral judgements they are to make," but rather "is an attempt to show what people are doing when they make moral judgements."[6] Some initiates in philosophy become disillusioned owing to this point of view when they study metaethics, since it lacks the moral guidance which they seek. Such objections do not arise in other areas of ethics or in the study of ethics as a "philosophy of life" in the German tradition, nor in the study of social ethics (ethics of a group, a society, or a nation), which has been the stepchild of ethics but is now rapidly maturing and commanding wide attention among philosophers. (The problems and issues discussed by social ethicists indicate the main subject matter of this field of study and are often alluded to in the title of such important books as *Moral Man and Immoral Society* by Reinhold Niebuhr, *The Open Society and Its Enemies* by Karl R. Popper, and *One Dimensional Man* by Herbert Marcuse.)

Definists, Noncognitivists, Cognitivists. According to definist philosophers, ethical terms represent properties of objects, and moral value judgments are therefore propositions or sentences that ascribe properties to the objects of moral concern. In succeeding chapters of this book which discuss the ideas of major philosophers, it will become clear that naturalists such as Ralph Barton Perry are definists, and that even intuitionists hold to a definist position (notwithstanding their belief that terms like 'ought' and 'good' are simple, unanalyzable, or indefinable), since those moral terms that are accepted by them as definable must be defined by nonethical ones. *Noncognitivists,* represented in this book by the metaethical philosophers Ayer and Stevenson, argue that moral judgments do not exist as realities or do not

4. Richard T. Garner and Bernard Rosen, *Moral Philosophy: A Systematic Introduction to Normative Ethics and Meta-Ethics* (New York: Macmillan, 1967), p. 213.

5. A. J. Ayer, "On the Analysis of Moral Judgements," *Horizon,* 20 (1949).

6. A. J. Ayer, *Philosophical Essays* (London: Macmillan, 1963), p. 246.

correspond to real things. The noncognitivists, who are sometimes regarded as a subgroup of the *nondescriptivists* (the two terms are used interchangeably by some philosophers), entirely reject definist theories and assert that so-called value judgments neither affirm nor deny moral properties to individuals or to their actions, that their logic is of a different order, conveying a different meaning. "Usually a distinction is made between those who hold that moral judgments are true or false, and those who deny it. The former are called *cognitivists;* the latter *noncognitivists*."[7] Ayer and Stevenson are among the most extreme exponents of the noncognitivist point of view, regarding moral judgments merely as ejaculations, evocations, or expressions of attitudes, whereas the philosophers of the Oxford language school (R. M. Hare, for example) take a more moderate position, viewing moral judgments as prescriptions, recommendations, and, possibly, evaluations. (See chap. 15 for an analysis of the noncognitivist theories.)

Ethics and Morals. The terms *ethics* and *morals* should not be used interchangeably. Perusal of American college bulletins describing the curricular offerings will reveal that the courses in this field of study are uniformly called ethics (or ethics in an extended title), not morals. *Ethics* is the term for the *study* of morals or moral issues; ethics consists of a theoretical or rational interpretation of moral phenomena. On the other hand, the term *morals* refers not to a study or discipline, but to the standards which individuals are enjoined to observe in their conduct. Whereas ethical activity would be "cerebral," suggested moral activity would pertain to individual or social reform.

There are two exceptions to the rule above. (1) The learned professions (medicine, law, theology) have formulated professional codes, either as formal declarations or as informal understandings. Thus, for a physician to transgress his established code makes him *unethical,* subject to disciplinary action because of his unethical practices. For a lay person to transgress his personal code of ethics, however, makes him immoral, not unethical. An unprincipled person is one who has no personal code of his own but exhibits behavior which transgresses the moral codes of others. (2) In Great Britain, courses in philosophy dealing mainly with ethical theory have carried the titles of "moral philosophy" or "moral science." *Moral* is coupled with *philosophy* or *science* to produce a new or synthetic term.

The terms *ethics* and *morals* derive from similar etymological sources, the former from the Greek (*ethikē*), signifying the science of character, the latter from the Latin (*mos,* plural *mores*), denoting customs or manners. Aristotle, who stated that ethics (*ethikē*) means the science of character,[8] added that "moral virtue comes about as a

7. Garner and Rosen, *Moral Philosophy,* p. 213.
8. Aristotle *Politics* 1261[a].

result of habit, whence also its name *ethikē* is one that is formed by a slight variation from the word *ethos* (habit)."[9]

Monistic, Dualistic, and Pluralistic Theories. In philosophy the terms *monism, dualism,* and *pluralism* refer respectively to: one, two, and many. Thus, the *metaphysical monist* believes that ultimate reality (the ontological makeup, or stuff of reality) is a single entity; an *epistemological dualist* believes that knowledge, or the process of knowing, involves two factors, namely, the knower and the object of his knowledge. Similarly, *ethical monism* is the view that the greatest good is a single entity such as pleasure, espoused by the hedonists, or God, as the Thomists held, or happiness (contemplation of good and beauty as a state of mind, *eudaimonia*) as Aristotle taught; *ethical dualism* is the view that there are two principal goods (or good co-existing with evil); and *ethical pluralism* is the view that many goods exist.

Hedonists have been historically the foremost exponents of ethical monism, particularly the quantitative hedonists, who maintain that the single entity *pleasure* is the sole good and that it varies only in quantity, since there are no qualitative distinctions. Ethical pluralists insist that there are other goods besides pleasure, such as knowledge, beauty, love, and friendship. Throughout the history of philosophy the attempt to determine whether ethical monism, dualism, or pluralism is true has created one of the major areas of deliberation. The relevant arguments and conclusions of leading philosophers will be discussed in succeeding chapters.

9. Aristotle *Nichomachean Ethics* 1103[a].

2

Cynicism and Stoicism: Freedom from Passion and Indifference to Pain

Secular ethics in the Western world originated with Socrates. Indeed, it is to Socrates that four ancient schools of ethical thought trace their origin: (1) the *Megarian* school, which under the leadership of Euclid (ca. 450–380 B.C.) synthesized the Eleatic concept of 'being' with the Socratic concept of the 'good', identifying them as one and the same; (2) the *Platonic* school; (3) *Cynicism;* and (4) the *Cyrenaic* school. Each school accepted the Socratic theory that man's most prized possession is knowledge and that knowledge of the highest good (*summum bonum*) should be his primary goal.

For these ancient schools the significant terms were *knowledge, virtue, happiness.* It is ironic that schools as divergent in their philosophical outlook as Cynicism and Cyrenaic hedonism should find their common roots in the same fundamental Socratic principle: *Knowledge is virtue, and virtue issues in happiness.* While both schools attached great importance to knowledge, whereas the latter emphasized its relationship to virtue, the former regarded it as a means for the pursuit of happiness. Socrates did not define good, and by leaving it an open issue, paved the way for discussion and interpretation, accordingly causing the Cynics and Cyrenaics to implement (or diverge from) his point of view in opposite directions.

Both schools were vitally interested in determining precisely what constitutes the true happiness of the "Wise Man" (a common expression of that time which could be understood as "philosopher"), but the Cynic sought for it in virtue, while the Cyrenaic found it in pleasures of the moment. The Cynics sought *apathē* (indifference to feeling), whereas the Cyrenaics pursued *pathē* (feeling). The two schools, however, were in agreement that the laws of the state were improper restrictions on the rights given to man by nature. The cosmopolitanism of the Cynics, which made them feel superior to and independent of any single state, and the selfish egoism of the Cyrenaics that forbade them to inconvenience themselves for the good of anyone else (including the state) caused both groups to be indifferent to patriotism and the obligations of citizenship.

SOCRATIC ETHICAL THEORY

Inasmuch as Socrates (469–399 B.C.) left no writings by his own hand, subsequent generations depended chiefly upon oral statements attributed to him by his most illustrious student, Plato, and upon the *Memorabilia of Socrates,* recorded by Xenophon. Unlike Plato and Aristotle, his intellectual beneficiaries, Socrates was not connected with a university, such as Plato's Academy or the Lyceum of Aristotle, but taught the public at large in the marketplace and without financial remuneration. When he was convicted by the state for allegedly corrupting Athenian youth and showing disrespect for deities of Athens, he accepted the death penalty and willingly drank the fatal hemlock.

Virtue Is Knowledge. For Socrates, virtue is knowledge (knowledge of the good); the two are equated. A person who *knows* what is right will by virtue of such knowledge *do* what is right; conversely, to do wrong stems from ignorance, evildoing being an involuntary act. While virtue and knowledge are identified as one, in a sense, actually virtue is the *result* of knowledge and dependent upon it. Genuine knowledge as Socrates understood it was *moral insight,* which he assessed as the best thing in the world. Virtue (*aretē*) is excellence, ability, or efficiently functioning at one's task. Since all knowledge is virtue, then it follows that knowledge is the most excellent of all possessions. Taylor observed that when Aristotle has occasion to refer to the ethics of Socrates, he ascribes three special tenets to him:

> (*a*) virtue, *moral* excellence, is identical with knowledge, and for that reason, *all* the commonly discriminated virtues are one thing; (*b*) vice, bad moral conduct, is therefore in all cases ignorance, intellectual error; (*c*) wrong-doing is therefore always involuntary, and there is really no such state of soul as that which Aristotle himself calls "moral weakness" (*acrasia*), "knowing the good and yet doing the evil."[1]

Knowledge not only results in right conduct, but knowledge per se *is* good conduct. "No man errs of his own free will" implies that while men seek what is good, moral disagreement among individuals results from the different degrees of knowledge that each possesses.

Inasmuch as virtue is knowledge, then it is teachable and can be conveyed to other persons merely through instruction; and since knowl-

1. A. E. Taylor, *Socrates: The Man and His Thought* (New York: Doubleday, 1954), p. 141.

edge is a single body of learning, the seemingly multiple virtues are ultimately not many, but one entity.

Know Thyself. The preceding discussion implies that the only person capable of performing moral behavior is one who has accurate knowledge of both himself and his relation to things in the world around him. ("The unexamined life is not worth living.")

"Know thyself," a Delphic oracle, is an important Socratic dictum.

> Socrates then said, "Tell me, Euthydemus, have you ever gone to Delphi?" "Yes, twice," replied he. "And did you observe what is written somewhere on the temple wall, KNOW THYSELF?" "I did." "And did you take no thought of that inscription, or did you attend to it, and try to examine yourself?". . . "I did not indeed try, for I thought that I knew that very well already. . . ." "But whether does he seem to you to know himself, who knows his own name merely, or he who, . . . having ascertained with regard to himself how he is adapted for the service of mankind, knows his own abilities? . . . For they who know themselves know what is suitable for them, and distinguish between what they can do and what they cannot; and, by doing what they know how to do, procure for themselves what they need, and are prosperous, and, by abstaining from what they do not know, live blamelessly, and avoid being unfortunate."[2]

Knowledge, virtue, which is defined as *moral insight,* is a necessary prerequisite to good action. Knowledge of self is of paramount importance, for it will benefit a person little to know facts about the universe which have a negligible or remote relation to the self, without first knowing himself. Righteousness is health, and unrighteousness is a diseased state of the soul. Self-improvement has primacy over scientific advancement. Success and happiness lie in self-knowledge, because, if a man could know precisely his nature, his motives (conscious and unconscious), his limitations, handicaps, talents, abilities, the purpose and goal of his life, then success would be assured by intelligent living in accord with such knowledge.

The Intellective Will. Underlying the theory that a man who knows what is good will necessarily pursue it is the Socratic premise that a person will never knowingly or purposely harm himself. For example, an individual will never permit a poisonous snake to bite him, because he is aware of the possible ill effects, and a person will never allow his mind to entertain delusions of persecution if he knows that it will lapse into paranoia. "They who do not know themselves, but are deceived in their own powers, are in similar case with regard to other men, and other human affairs, and neither understand what they

2. Xenophon *Memorabilia of Socrates,* bk. 4, chap. 2, secs. 24–26.

require, nor what they are doing, nor the characters of those with whom they connect themselves, but, being in error as to all these particulars they fail to obtain what is good, and fall into evil."[3] No one is voluntarily evil. "He who knows the beautiful and good will never choose anything else, he who is ignorant of them cannot do them, and even if he tries, will fail."[4]

The Utilitarian Element in the Socratic Ethic. There is some utilitarianism in the ethics of Socrates; he maintained not only that virtue is knowledge of the good but also that the good is useful, beneficial, helpful, and advantageous (i.e., appropriate to the person in question, to his end in view), and that its attainment results in happiness. Thus, the good must be good for something; it must possess utilitarian value. Socrates defined good as that which is capable of perfectly satisfying man's yearnings, capable of providing happiness.

Knowledge alone is sufficient to cause a person to do good and bring about its accompanying effect, happiness. Knowledge possesses the power necessary to control the will and direct it to choose the good, the beneficial, the useful, the profitable. *Will,* therefore, is subject to intellectual determination, to the power or force of knowledge, which motivates it.

Virtue. The virtues, as aspects of knowledge, are effective in producing good and happiness. Virtue is one entity; the various virtues are simply elements of the one virtue, *wisdom*. Self-control is, according to Socrates, one of the more important virtues, for by it one's life is carefully directed in that course of action that is most beneficial; self-control means moderation, the avoidance of extremes, or (as Socrates worded it) "nothing too much." Other virtues aid similarly, hence for this reason have the right to be considered virtues. Accordingly, virtue (that ability to act properly and intelligently which is based upon man's capacity to know what is truly good, useful, beneficial) is the goal upon which a person should set his sights.

Contrariwise, evil stems from error, ignorance, vanity, uselessness, disadvantageousness, harm, erroneous judgment. No one would do evil knowingly—"no one sins deliberately"—for it is tantamount to self-injury. Permanent misery lies in immorality, while lasting happiness is found in a life morally ordered. Philosophy was regarded by Socrates as a form of meditation in which a person reasons about the law of goodness, a law which holds valid for all persons alike.

Criticism of the Socratic Ethic. Although much evil is committed out of ignorance, such as the evil stemming from racial prejudice, it is another matter to contend that *all* evil is attributable to ignorance. The

3. Ibid., bk. 4, chap. 2, sec. 27.
4. Ibid., bk. 3, chap. 9, sec. 5.

criticism that men knowingly commit evil was familiar to Socrates, for in the *Protagoras* (352d–e) he acknowledged that most men did not agree with him. Moreover, in the *Hippolytus,* Phaedra asserted that men know what is right, yet do not do it, either through idleness or because they prefer pleasure to good. *Medea* pointed out that passions often cause us to commit evil despite our better judgment; and many people in our own time have had the experience of impulsively committing wrongs which they later regret. Aristotle objected that Socrates failed to recognize the role played by the will in human moral deficiencies.[5] For Aristotle, the irrational part of the soul exists and is responsible for bad choices.

Today, we are well aware of neurotic persons who find themselves often behaving contrary to their intelligence and understanding, even though they are willing to do what they know is the preferred behavior but are inhibited by their inability to cope with their emotions. Furthermore, persons ordinarily considered normal become victimized by their emotions, as, for example, when their sexual drives cause them to behave contrary to their wise judgment. Often people remain subject to irrational phobias despite their knowledge that they are groundless and their desire to dispel them.

Most persons have had the experience of eating foods that they knew were detrimental to health, but knowledge of the fact did not deter them; the same is true of many cigarette smokers and drug addicts. On innumerable occasions men who know the better course resort to the worse. Alcoholics drink themselves into unconsciousness despite their knowledge of the disastrous consequences.

To all these arguments Socrates could reply that the persons involved do not have sufficient knowledge about the workings of the emotions and the appetite and lack the information required for gaining mastery over oneself.

If Socrates is right in believing that we have only an intellective will, then what we call will is merely the understanding or an aspect of it, and the personality is devoid of genuine choice. Yet, experience in everyday living testifies that we make choices independently of our intellect. Often we make a decision on impulse, and only later use our intelligence to find the best way of executing it. Hence, in a sense the will directs the intellect.

The statement that "virtue is knowledge" is not fully satisfactory because, in order to develop a particular virtue by obtaining knowledge, one must first possess another virtue, namely, the ability to gain such knowledge (*aretē*) about the virtue. Socrates also failed to give us a specific goal in life. Guthrie comments, " 'Virtue is knowledge.' But what sort of knowledge? Actual, potential, universal, particular?

5. See Aristotle *Nicomachean Ethics,* bk. 7, chap. 2.

And is knowledge the whole of virtue, or an essential integrating element in it?"[6]

CYNICISM: THE GOOD (VIRTUE) AS SELF-CONTROL AND INDEPENDENCE

Among the lesser Socratics were Antisthenes, Diogenes, and Crates. Antisthenes of Athens (ca. 445–ca. 360 B.C.), an outstanding Cynic and devotee of Socrates, upheld the antithetical position to the hedonists, who emphasized pleasure and happiness in Socratic philosophy; the Cynics, on the other hand, chose virtue as the goal.

Antisthenes: The Pursuit of Virtue. Pleasure, in the estimation of Antisthenes, was an evil, and he declared, "Better madness than surrender to pleasure"; that is to say, he would rather be a victim of madness than of desire. According to him, the Wise Man pursued *wisdom* and *virtue;* furthermore, this pursuit involved two requisites, namely, resistance to personal superfluous appetite and emancipation from the prejudices and conventions of other men. While conventions (civil law and social morality) are repudiated as irrational prejudices, the laws of nature, those dictated by wisdom, are embraced and accepted as valid for all persons. Consequently, the Cynics advocated a return to nature and viewed the influence of civilization as pernicious. Their rejection of conventional morality, including patriotism, elevated them to a lofty role as citizens of the world, or *cosmopolites,* an appellation which they proudly accepted.

For Antisthenes, *virtue was the greatest good.* Cynics not merely viewed virtue as the highest good, but it was for them the only good, and the *conditio sine qua non* of happiness. Not only is virtue the indispensable condition of happiness, but it is sufficient for the satisfaction of any desire for happiness. Thus, virtue is the supreme and sole good. On the other hand, evil is to be shunned, and anything else that exists besides good and evil is of minor consequence and should simply elicit an attitude of indifference.

Negatively stated, the Cynic's goal is the repudiation of all avoidable desire. This goal is accomplished through virtue, inasmuch as virtue renders a man independent of the circumstances that wield his fortune. Hence, virtue is essentially freedom from want, need, desire, and passion. The basic task of human life is to reduce man's wants to the barest minimum and to make him indifferent to all other desires so that he will regard all unnecessary striving as evil.

The values of civilization were eschewed by the Cynics as superfluous; wealth, refinement, fame, honor, and the like were deemed as

6. W. K. C. Guthrie, *A History of Greek Philosophy* (Cambridge: Cambridge University Press, 1969), 3:459.

needless as sensual satisfaction. Even art, science, family, and nationality were matters of indifference.

Diogenes: Contempt for Common Goals. Cynics had assigned for themselves a dual vocation: practicing virtue and assisting the morally corrupt. They were relentless preachers of morality whose vehement denunciations of the follies of society reached the heights of invective as they displayed supercilious contempt for their fellow men. It was this contemptuous attitude that converted the essentially constructive term *cynicism* into an opprobrious one.

Influential among the Cynics was a disciple of Antisthenes, Diogenes of Sinope (ca. 400–ca. 325 B.C.), about whom numerous fascinating tales have been recorded. It is said that he used a tub to shelter himself from the weather, and with a lighted lantern went out at midday in search of an honest man. When he saw a peasant child drink water by cupping his hands, he rid himself of the only wooden bowl he possessed. When sold into slavery, he received an inquiry from his master concerning his trade, to which he responded that the only trade he knew was that of governing men, and consequently wished to be sold to a man who needed a master. His forte was the preaching of self-control, a doctrine to which he devoted his life. He accepted the appellation *kuon* (dog), from which the word *Cynic* probably derives, although it could have been a pun, a play on the word *Cynosargus,* the seat of the school (or gymnasium) in which the Cynics taught.

Crates: The Happiness of Poverty. Crates of Thebes, a student of Diogenes, abandoned a life of wealth and fortune for the poverty afforded by the life of a Cynic. His kindly attitude won him popularity and acceptance, and unlike the sarcasm of Diogenes, his humor did not have a bite to it. He taught that life's ideal is the happiness attainable through poverty.

STOICISM: A PHILOSOPHY OF INDIFFERENCE AND TRANQUILLITY

Zeno of Citium (335–263 B.C.), in Cyprus, was the recognized founder of Stoicism in 308 B.C., a philosophy named after the painted porch (*stoa poikile*) which was found on the north side of the marketplace in Athens, the gathering area of philosophers interested in disseminating their doctrines. Other than initiating Stoical thought, he designated life's ultimate goal as wisdom, and endorsed the permissibility of suicide.

Other illustrious Stoics were Cleanthes of Assos (331–232 B.C.), Zeno's most outstanding student and successor, and Chrysippus of Soli or Tarsus (ca. 280–ca. 207 B.C.) in Cilicia, successor of Cleanthes and regarded as a second founder of the school. Other major Stoics were

Seneca (A.D. ca. 4–65), Epictetus of Hieropolis (A.D. ca. 55–ca. 135), and Marcus Aurelius (A.D. 121–180).

Ethics of Zeno and Early Stoics. The philosophy of Zeno advocated the goal of freedom from passion, complete indifference to joy and grief. For the Stoic, virtue consisted of "living harmoniously with nature." Zeno was the first to proclaim that life's chief good is living according to nature, i.e., according to one's own nature, and shunning that which is forbidden by the "common law of man." Common law he identified with right reason and God (Zeus), who regulates and directs all things.

VIRTUE, GOOD, AND REASON. Such also is virtue and the happiness of man. One must flow with the current of life and be in harmony with the will of the universe, that is, with its governor and director. In his *Hymn to Zeus,* Cleanthes wrote:

> *God's universal law, which those revere,*
> *By reason guided, happiness who win.*[7]

In other words, the prime good is acting in accord with sound reason, which impels one to choose goals that comport with nature. Generally speaking, virtue is perfection. From this point of view, good is "advantage," and, particularly, it is usefulness.

> They define the good in a peculiar manner, as being what is perfect according to the nature of a rational being as rational being. And, secondly, they say that it is conformity to virtue, so that all actions which partake of virtue, and all good men, are themselves in some sense the good. And in the third place, they speak of its accessories, joy, and mirth, and things of that kind.[8]

Similarly, vices—namely, folly, cowardice, injustice, and the like—have their accessories, such as despondency and melancholy.

INTERNAL AND EXTERNAL GOODS. Some goods are within us, others external; internal goods are the virtues, while external goods are typified by friendship. A perfect good is one that is perfectly harmonious. The four perfect goods are justice, courage, temperance, and knowledge. Since the goods are virtues, all are equal. Every good possesses beneficial qualities, never injurious ones. Inasmuch as health and wealth are not of themselves beneficial or injurious, they cannot be regarded as goods; pleasure, too, is not a good, the reason being that there are disgraceful pleasures. "To benefit a person is to move or keep him according to virtue, but to injure is to move him or to keep him according to vice."[9]

7. Cleanthes *Hymn to Zeus,* in *Essential Works of Stoicism,* ed. Moses Hadas (New York: Bantam, 1961), p. 51.
8. Diogenes Laertius *Life of Zeno,* in *Essential Works of Stoicism,* p. 27.
9. Ibid., p. 30.

DUTY. Duty, defined as that which "reason elects to do," includes the obligation to one's parents, brothers, and country, and to bring pleasure to one's friends, but does not mean approval of everything done from impulse or inclination.

Epictetus: Stoical Indifference to Pain. Stoicism, essentially a practical philosophy, drew its concept of the Wise Man from the lives and personalities of Socrates and Antisthenes, who were regarded as outstanding Cynics (in the finest sense of that word). The ideal of Stoicism is absolute mental freedom from the vicissitudes of life. Inner peace of soul is maintained despite external tempestuous changes transpiring in the outer world.

Initially, independence was thought of as emancipation from passions, an apathetic state capable of removing a person from four basic evils or unnatural forms of emotional stimulation: (1) pleasure, (2) sorrow, (3) desire, and (4) fear. These four, regarded as diseases, must be expunged from the personality in order for the 'Man of Wisdom' to maintain true health. "The only real thing is to study how to rid life of lamentation, and complaint."[10]

VIRTUE AS THE HIGHEST GOOD. The *summum bonum,* man's principal goal in life, is *virtue,* because virtue alone is sufficient for happiness. Virtue is understood to be a life in full accord with the laws of nature, and to the Stoic meant a human will attuned with that of the divine will. The only good is virtue, and the sole evil, vice; all else lies in an intermediate position between these two. Some of the intermediates are acceptable, while others are objectionable, the remainder being inconsequential or a matter of indifference.

A rationally well-ordered soul, which achieves coherent integration of the cardinal virtues within the personality, makes an individual truly virtuous. The virtues consist of practical wisdom (meditation), courage, discretion (self-control), and justice. Cleanthes, however, replaced meditation with endurance. The Wise Man, possessing virtue, performs right action prompted by a virtuous disposition characteristic of his nature.

THE INVINCIBLE WILL. The virtuous sage is an emancipated individual, free from emotional entanglement, yet not without feeling. As such he is master over his own life because it is under the control of his will. "Only consider at what price you sell your own free will, O man!"[11] One must never surrender his will or permit anyone to break his spirit—his will.

Peace of mind is not contingent upon external circumstances but upon the inner spirit, an unconquerable will. "But the tyrant will chain—what? A leg. He will take away—what? A head. What is there,

10. Epictetus *Discourses,* bk. 1, chap. 4.
11. Ibid., chap. 2.

then, that he can neither chain nor take away? The free will. . . . Who, then, is unconquerable? He whom the inevitable cannot overcome."[12] No one is imprisoned who elects to be there, no one lonely except he who resists it. One may be master over your "carcass," but never over you unless you allow him to break your will. "Thus Demetrius said to Nero: 'You sentence me to death; and Nature you.' "[13] When Socrates' accusers attempted to break his will and make his spirit yield, his reply to his enemies was: "Anytus and Meletus have power to put me to death, but hurt me they cannot."[14] By not allowing his will to be broken, Socrates gave his enemies no satisfaction. If you rely on things beyond the control of your will, then you will court disaster.

RESIGNATION, ACCEPTANCE, AND CONTENTMENT. Epictetus taught that the Wise Man should be resigned to that which cannot be changed, for life's goal is tranquillity or eternal calm of the spirit within. Much depends upon one's philosophical attitude. "In life too, this is the chief business, to consider and discriminate things, and say, 'Externals are not in my power; choice is. Where shall I seek good and evil? Within; in what is my own.' "[15]

One must take death in his stride "as one who knows that what is born must likewise die. For I am not eternity, but a man—a part of the whole, as an hour is of the day. I must come like an hour, and like an hour must pass away."[16] In the face of catastrophe, one must not murmur but utilize God's gifts, such as fortitude, patience, and magnanimity.

Epictetus even provided a prescription for dealing with and attenuating one's emotionally disturbed state:

> If you would not be of an angry temper, then, do not feed the habit. Give it nothing to help its increase. Be quiet at first and reckon the days in which you have not been angry. I used to be angry every day; now every other day; then every third and fourth day. . . . For habit is first weakened and then entirely destroyed.[17]

Another comment deals with sexual impulses:

> To-day, when I saw a handsome person, I did not say to myself, Oh, that I could possess her! and how happy is her husband, . . . nor did I go on to fancy her in my arms. On this I stroke my head and say, Well done, Epictetus.[18]

12. Ibid., chap. 18.
13. Ibid., chap. 25.
14. Ibid., chap. 29; also, Plato *Apology* 30c.
15. Epictetus *Discourses,* bk. 2, chap. 5.
16. Ibid.
17. Ibid., chap. 18.
18. Ibid.

Epictetus advised men to choose the best life, for habit will make it pleasant.

LIVING IN ACCORDANCE WITH VIRTUE. A life comporting with nature conforms to reason, for virtue means obedience to reason (insight), to the laws of nature. "To a reasonable creature, that alone is unsupportable which is unreasonable."[19] The irrational life, emotionally disorganized, with the soul in a diseased state, is evil. Mastery of life is identified with mastery of one's passions. Only virtue, the subordination of passions to reason, can give man genuine happiness. The fool, whose soul is in a diseased state, lacking emotional control, is evil. His spirit lacks integration, and his life is discordant with nature.

THE STOICS' PHILOSOPHY OF LIFE. Epictetus viewed philosophy as rigorous training in virtue, the removal of moral defects. His ethical philosophy was based on theism, on faith in God's providential care and concern for man, in the affinity of the human mind with the divine, in the rationality of nature. He repudiated the belief in irrational evil, the theory that evil exists which serves no good purpose whatever; all evil is instrumental, subserving some good end or purpose. An evil such as a toothache he would probably explain as an instrumental good because it summons one to attend his aching tooth before irremediable damage occurs.

The Stoic faces and accepts the vicissitudes of life as spiritual tasks or exercises ordained by God. His security grounded in self-respect, he harbors no anger, wrath, envy, pity, nor is he desirous of a fine reputation, a beautiful woman, or sumptuous foods; rather he enjoys a "free open-air spirit." As God's ambassador to the world at large, he exemplifies and teaches how one should live. Surrendering his life to God, he is prepared to accept whatever fate is in store, including death, and this without flinching. He meets all challenges and situations with a cynical or stoical stance, with full acceptance of his mortal nature—a body subject to destruction. " 'When did I ever tell you that I was immortal? You will do your part, and I mine; it is yours to kill, and mine to die without quailing; yours to banish, mine to depart untroubled.' "[20]

Shunning sexual cravings as undesirable, the Stoic prefers abstinence, for sex and women are enslaving. One is a "poor wretch to be a slave to a paltry girl."[21] Again he wrote, "A worthless girl has made a slave of me, Whom never foe subdued."[22] Often women are too much for men to cope with, and punishing results ensue. Spiritual tranquillity is correlated with sexual continence and to the degree that one is liberated from sexual obsession.

19. Ibid., chap. 2.
20. Ibid.
21. Ibid., bk. 4, chap. 1.
22. Ibid.

According to Epictetus, moral principles are innate in man; the only powers which man possesses are his will and the use of rational ideas. He regarded the *summum bonum* as virtue, defining it as living according to nature, and designated *endurance* as the supreme virtue. We must "make the best of what is in our power, and take the rest as it occurs."[23]

Men should be self-sufficient, said Epictetus, depending only on their own reason for guidance, and should meet with equanimity the consequences of their decisions, including the suffering they may experience; they are powerless to alter the course of undesired events and should therefore assume an attitude of indifference toward them. This state of mind can be achieved by the will, which, if properly disciplined through self-control, is both autonomous (independent of externals) and unconquerable (inviolable). The goal of life is eternal calm, tranquillity, contentment, freedom from perturbation; it is the function of logic or science to facilitate this end. "What, then, is the punishment of those who do not so accept them? . . . Shall we throw him into prison? What prison? Where he already is; for he is in a situation against his will, and wherever any one is against his will, that is to him a prison,—just as Socrates was not truly in prison, for he was willingly there."[24]

Epictetus advocated *stoical pessimism*, an attitude or doctrine of last resort which permitted suicide should life reach the point of unendurability. At least a person never need be concerned about how severe, unfortunate, or intolerable his future existence may be, since nature has provided an escape—death's perennial open door. Since the worst that life affords is death, one need not be overly concerned.

Inasmuch as they are beyond man's power to control, Epictetus urged the necessity of keeping the mind independent of all external or material goods. Accordingly, it is necessary to forgo objects of desire, even annihilating desire by the acceptance of one's lot in life.

> Why are we thus enraged? Because we make idols of those things which such people take from us. Make not an idol of your clothes, and you will not be enraged with the thief. Make not an idol of a woman's beauty, and you will not be enraged with an adulterer. Know, that thief and adulterer cannot reach the things that are properly your own; but those only which belong to others, and are not within your power. If you can give up these things, and look upon them as not essential, with whom will you any longer be enraged?[25]

23. Ibid., bk. 1, chap. 1.
24. Ibid., chap. 12.
25. Ibid., chap. 18.

True or valid goods are those of the soul, those that are found within oneself. A person need not fear externals, including death; rather, he should fear God or the divine which dwells within himself.

Marcus Aurelius: Summary View of Stoicism. All the great Stoics believed in obedience to nature—to inner nature, or reason, and to outer nature, or natural law. Marcus Aurelius, the last great Stoic, reiterated that man must live in accordance with reason, for his soul is identical with it.

A harmonious life is one that is in tune with nature. Emotional upheaval and depression stem from the element of surprise, and their attendant distress or one's lack of adjustment to them is due to inadequate foresight. Emotions, the cause of misery, erode as understanding increases. Attitude, too, is important: "Take away your opinion, and then there is taken away the complaint, 'I have been harmed.' Take away the complaint, 'I have been harmed,' and the harm is taken away."[26]

To understand is to forgive those who offend. In passion-free wisdom, one lives above his circumstances of pain and misery. Worry is dispelled by gaining a larger perspective of things.

> Do not disturb yourself by thinking of the whole of life. Let not your thoughts at once embrace all the various troubles which you may expect to befall you: but on every occasion ask yourself, What is there in this which is intolerable and past bearing? for you will be ashamed to confess. In the next place remember that neither the future nor the past pains you, but only the present. But this is reduced to very little.[27]
>
> Let not future things disturb you, for you will come to them, if it shall be necessary, having with you the same reason which now you use for present things.[28]

Compare the above admonition with the admonition of Jesus: Take no thought for tomorrow, for the present day's evils are sufficient with which to contend; one is advised to live one day at a time. For Marcus Aurelius, anxiety is due to ignorance and partial knowledge, but for Jesus it is a sign of lack of faith in the providential care of God.

According to Marcus Aurelius, the natural is necessary, the necessary is reasonable, and the reasonable is good.

Evaluation of Stoicism. Stoicism is one of the most commanding, appealing, and lasting philosophies in human intellectual and moral history. For two centuries it posed as a worthy and potent rival to Christianity. During that time and ever since, some of its doctrines have been assimilated into Christian theology as well as the thought

26. Marcus Aurelius Antoninus *Meditations* 4.7.
27. Ibid., 8.6.
28. Ibid., 7.8.

of Christian and secular philosophers, including Kant, Spinoza, and a host of others.

What a commendatory achievement it would be for one to be able to contain his emotions so that they respond to the dictates of his intellect! To be in harmonious tune with nature is a state devoutly to be coveted; but alas, Stoicism, like all philosophies constructed by the mind of man, has its deficiencies.

Everyone knows that emotions can make man miserable, but eliminating them in toto would not bring happiness, nor would it be possible or psychotherapeutically desirable to do so. How opaque, dull, and neutral life would be without feelings and emotions, which add richness and color to human experience! Imagine how unfortunate a person would be who could not react with feeling to stirring masterpieces of literature or to the artistic creations of the world's foremost artists and sculptors or to the sweet sounds of great music. Only a spiritually crippled person, virtually blind in the sphere of values, could be totally emotionless in the presence of aesthetic, moral, religious, and philosophical truths. Without feeling, man would have no interest whatever, either in his career, science, individual and social affairs, or indeed in life itself.

Curiously enough, a lack of interest or a boredom regarding life became a critical problem for some of the Stoics, owing to the Stoic tenet of *taedium vitae* or the belief that suicide was indicated and permitted when one became weary of his existence. Several Stoics availed themselves of this vehicle out of life, for figures no less than Zeno, Cleanthes, and Seneca in cold and dispassionate deliberation exited this life in the spirit of Epictetus' and Marcus Aurelius' tutelage. "Suppose someone made the room smoke. If the smoke is moderate I will stay: if excessive, I go out: for one must remember and hold fast to this, that the door is open,"[29] advised Epictetus, intimating suicide. Marcus Aurelius reiterated: "It is in thy power to live here. But if men do not permit thee, then get away out of life, yet so as if thou were suffering no harm. The house is smoky, and I quit it."[30]

Such instruction and behavior seem contradictory and inconsistent with Stoical thought, especially when we recall that Epictetus, a slave and a cripple, dispassionately warned his cruel master that if he continued to twist his leg (which was being done out of a perverted or sadistic sense of humor), it would break. Another Stoic, Posidonius, confronted his intense pain when it interrupted his discourse on good by addressing the pain with the words that he would never admit it to be an evil, despite its attacks.

Nevertheless, very few of us, if any, would regard the pain of a

29. Epictetus *Discourses,* bk. 1, chap. 25.
30. Marcus Aurelius Antoninus *Meditations* 5.29.

broken leg as unreal. The Stoics taught that evil consists of ignorance and lack of understanding. But if evil is lack of understanding, how can one be sure that goodness is not the same also? Since the Stoics offer no proof of their assertion, it is based on an *argumentum ad ignorantium* fallacy, that is, the error of pleading for an argument from ignorance instead of advancing facts in support of one's contention. Understanding does not always solve problems or avert evil. A psychiatrist may understand and readily explain why a homicidal maniac committed a murder, but, although we should feel sorry for both the madman and his victim, the tragedy could not be thus eradicated. Perhaps the most that can be acceded to the Stoic is that understanding the roots of evil may sometimes diminish its consequences. Man is indeed fortunate that understanding the role of goodness and beauty in life does not detract from but rather enhances them; it is his good fortune also that life commands interest, for it is only in transient moments as in some cases of mental illness that *joie de vivre* is lost.[31]

Some of the goals of the Stoics are so extremely "idealistic" that they exceed the ability of man to achieve; as such, they could engender disappointment to the point of despair. The psychiatrist Alfred Adler contended that neurosis can occur when one sets his goals far beyond his abilities to achieve. Apparently the only way to make Stoicism workable would be to moderate its goals, bringing them within the reach of a person's capabilities. In fact, attainment of the Stoic ideal of complete indifference to one's circumstances would indicate a state of psychosis, for only schizophrenics exhibit such extreme indifference to their environment.

31. Acknowledgment is made to Brand Blanshard, *Reason and Goodness* (New York: Macmillan Co., 1961), chap. 2, for generating some of the ideas expressed above.

3

Hedonism: The Pursuit of Pleasure

The term *hedonism,* derived from the Greek *hēdonē,* signifying pleasure, has acquired two meanings in the history of philosophy, one pertaining to the psychology of personality, the other to normative ethics. It is in the second sense that the term has relevance in this and succeeding chapters. When used in reference to moral values, it is termed *ethical hedonism,* and is defined as the view that pleasure, and only pleasure, is intrinsically good, and that pain is evil.

In ancient Greece the leading exponents of hedonism were Aristippus and Epicurus. In modern times the most prominent hedonists have been the famous British philosophers Jeremy Bentham and John Stuart Mill, known as hedonist utilitarians.

CYRENAIC HEDONISM: THE PURSUIT OF MOMENTARY PLEASURES

In the last half of the fourth and the early quarter of the third centuries B.C., a new school of ethical philosophy known as the Cyrenaics, or *Cyrenaic hedonism,* made its appearance in Cyrene, chiefly through the efforts of Aristippus of Cyrene, a friend and admirer of Socrates. His grandson (also called Aristippus) formulated his grandfather's ethical position toward the end of the fourth century B.C.; important modifications in hedonist doctrine were introduced by some of his followers, including Theodorus, Hegesias, and Anniceris.

Hedonism began with Aristippus' declaration that pleasure is the only good, but he referred mainly to momentary pleasures, and eventually all of his tenets were repudiated by his followers. The latter moved Cyrenaic philosophy in the direction of pessimism, and their contributions, especially those of Anniceris, introduced considerable refinement and sophistication into hedonist doctrines.

Aristippus: The Immediate Gratification of Pleasure. Aristippus of Cyrene (ca. 435–ca. 356 B.C.), founder of what became known as the Cyrenaic form of hedonism, came under the influence of Socratic teaching, but, unlike the Stoics and Cynics, emphasized the element of *happiness* which accrues to the virtuous man. Aristippus defined virtue as the capacity for enjoyment, and enjoyment was to him a state of happiness resulting from a satisfied will with its attendant pleasures fulfilled. Pleasure becomes the sole good and *summum bonum* (the highest good). Pleasure is of one kind only, and differs merely in intensity, degree, and purity, the finer pleasures being those unadulterated with pain. A sensation of gentle motion (rather than emotion), is his definition of pleasure; it is that feeling of pleasant satisfaction which ensues with the gratification and abatement of appetite. Pain he regarded as violent emotion, disturbing to the personality, while rest is a mental state of indifference. Aristippus was persuaded that all things work toward a good end or purpose.

Cyrenaics stressed sensual or physical enjoyment of the immediate present, since only the present is in a person's power; the future is beyond one's control. Yet, the indiscriminate gratification of pleasures must be eschewed. The Wise Man (philosopher) knows how to enjoy the present wisely; he masters his pleasures, that is, he enjoys them without becoming their slave. "I possess, but am not possessed." The ideal, then, is the control of pleasure in the midst of enjoyment with appetite pleasingly fulfilled, yet rightly, wisely, and with a measure of self-control. Wisdom, an instrumental value, is not an intrinsic good, an end in itself. While Cynic discretion shunned pleasure as an unintelligent course of action, Cyrenaic hedonism sought to exercise command over pleasure. The statement, "My machine is so happily compounded that I am sufficiently sensitive to things to enjoy them, but not to suffer from them," is attributed to Aristippus.

Theodorus: Egoistic Hedonism. Theodorus, "the atheist," repudiated all altruistic propensity and all institutions, both political and religious, and pursued a course of complete devotion to sensual enjoyment. Cyrenaic philosophy in practice degenerated into *egoistic hedonism,* in which each person is interested solely in his own private pleasures, oblivious to social responsibilities, friendship, and the welfare of others. Laws and moral codes were looked down upon as mere conventions of society and were tolerated only if unavoidable. The enjoyable fruits of civilization were accepted, but repayment by way of social and political duties was left to others, as were sacrifice, patriotic gestures, and other altruistic behavior. Egoistic hedonists regarded sadness as the great evil, a happy disposition as the *summum bonum.*

Hegesias: Hedonistic Pessimism. With Hegesias, Cyrenaic hedonism further deteriorated into *hedonistic pessimism,* the position that the hedonistic goal is impossible to fulfill, since the majority of people fail to realize a life of pleasure. Without pleasure, life becomes worthless and should be discarded as a valueless endeavor. The greatest achievement possible is escape from pain. Wealth and affluence do not render us immune to pain; death is to be embraced as the only certain path to the state of painlessness. The blessed man is the one who escapes discomfort and attains painlessness, namely, a dead man. Pleasure and pain are contingent upon one's attitude, and the Wise Man is indifferent to life itself, as well as to external conditions. How ironic that hedonism should thus finally revert to the goal of its opposite philosophy, accepting indifference as the supreme good, similar to that independence of externals advocated by the Cynics.

Hedonistic pessimism is a self-defeating philosophy which destroys itself. Hegesias, called "the counsellor of death," has been charged with responsibility for numerous suicides inspired by his teachings. Cyrenaic hedonism gradually dissipated, merging into the ordinary philosophical outlook of the time.

EPICUREANISM: THE GOOD LIFE AS INTELLECTUAL PLEASURE AND CONTENTMENT

In response to a refinement of hedonism, Epicureanism arose and flourished with its emphasis on the superiority of mental pleasures over the sensual or material. Expression was given to the pleasures of a cultured and noble individual, mental joys over which one can exercise some control. Epicurean ideals included pleasures ensuing from friendship, contentment, peace, morality, and aesthetic pursuits. The school flourished from the fourth to the first centuries B.C.

Epicurus of Athens. The school of *Epicurean hedonism* was founded in 306 B.C. in the Garden in Athens by its esteemed head, Epicurus (341–270), who remained there in that capacity until his death. Although he considered pleasure to be the supreme goal of life, his own life was marked by simplicity, for he believed that happiness was possible on a plain diet of bread and water and the minimal satisfaction of other bodily needs.

RELATION OF EPICUREANISM TO CYRENAICISM. As Stoicism was the offshoot of Cynicism, so was Epicureanism the outgrowth of Cyrenaic hedonism. Epicureanism introduced a refinement upon Aristippan hedonism by adding mental or spiritual pleasures to physical satisfactions. Whereas Aristippus emphasized momentary pleasure, Epicurus preferred the ideal of permanent pleasure, coupling repose with pleasure so that one would be free from pain while enjoying both physical health and mental tranquillity.

THE ABSENCE OF PAIN. If a person succeeds in avoiding all physical pain and mental anguish, he will discover that a simple and ordinary life is pleasant in itself. Enormous quantities of pleasure are unnecessary for the good life; continence followed by moderate satisfaction will suffice; danger lurks beyond moderation. Often, suffering for the promise of greater future goods is advisable, while spiritual pleasures is preferable to sensual indulgence. The pleasant life, in the opinion of Epicurus, is one marked by freedom from anxiety, the sweetness of mental serenity. Positive happiness is inaccessible; hence, quiet contentment is to be sought.

Anxiety is the greatest threat to peace of mind, and the worst fear is that of death. Accordingly, fear of death must be abolished, and Epicurus makes use of the following dilemma to prove that this end can be achieved. While we are alive, he said, we need not fear death, but when death comes, either of two alternatives will be possible for us: the first alternative is an afterlife, and if this is the case, then fear of death is needless; the second alternative is death (defined as absence of sensation), a state in which we are incapable of worrying; consequently, fear of death is vain, foolish, and unnecessary.

Each pleasure is evaluated with respect to its ability to produce unmitigated satisfaction. Although painlessness is a most desirable kind of pleasure, satisfaction of needs is the preferred type of pleasure because it alone brings perfect happiness, namely, the state in which every want becomes quiescent through fulfillment. The Stoics underscored the virtue of indifference to passions, whereas the Epicureans espoused the absence of passion as that state in which all needs or wants have been suitably fulfilled, resulting in constantly pleasant contentment.

THE GREATEST GOOD. The Epicurean *summum bonum,* prudence or insight, was deemed necessary for the proper exercise of virtues leading to the pleasant or good life. In order to be "as free as the gods," happiness must be located within oneself, and in one's virtue. The hallmark of virtue is tranquillity, the more desirable virtues being cheerfulness, simplicity, and moderation. Accordingly, refined pleasures or spiritual values supersede physical gratification. The mind builds a reserve of pleasure both in anticipating future pleasures and in retaining past pleasures in memory. With such spiritual pleasure resources, one can cope with present miseries.

EPICUREAN SOCIAL ETHICS. With the exception of friendship, social involvements were greatly de-emphasized by the Epicureans. Marriage, because of its concomitant worries and responsibilities, was discouraged, as were all forms of public service. Despite their philosophy of hedonism, Epicureans believed it more pleasant to extend kindnesses than to receive them. The exchange of an altruistic public life for an egoistic private one was recommended, provided it resulted in personal benefits. But friendship, because it adds measurably to the life worth living, was considered highly desirable, perhaps the only worthwhile social relationship. The personal ideal of contentment was matched with the social ideal of friendship.

CRITICISM OF HEDONISM

Hedonism has been the object of criticism from many quarters and for numerous reasons. The following are some of the major objections to this philosophy of pleasure.

Lack of Evidence. Hedonists, by definition, assume that pleasure is good, without adequate supporting evidence. This is the same error committed by some utilitarians, who believe that the object of desire is by virtue of that fact desirable. Not only are many objects that a person actually desires undesirable, such as food that is detrimental to health, but pleasures per se are not necessarily good. Furthermore, there are a number of goods which cannot properly be classified as pleasure, such as arduous study leading to a successful and satisfying career.

Some Pleasures Unworthy. Wilbar Marshall Urban contended that pleasure must not be severed from value, if it is to be regarded as good. Pleasures must be qualitatively distinguished from one another, as John Stuart Mill insisted; otherwise, the pleasures of a madman—a Nero or a Hitler—would be equated with those of a rational man living sanely. G. E. Moore repudiated equating a drunkard's pleasure in breaking pottery with that of an individual's pleasure in watching a Shakespearean play.

Some Pleasures Unsatisfying. Pleasure is not necessarily satisfying, as is often the case with sexual pleasure. Schopenhauer noted that sexual pleasures are not fulfilling, but only momentarily alleviating. According to Erich Fromm, many persons who seek the satisfying experience of love confuse it with sex, believing that a sexual experience will provide the fulfillment derived from love. C. I. Lewis cited the confusion of desire or want with pleasure and satisfaction, asserting that "at least half of the world's avoidable troubles are created by those who do not know what they want and pursue what would not satisfy them if they had it." Pleasures also vary with one's physiological state and with one's previous experience of them.

The Irony of Pleasure. It is ironic that many of the good things in life are unpleasant or unwanted by most persons, such as a course of study leading to the M.D. degree. Yet, despite the overwhelming evidence to the contrary, hedonists believe that pleasure is the sole good.

4

Utilitarianism: The Greatest Happiness of the Greatest Number

The philosophy of utilitarianism is based upon the doctrine of utility, which states that the right act is that which produces the greatest amount of pleasure or happiness with the least amount of pain. This philosophy developed in England with the writings of John Gay (1699–1745) in his *Dissertation concerning the Fundamental Principle of Virtue or Morality* (1731), and William Paley (1743–1805) in his *The Principles of Moral and Political Philosophy* (1785), both of whom expounded its doctrines from a theological point of view. The leading exponents of utilitarianism were the British philosophers Jeremy Bentham, John Stuart Mill, Henry Sidgwick, Hastings Rashdall, and George Edward Moore.

CLASSICAL UTILITARIANISM

The better part of two millennia passed before any important development in the philosophy of hedonism took place. The change occurred when British philosophers found in hedonism an individual ethic capable of social application. *Utilitarianism,* which arose in antithesis to ethical intuitionism, viewed ethical actions as those resulting in happiness: the greater the happiness, the greater the moral merit of the act; furthermore, the more persons made happy, the more praiseworthy the act. Investigation into the circumstances and consequences of behavior was regarded as the basis for moral value judgments. Thus, Bentham asked the same question about a moral principle that he asked about legal statutes, namely, "What is the use of it?" and justified adherence to it only to the extent that it was capable of producing happiness. Mill, living during a period of increasing skepticism or indifference to religion, adopted the same inquiring attitude as he sought to provide a humanistic philosophy devoid of supernaturalism to replace the void.

Bentham: Quantitative Hedonist. One of the most influential of these British utilitarians was Jeremy Bentham (1748–1832), a philosopher renowned for his devotion to the advancement of human welfare. He became concerned with ethical theory through his interest in law and government, his disgust with injustice, and his desire for social and legal reform. He developed a new science of moral law, based on Richard Cumberland's "greatest good" or "greatest happiness" principle, to distinguish between good and bad laws for society.

Bentham's main work, *An Introduction to the Principles of Morals and Legislation* (the first part appeared in print in 1780, but the entire work was not published until 1879), opens with a statement that man is naturally motivated by pleasure and pain, whether or not he is aware of it. This is the theory of *psychological hedonism* or, as Bentham called it, the principle of self-preference; based upon it is *ethical hedonism,* the principle that we *ought* to pursue a life of pleasure.

Bentham went on to define the *principle of utility* as "that principle which approves or disapproves of every action whatsoever, according to the tendency which it appears to have to augment or diminish the happiness of the party whose interest is in question: or, what is the same thing in other words, to promote or to oppose that happiness."[1] In a later edition of this work, he called the principle of utility the *greatest happiness* or *greatest felicity principle,* or "that principle which states [identifies] the greatest happiness of all those whose interest is in question, as being the right and proper, and only right and proper and universally desirable, end of human action."[2] Thus, the principle of utility was renamed the greatest happiness principle by Bentham.

QUANTITATIVE HEDONISM. Bentham's is a "quantitative" hedonism, the theory that pleasure is of one kind only, differing merely in its quantitative aspects, not in quality. The "quantity of pleasure being equal, push-pin is as good as poetry."[3] Pleasure is enjoyable, and it matters not whether it proceeds from listening to the music of Beethoven, on the one hand, or "sticking pins in baby's bottom" on the other. Each person is his own best judge as to what is pleasurable to himself. Duty, obligation, or moral injunction is a question of what results in personal happiness.

THE HEDONISTIC CALCULUS (OR FELICIFIC CALCULUS). Influenced by the success of scientific method in other fields, Bentham tried to

1. Jeremy Bentham, "An Introduction to the Principles of Morals and Legislation" (1879), in *The Works of Jeremy Bentham,* ed. John Bowring (New York: Russell & Russell, 1962), 1:2.
2. Ibid., 1:1, footnote.
3. This widely used quotation is from John Stuart Mill's *Essays of Ethics, Religion and Society* (vol. 10, p. 13 of his *Works*). The nearest quotation to that of Mill's which could be found is: "Prejudice apart, the game of push-pin is of equal value with the arts and sciences of music and poetry;" in John Bowring's edition of *The Works of Jeremy Bentham,* vol. 2 (New York: Russell & Russell, 1962), p. 253.

apply it to ethics. He asserted that pleasures can be evaluated solely in terms of quantitative differences. The elements to be measured are (1) *intensity,* (2) *duration,* (3) *certainty,* (4) *propinquity,* (5) *fecundity,* (6) *purity,* and (7) *extent.* These seven points of the *hedonistic,* or *felicific, calculus,* as they are termed, are used to estimate the value of a particular pleasure or pain, or the good or bad tendency of the act that produced it.

BENTHAM'S MNEMONIC VERSE. In a revision, Bentham, in order to insure the retention of the fundamental principles of his moral philosophy, issued the following mnemonic lines:

> Intense, long, certain, speedy, fruitful, pure—
> *Such marks in* pleasures *and in* pains *endure.*
> *Such pleasures seek, if* private *be thy end:*
> *If it be* public, *wide let them* extend.
> *Such* pains *avoid, whichever be thy view:*
> *If pains* must *come, let them* extend *to few.*[4]

Note the comprehensiveness of these lines: how well they include the hedonistic calculus and its use, and even intimate the definition of utilitarianism!

BENTHAM'S FOUR SANCTIONS. In addition to the hedonistic calculus, Bentham introduced *four sanctions,* sources of pleasure and pain that serve as motives or that "are capable of giving a binding force to any law or rule of conduct." The four sanctions are: (1) *physical,* (2) *political,* (3) *moral,* or *popular,* and (4) *religious.*

EGOISTIC HEDONISM. To Bentham, the only pleasure is that which is capable of gratifying an individual for his own personal benefit without the slightest sacrifice that deference to others would involve; accordingly, Bentham's is an *egoistic hedonism.* Some authorities, such as A. J. Ayer, however, assert that Bentham identified self-interest with happiness, but not in a strict egoistic sense, for the "principle of benevolence" prompted a concern for the happiness of others.[5]

Bentham's disciples, accused of restricting their pleasurable pursuits to the physical, to the virtual disregard of cultural values, were opprobriously termed "Benthamites," and their philosophy was alluded to as "the pig philosophy." The pursuit of pleasure as the sole good could only lead to the neglect of spiritual and cultural refinement.

THE CRITERION OF MORALITY. Two important democratic principles followed as corollaries of Bentham's philosophy: (1) *the greatest happiness of the greatest number,* and (2) *everybody to count for one, nobody for more than one.* The former became the definition of utilitarianism, and its criterion of the right act; the latter, which Mill

4. Ibid., footnote to 4:2.
5. A. J. Ayer, "The Principle of Utility," *Philosophical Essays* (London: Macmillan, 1963), p. 250.

termed *Bentham's dictum,* was regarded as an explanatory commentary on the principle of utility.

The first principle was phrased by Bentham as: "The right and proper end of government in every political economy is the greatest happiness of all the individuals."[6] As early as 1725, Hutcheson had formulated the principle of "the greatest happiness for the greatest numbers."[7] The principle is ambiguous, however, because, from the statement as it stands, it is impossible to determine whether the emphasis is to be placed upon *good* (happiness) or *number.* The difference in meaning is critical, since if we weigh the emphasis in favor of the number involved, the good of the minority must be sacrificed in favor of the good of the majority, regardless of how minutely the majority benefit by the good or how much the minority is required to sacrifice. Placing the emphasis upon *good* implies the possible sacrifice of the pleasures of the majority in favor of the minority when the minority stand to benefit immensely and the majority's sacrifice is but small. It is true that some allowance was made by Bentham for *principles of benevolence,* which would elicit concern for another's happiness, and which signified enlightened self-interest. Nevertheless, inasmuch as society is a fictitious body, "the interest of the community" is merely the "sum of interests of the various members who compose it." A. J. Ayer claimed that Bentham's utilitarianism is not to be interpreted as a personal, but as a social, standard, for in his *Deontology* Bentham argued that actions that are conducive to general happiness always harmonize with those conducive to the individual's happiness.

The second principle, a socialization of utilitarianism, was interpreted by Mill as the "equal claim of everybody to happiness." It implies that each individual's pleasure is equally as important to himself as anyone else's may be to that person; it is, therefore, a principle of fairness and the recognition of equality respecting individual rights.

CRITICAL COMMENTS ON BENTHAM'S ETHICS. The term "utility" is a misleading one, because, although it is generally understood to mean usefulness, for Bentham it meant that property of an act that produces happiness. He used a circuitous, if not a devious, route to derive happiness from utility. According to his philosophy of utilitarianism, the useful is the good, the good consists of the best consequences of our actions, the best consequences are happiness, and happiness must be interpreted in terms of pleasure and pain.

The pleasures approved by Bentham were not those of quality nor those which are commonly referred to as values, and yet in his *Intro-*

6. Jeremy Bentham, "Introduction to the Constitutional Code," in *The Works of Jeremy Bentham,* ed. John Bowring (New York: Russell & Russell, 1962), 2:2.

7. Francis Hutcheson, *An Inquiry concerning Moral Good and Evil* (London, 1725), Steph. 121.

duction to the Constitutional Code he expected legislators to find their greatest happiness in promoting the happiness of their constituents. How this is possible for anyone pursuing only his self-interest is difficult to see. He believed that this result can somehow be achieved through education and other means of encouragement. To go from self-interest to idealistic altruism is a jump that is not even allowed ethical idealists. The most that Bentham could expect (and he did) is that individuals would not interfere with the happiness of others in pursuit of their own.

Some scholars criticize Bentham's definition of utility, the "greatest happiness principle," as being *prescriptive,* persuasive, or simply a recommendation; hence it cannot be predicated as true or false since it is not *descriptive.* Accordingly, there is no way for Bentham to prove his ethical premises.

One of the more common objections to Bentham's theory is that it is based on a false psychology. It assumes that all of one's actions are purposive, but this assumption is obviously not valid when actions are prompted by impulse, nor is it true when actions fail to bring a person his anticipated happiness. Occasionally, choices that are expected to bring happiness terminate in calamity; for example, we may enjoy a sumptuous dinner and later become ill as a consequence. Psychologists, such as O. H. Mowrer, Neal Miller, and John Dollard, have shown that bad judgment is often responsible for neurotic behavior.[8] Viktor Frankl and other psychiatrists claim that happiness is not the product of direct choice, but is attained as a concomitant of other actions—for example, actions in pursuit of a meaningful life.[9] Critics have also pointed out that the conscious pursuit of happiness leads a person to the *hedonistic paradox,* the inability to find happiness by direct pursuit of it, since happiness is a by-product of an activity which in itself cannot be said to be happiness per se. Moreover, there is no object which can be said to elicit happiness for any and all persons alike.

Close scrutiny of the principle of utility reveals its circularity. It is based on the rationalization that whatever one does results in happiness because that is why one does it. Even if the action results in misery, the misery is explained as happiness on the mere assumption that one does only what results in happiness. Consequently, catastrophic consequences must be explained as masochism, and masochism as a form of happiness. Or, as A. J. Ayer said of this principle, "It is to say no more than every man does what he does."[10] It is tantamount to saying

8. See John Dollard and Neal Miller, *Personality and Psychotherapy* (New York: McGraw-Hill, 1950), chap. 2.

9. See Viktor Frankl, *The Will to Meaning* (New York: World, 1969), pp. 33–38.

10. A. J. Ayer, *Philosophical Essays,* p. 265.

that what a person intends is (by virtue of that intention) his own greatest happiness. Thus, it can be said that the ascetic is deriving as much pleasure from his life as the hedonist. Either this statement is false or the term "pleasure" becomes meaningless. One could indeed maintain that the ascetic's life of deprivation is at least as satisfying as the hedonist's and more worthwhile. Pleasure, for Bentham, simply means whatever a man wills, and whatever a man wills is pleasurable, but this conclusion would be categorically false in the case of an angry man who chose to harm himself. Sidgwick notes that it makes no sense for Bentham to persuade others of his ethics if it is true that each man because of his psychological makeup pursues his greatest apparent happiness.[11]

Even Bentham's dictum, "Each is to count for one, nobody for more than one," has come under criticism. Rashdall incisively notes that "to reward the idler as much as the industrious . . . would be to make him count not for one but for several; since his support would impose additional labor on the industrious members of the community."[12]

Carlyle: Altruistic Utilitarianism. Bentham's egoistic hedonism was challenged by other British philosophers who sought to champion the cause of utilitarianism by rendering it altruistic. Thomas Carlyle (1795–1881), who denounced Benthamism as a "pig philosophy," supplanted the "greatest happiness principle" of Bentham with the "greatest nobleness principle," which enjoins us to look to the heroes for our ideals and to find our happiness in our work. The mind's pleasures are superior to those of the stomach, and culture is superior to sensuality. "The shoe-black also has a soul quite other than his stomach, and would require for his permanent satisfaction and saturation *God's Infinite Universe.*" According to Carlyle, Bentham's hedonism with its egoistic motivation contributes to the deterioration of the times, and persons so motivated merely increase the number of "knaves and dastards arrested."

Mill: Qualitative Hedonism. It remained for John Stuart Mill (1806–1873), Bentham's disciple and intellectual successor, to embellish utilitarianism with certain idealistic characteristics in order to rescue it from its uncouth lapse into a "pig philosophy." Bentham's basic premise was that the greatest and sole good is pleasure, a pleasure of a single quality which is calculable in quantity only, not in kind. Mill reasoned that if this is so, then it is of little consequence who the sentient being happens to be that is presently enjoying pleasure, an animal or a human being. Therefore, as long as one is enjoying life's *summum bonum,* it matters not what he is, except that if he is a

11. Henry Sidgwick, *The Method of Ethics* (New York: Dover, 1966), pp. 84–85.

12. Hastings Rashdall, *The Theory of Good and Evil* (London: Oxford University Press, 1907), 1:230.

miserable human being, it would be preferable for him to be a happy pig instead.

Nevertheless, Mill refused to cast his lot with porcine pleasures. He preferred to be a miserable man rather than a contented pig. Now he was confronted with the question of why he would not choose to be a pig, and he resolved the issue by introducing the concept of *qualitative hedonism,* the theory that pleasures differ in kind as well as quantity. A small amount of pleasure of high quality is preferable to an enormous amount of pleasure of inferior quality. We may illustrate this point by comparing a ton of coal to an ounce of diamond; all things being equal, a ton of coal is less valuable than a tiny diamond, despite the fact that both are composed of carbon atoms.[13] "The only true or definite rule of conduct or standard of morality is the greatest happiness, but there is needed first a philosophical estimate of happiness. Quality as well as quantity of happiness is to be considered; less of a higher kind is preferable to more of a lower. The test of quality is the preference given by those who are acquainted with both. Socrates would rather choose to be Socrates dissatisfied than to be a pig satisfied. The pig probably would not, but then the pig knows only one side of the question; Socrates knows both."[14]

CRITERION OF MORALITY: THE HEDONIC EXPERT. Should the fool or the pig object to this conclusion, claiming their own opinions equally valid, they would find themselves mistaken, because they are not in a position to make a judgment of value concerning an experience they can never have. But the human being can know the pig's pleasure, for man has had the experience of satisfying his sensual appetites, which are like those of the pig. Similarly, the intelligent man can know an ignorant person's state of mind, since all intelligent persons have experienced moments when they were themselves in a state of ignorance, and he can appreciate how much more desirable it is to be enlightened.

Decisions as to which pleasures are more valuable must be made by the *hedonic expert,* who is in a position to do so because he has had adequate experience with both types of pleasure and knows how to evaluate them. To be sure, a euphoric idiot would refuse to trade places with an intelligent person, because the idiot considers himself happier; but the intelligent individual, though he may concede that the idiot is happier, would never choose to exchange places with him, for he knows that being an intelligent person is more valuable than being an idiot. This kind of reasoning applies to comparisons between deprived, unhappy human beings and well-fed, happy lower animals. The hedonic expert knows that it is still preferable to be the human

13. This illustration is the author's.

14. John Stuart Mill, "Mill's Journal," in *Mill's Ethical Writings,* ed. J. B. Schneewind (New York: Collier, 1965), p. 343.

being because there is an important qualitative pleasure (value) in merely being a man which vastly outweighs all the physical pleasures afforded an animal; there is a qualitative difference in value. "A being of higher faculties requires more to make him happy, is capable probably of more acute suffering, and is certainly accessible to it at more points, than one of an inferior type; but in spite of these liabilities, he can never really wish to sink into what he feels to be a lower grade of existence."[15] Superior types of being have greater worth, dignity, than lower types.

MILL'S TWO SANCTIONS. Mill reduced Bentham's sanctions to two: (1) internal and (2) external, the former having the far greater import. External sanctions are those extraneous forces brought to bear upon the individual, such as adverse public opinion and fear of "divine" retribution (Bentham's moral and religious sanctions), while the internal sanction is the call of duty, an inner sense of obligation.

PROOF OF UTILITARIANISM. Now that Mill has presented his case, what proof does he offer for his assertions? He adduces: "The only proof capable of being given that an object is visible is that people actually see it. The only proof that a sound is audible is that people hear it; and so of the other sources of our experience. In like manner, I apprehend, the sole evidence it is possible to produce that anything is desirable is that people do actually desire it."[16] Mill's proof of utilitarianism is comparable to that of Bentham, who argues that when a person is experiencing a pleasure, he cannot deny that he likes it. While the pleasure is being experienced, an individual must admit that he is in fact enjoying it.

According to Mill, something is desirable merely on the grounds that it is capable of stimulating desire. Logicians term Mill's error regarding this point a *figure-of-speech fallacy*. The suffix *ble* does not have the same meaning in each case: visi*ble,* audi*ble,* and desira*ble.* The first two terms signify something that can be or actually is seen or heard, whereas *desirable* connotes "ought to be desired." The studious reading of the *Encyclopaedia Britannica* is highly desirable, but a person actually engaged in its reading may not possess any desire at all. Your heart surgeon may inform you that in your particular case, open-heart surgery is highly desirable, yet instead of jumping for joy, you may feel nauseous.

BENTHAM'S DICTUM. As for Bentham's dictum, "Each to count for one, nobody for more than one," Mill not only accepted it, but also made good use of it. Furthermore, he felt that, inasmuch as a person pursues his own happiness, he should seek the happiness of others as well.

15. John Stuart Mill, *Utilitarianism,* 12th ed. (London, 1895), chap. 2.
16. Ibid., chap. 4.

Critical Comments on Mill's Ethics. Mill, like Bentham, adopted psychological hedonism. Even granting the validity of psychological hedonism, ethical hedonism does not necessarily follow from it. A person may indeed seek his own greatest happiness, but this does not mean that he ought to, for this would be tantamount to saying that because a person has a natural disposition to kill, he should do so. The error arises from the mistaken notion of identifying pleasure with good.

Act-utilitarianism, which holds that the right action is that which will produce the greatest good, is constantly plagued with the problem of the foreseeable outcome of one's actions. If acts are good according to their outcome, then one never knows his moral score, inasmuch as the consequences of acts are endless, like the ripples created by a pebble dropped in water. Aware of this difficulty, Mill tended to favor *rule-utilitarianism*—"living according to maxims of prudence wholly founded on foresight of consequences."[17] Alas, even a rule does not rescue one from this predicament, although it may be a welcome aid.

Mill, and Bentham also, lack proof of their principle of utility, a matter that was pointed out as early as the publication of Spencer's *Social Statics.*[18] While the two thinkers objected to the ethical intuitionists for resorting to a "moral sense" as the criterion of moral right, their own utility principle ultimately rests on a moral sense, or intuition, as its proof.

Sidgwick: Universalistic Hedonism. Henry Sidgwick (1838–1900) wrestled with the problem of individual happiness versus the happiness of others; since happiness is experienced subjectively by an individual, is there any reason why the happiness of the rest of mankind should be incumbent upon him? Why should he care about the happiness of others, when the only happiness that he can possibly experience is his very own?

The above questions must be answered on the utilitarian premise that happiness is the sole good, not duty or virtue, since the only duty is to acquire happiness, and the only virtue is the ability to obtain it. Sidgwick's final conclusion combines *Kantian intuitionism*[19] with the utilitarianism of Mill, producing *intuitional utilitarianism.* Convinced of the validity of Mill's ethical hedonism, Sidgwick asserted that happiness is unquestionably the ethical goal of man, and equally persuaded by the truth of Kant's *categorical imperative,* he maintained that a person has the *duty* to promote universal happiness. The "natural

17. John Stuart Mill, "Professor Sedwick's Discourse on the Studies of the University of Cambridge," in *London Review* (1835). Reprinted in *Mill's Ethical Writings,* ed. J. B. Schneewind (New York: Collier, 1965), p. 93.

18. Herbert Spencer, *Social Statics,* rev. ed. (New York: D. Appleton, 1896), pp. 17–19.

19. See the section on Kant's intuitionism in chapter 8.

end of action" is "private happiness, and the end of duty, general happiness."[20]

THE COMMON-SENSE CALCULUS AND THE PRINCIPLE OF JUSTICE. To prove his position, Sidgwick did not use the hedonistic calculus, which he regarded as faulty and suitable only for egoistic hedonism, but instead used the *calculus of common sense,* reason. "Reason shows me that if my happiness is desirable and good, the equal happiness of any other person must be equally desirable."[21] Thus, we have the Sidgwickian rendition of the Kantian principle: What is right for one is right for all. Sidgwick's principle of justice reads: "It cannot be right for A to treat B in a manner in which it would be wrong for B to treat A, merely on the ground that they are two different individuals, and without there being any difference between the natures or circumstances of the two which can be stated as a reasonable ground for difference of treatment."[22]

The reconciliation of the problem not only called for the marriage of utilitarianism with intuitionism, but implied theism as well, for the concept of duty entails the moral government of the world, and consequently, its Governor.

HAPPINESS AS THE ULTIMATE GOOD. Terming his system *universalistic hedonism,* Sidgwick considered the *summum bonum* (or *ultimate good,* as he preferred to call it) to be the promotion of happiness as the common end of man. All right conduct is determined by the ultimate good—happiness—and virtue must be defined in accordance with this ultimate good. The *right act* is defined as follows: "The conduct which, under any given circumstances, is objectively right, is that which will produce the greatest amount of happiness on the whole: that is taking into account all whose happiness is affected by the conduct."[23] Although right conduct is the pursuit of only that private happiness to which a person is rightfully entitled, duty is the enhancement of general happiness, which at times may incur self-sacrifice when reason dictates. "It may yet be *actually* reasonable for an individual to sacrifice his own Good or happiness for the greater happiness of others."[24]

IDEAL UTILITARIANISM—AN ETHICS OF CONSEQUENCES

Ideal utilitarianism is a school of philosophical thought which emerged from the later developments of utilitarianism, utilizing its

20. Henry Sidgwick, *The Methods of Ethics,* 6th ed. (London: Macmillan, 1901), bk. 3, chap. 14.
21. Ibid.
22. Ibid., chap. 5.
23. Ibid., chap. 14.
24. Ibid.

refinements and discarding its weaknesses. However, it is not strictly utilitarian in the early sense of the term, but a synthesis of the idealism of Thomas Hill Green (whose system of ethics is treated in the chapter on self-realizationism) and the utilitarianism of Henry Sidgwick. It differs from utilitarianism mainly regarding the question of hedonism; it is teleological but not hedonistically oriented. The term *ideal utilitarianism* was coined by Hastings Rashdall (1858–1924), a prominent proponent of this school of thought.

Hastings Rashdall: Ethics as the Maximum Production of Good Consequences. Rashdall held that the primary concern of ethical philosophy was the investigation and evaluation of the meanings of the terms *right* and *wrong,* with the end of determining precisely what actions are right and wrong. In such an investigation, unless a person is unbiased, he may easily fall prey to some form of the hedonistic theory which traces all human conduct to the function of a single motive, the desire for pleasure. Such a conclusion will predetermine the nature of right action, as follows: that act is morally right which is conducive to pleasure, and that act is morally wrong which leads to pain or diminishing pleasure. This view rests upon psychological hedonism, the theory that man by natural disposition seeks pleasure and avoids pain.

Rashdall's ideal utilitarianism is not so much a compromise of the two conflicting systems, intuitional idealism and utilitarianism, as it is the encompassing and harmonizing of them, the elimination of their errors, and the avoidance of extremes to which each has fallen prey. Not merely right conduct, but virtues as well may be explained on the basis of this synthetic position.

CALCULUS OF CONSEQUENCES. Perhaps the chief task confronting the philosopher of ethics is that of determining the *moral criterion,* a criterion capable of indicating exactly whether an act is moral or immoral. For ideal utilitarians, the right act is that act which has the best consequences. Good, although not divorced from pleasure or happiness, is calculable in terms of the consequences taken as a whole. Neither a hedonistic calculus, such as the one devised by Bentham to discriminate among mere quantitative pleasures, nor recourse to the judgment of the hedonic expert, as proposed by Mill, is an adequate test, but there is one, namely, a *calculus of consequences,* which treats the situation as a whole, not merely the pleasure or necessarily the happiness of the individual in question. "The right action is always that which (so far as the agent has the means of knowing) will produce the greatest amount of good upon the whole. This position implies that all goods or elements of the good are in some sense and for some purposes commensurable. . . . This view of Ethics, which combines the utilitarian principle that Ethics must be teleological with a non-hedonistic view of the ethical end, I propose to call Ideal

Utilitarianism. According to this view actions are right or wrong according as they tend to produce for mankind an ideal end or good, which includes, but is not limited to, pleasure."[25] Therefore, according to the ideal utilitarian, *the good determines the right act.*

RASHDALL'S AXIOM OF EQUITY. According to Rashdall, in order to know whether an action is right, one must consider its relation to that object which is recognized as desirable, namely, the *summum bonum.* The right act is not good in itself, in the sense of duty for duty's sake, but is good because it contributes to consequences which may be deemed good. The consequences considered good need not be restricted to pleasure, though the good includes pleasure. Nevertheless, my personal good may not be obtained at the expense of another individual. Indeed, altruism may be indicated when the good of another person is of sufficient import for me to sacrifice my own immediate and minor good for his benefit, especially when his good contributes measurably to the good of the whole of mankind. All things being equal, however, and provided that my good does not impede the good of another, then the consideration of my own personal good reigns paramount. Rashdall's *axiom of equity* reads: "It is self-evident to me that I ought (where it does not collide with the greater good of another) to promote my own greatest good, that I ought to prefer a greater good on the whole to a lesser, and that I ought to regard the good of one man as of equal intrinsic value with the like good of any one else."[26] *Any one else* implicitly includes myself as well; accordingly, there may be occasions when I must altruistically subordinate my pleasure to that of another person.

JUSTICE, VIRTUE, BENEVOLENCE, AND THE IDEAL LIFE. Having defined ideal utilitarianism as "our view that acts are right or wrong according as they tend or do not tend to promote a Well-being or *εὐδαιμονία* or good consisting of various elements, the relative value of which is intuitively discerned,"[27] Rashdall then proceeded to explain its relationship to justice, virtue, and benevolence. *Justice* is the impartial treatment accorded to individuals on the basis of an established system of distribution, while "ultimate justice would mean the distribution of true good in accordance with the principle that one man's good is of as much intrinsic value as the like good of another's."[28]

In the light of the foregoing, *virtue* may be defined in terms of rational *benevolence* (or love) regulated by justice, or benevolence consistent with justice. Despite the opinion of hedonistic utilitarians, virtues, including those which are obviously altruistic, possess a value of their own surpassing the mere value of the pleasure which they

25. Rashdall, *Theory of Good and Evil,* 1:2.
26. Ibid., p. 185.
27. Ibid., p. xvii.
28. Ibid.

produce. "The end which the benevolent man is to promote must include many other kinds of good besides pleasure, many dispositions, emotions, activities, states of consciousness which are valued for their own sakes and not merely as a means to some further good."[29]

Virtues are those things which contribute to general or social good, such as honesty, industry, family affection, kindliness, compassion, loyalty, orderliness, and courage. Morality, pleasure, virtue, and other things designated good are constituent aspects of an ideally good life, a life which becomes "the duty of each to promote for all."

Value, pleasure, and happiness are the three categories of the ideal life. Although values are found in the personalities of individuals, their objective basis is grounded in God. Accordingly, morality originates with persons, but terminates in God and immortality. However, owing to the presence of *surd evil* (ultimate or intrinsic evil) in the world, God must be limited in power, and the optimism of the absolutists who adhere to an omnipotent God must be replaced with *meliorism* (the view that the world is not absolutely good, but increasingly becomes better) and *theistic finitism* (the belief that God is limited in power). Finding it necessary to ground his ethics in metaphysics, Rashdall developed a philosophy of personal idealism with God the supreme person.

EVALUATION OF RASHDALL'S POSITION. In his ideal utilitarianism, Rashdall has gained the advantage of taking into account the quality of the act itself as well as its consequences in determining ethical judgments. One's attitude or concern in enhancing the common good is to be regarded as a portion of the total good to be augmented.

G. E. Moore: Good as Indefinable and Real. George Edward Moore (1873–1958), more than any other English philosopher during the first half of the present century, has influenced the direction of British, and perhaps even American, philosophy. From 1920 to 1947 he edited *Mind,* a major British philosophical journal; he also held the chair of philosophy at Cambridge University (1925–1939). Moore's ethical philosophy is found in a number of writings, but two rich sources are his books *Principia Ethica* (1903) and *Ethics* (1912).

Moore sired a number of schools of philosophical thought: British neorealism, the analytic school (which dominates the British philosophical scene and has a firm hold in America), and ideal utilitarianism, since he published his views on ethics before Rashdall. Occasionally Moore's ethical theory is termed *agathistic utilitarianism* in order to differentiate it from hedonistic utilitarianism, the theory that pleasure is the sole intrinsic good.

THE NATURE OF ETHICAL QUESTIONS. According to Moore, ethics

29. Ibid., p. 188.

is concerned with two fundamental questions: (1) "What kind of things ought to exist for their own sakes?" (i.e., What is good?) and (2) "What kind of actions ought we to perform?" (i.e., What is good conduct?). While the first inquires as to the nature and definition of intrinsic good, the second seeks a moral criterion.

GOOD AS INDEFINABLE. To Moore, the fundamental question in ethics is how *good* is to be defined. Not what things are good, but the definition of good per sè, is the problem. But the investigation yields a seemingly disappointing conclusion, for "If I am asked 'What is good?' my answer is that good is good, and that is the end of the matter. Or if I am asked 'How is good to be defined?' my answer is that it cannot be defined, and that is all I have to say about it."[30]

Propositions concerning the good are not analytic, but synthetic; accordingly, they can be broken down into their component parts. But good itself is a simple idea, an ultimate which cannot be broken down because there is nothing beyond it into which it may be divided. "My point is that 'good' is a simple notion, just as 'yellow' is a simple notion; that, just as you cannot, by any manner of means, explain to any one who does not already know it, what yellow is, so you cannot explain what good is."[31] If a person has never experienced yellow, there is no way in which you can convey the experience to him. A horse, for example, is not in the same category, for it is complex; hence you may define "horse" in terms of its many different properties and qualities until you arrive at *horse* reduced to its simplest terms, which are no longer definable. Simple terms, owing to their ultimate nature, must be thought or perceived by the person capable of thinking or experiencing them, but to a person incapable of thinking them or even perceiving them, they can never be explained, nor can you make their nature known by any definition. Complex objects, can, however, be described to a person who has never experienced them by defining them in terms of their parts.

> And so it is with all objects, not previously known, which we are able to define: they are all complex; all composed of parts, which may themselves, in the first instance, be capable of similar definition, but which must in the end be reducible to simplest parts, which can no longer be defined. But yellow and good, we say, are not complex: they are notions of that simple kind, out of which definitions are composed and with which the power of further defining ceases.[32]

30. G. E. Moore, *Principia Ethica* (Cambridge: Cambridge University Press, 1903), p. 6.
31. Ibid., p. 7.
32. Ibid., pp. 7–8.

Moore then explains that it is not *the* good (that which is good) which is indefinable. *The* good is a substantive to which the adjective *good* applies. *The* good may be said of a number of things, such as pleasure, a house, an education. "I believe *the* good to be definable; and yet I still say that good itself is indefinable,"[33] because *good,* that which signifies a quality which belongs to a thing, is simple, hence unanalyzable and indefinable. Although good remains indefinable, duty, virtue, right, and other ethical terms are definable—definable in terms of good.

THE NATURALISTIC FALLACY. Since good cannot be defined, if a person cannot experience good, then he can never know it. Yellow is a comparable ultimate term; if a person has never experienced the color yellow for himself, then there is no way in which the color yellow can be defined for him. Yellow can be defined in terms of the light vibrations responsible for its perception, but to equate the actual experience of yellow with these vibrations in space is to commit the *naturalistic fallacy*. Good is not a natural property like pleasantness or the quality of being the object of desire; it is simply good. The naturalistic fallacy is to claim that good is some natural property or combination of properties. "But far too many philosophers have thought that when they named those other properties they were actually defining good; that these properties, in fact, were simply not 'other,' but absolutely and entirely the same with goodness. This view I propose to call the 'naturalistic fallacy.' "[34] To say that good is but the object of desire or to offer any other form of ethical naturalism is to commit the fallacy in question. What we must determine is simply what *is* good, not how the word is commonly used or what kind of actions are approved. To assert that pleasure is good is to say merely that "pleasure is pleasure," and thus we are no nearer to good.

Good as indefinable is comparable to the experience of pleasure. The relation of pleasure to other things is possible to ascertain; it can be said that it is in the mind, that it causes desire, and that we are conscious of it, but to describe its relations to other objects is not to define it. For example, to define it as a natural object and say that pleasure means the sensation of red, and therefore pleasure is a color, is both ludicrous and an example of the naturalistic fallacy.

MOORE'S IDEAL UTILITARIANISM. The second major question confronting the ethicist is: What is good conduct? Or, what kind of actions ought we to perform? To this, Moore's answer follows the lines of ideal utilitarianism in stating that the right act is one which will produce the best actual consequences. Moore formulates this aspect of his system by the following two propositions:

33. Ibid., p. 9.
34. Ibid., p. 10.

> (1) that the question whether an action is right or wrong always depends upon its *total* consequences, and (2) that if it is once right to prefer one set of *total* consequences, A, to another set B, it must always be right to prefer any set precisely similar to A to any set precisely similar to B.[35]

Note that right action does not depend upon the best foreseeable consequences, the best predictable, or the best probable, but upon the best *actual* consequences. What a person has reason to expect will result from his actions may not be what actually transpires, yet it is the actual consequences which determine the rightness of an act; although a person had the best of intentions, his action would, nevertheless, be ruled as wrong if it did not produce the best actual consequences. Intentionally to bring about undesirable or deleterious consequences is always wrong. "It seems to me to be self-evident that knowingly to do an action which would make the world, on the whole, really and truly *worse* than if we had acted differently, must always be wrong."[36] This being the case, a duty as universally binding as the categorical imperative of Kant cannot conceivably be valid and morally good if consequences resulting therefrom are bad. There are no universal moral laws in the Kantian sense. Moral laws are statements that particular kinds of actions will have good consequences.

To judge an act as good is to consider its value as means; it is good as means, and as means it becomes right when it secures the greatest possible total good. "In other words, to judge that an action is generally a means to good is to judge not only that it generally does *some* good, but that it generally does the greatest good of which the circumstances admit."[37]

To make a judgment of absolute right and duty, it is necessary to determine that the "course of action in question is *the* best thing to do; that, by acting so, every good that *can* be secured will have been secured. . . . In asserting that the action is *the* best thing to do, we assert that it together with its consequences presents a greater sum of intrinsic value than any possible alternative. . . . In short, to assert that a certain line of conduct is, at a given time, absolutely right or obligatory, is obviously to assert that more good or less evil will be done instead."[38] To make judgments according to the above principle, one must assess the consequences not only of the act in question, but also of any other action that may rival it as a possible alternative. "Our 'duty,' therefore, can only be defined as that action which will

35. G. E. Moore, *Ethics* (London: Oxford University Press, 1912), p. 106.
36. Ibid., p. 112.
37. Moore, *Principia Ethica,* p. 23.
38. Ibid., pp. 24–25.

cause more good to exist in the Universe than any possible alternative."[39]

CRITICAL COMMENTS CONCERNING G. E. MOORE'S ETHICS. Several authorities have been unhappy with Moore's contention that the good is indefinable. Ralph Barton Perry claims that good is definable, and feels that he has proved that fact by defining it as any object of interest.[40] But Moore, it can easily be seen from his philosophical position, would counter that Perry has committed the naturalistic fallacy in so doing. A. C. Ewing has a severer criticism; he asserts that if a fundamental ethical term is indefinable, then it cannot be known.[41] He adds, however, that a person may know something by experience without being able to provide a definition of that experience; *good* and *ought* may fall into this category. Some philosophers, defining truth as the definition of the real, would regard good as unreal if it is incapable of being defined.

To assert that goodness is indefinable is regarded by W. K. Frankena as the "fallacy of begging the question."[42] Frankena maintains that Moore failed to prove goodness to be a simple and indefinable quality, and also failed to establish it as a nonnatural property. Moreover, Moore, the great antagonist of naturalistic ethics, did not quite explain his concept of a natural property, except to insist that an object's goodness and a descriptive analysis of its natural properties are not to be confused. Ironically, intuitionists (such as Moore) and *noncognitivists* or *emotivists* (such as Ayer and Stevenson) are allied in rejecting the view that ethical judgments are subject to the usual types of proof.

To compare good with yellow is an imperfect analogy according to Wheelright, for yellow is known by sense perception, while good lacks the sense qualities of color.[43] Nevertheless, Wheelright's criticism is not quite justified, since the phenomenologist Moore was addressing himself to subjective phenomena (or what is today termed phenomenological experience), and on that experiential level both yellow and good are equally subjectively experienced.

To apply Moore's ethics successfully would require omniscience; the limited mind of man is incapable of following the endless consequences of his own actions, much less being able to predict with accuracy the

39. Ibid., p. 148.

40. Ralph Barton Perry, *General Theory of Value* (Cambridge, Mass.: Harvard University Press, 1926), p. 183.

41. A. C. Ewing, *Ethics* (London: English Universities Press, 1953), p. 13.

42. William K. Frankena, "The Naturalistic Fallacy," *Mind* 48 (1939), pp. 468, 471.

43. Philip Wheelright, *A Critical Introduction to Ethics,* 3d ed. (New York: Odyssey, 1959), pp. 302–303.

ultimate outcome of his choices. According to Moore's system, it would be impossible to know whether one ever committed a right act.

ACT-UTILITARIANISM AND RULE-UTILITARIANISM

What is the criterion of moral decisions? Is it the acts committed or the rules adhered to or violated? An *act-utilitarian* would say an individual's actions are judged by their consequences; and should rules be considered at all (e.g., honesty is the best policy), their value is no more than a mere rule of thumb. But for a *rule-utilitarian* ethical principles are the basis for determining what action will result in the greatest good for the greatest number. It is not a question of "which *action* has the greatest utility, but which *rule* has."[44] Although the principle of utility is present in both types of utilitarianism, act-utilitarianism resorts to consequences as the basis for a decision of the right act, while rule-utilitarianism appeals to rules for guidance.

Whereas Bentham was essentially an act-utilitarian, Richard B. Brandt, who introduced the terms act- and rule-utilitarian, may also be classified as a rule-utilitarian, for in his article "Toward a Credible Form of Utilitarianism," he stated that

> an act is right if and only if it conforms with that learnable set of rules the recognition of which as morally binding—roughly at the time of the act—by everyone in the society of the agent, except for the retention by individuals of already formed and decided moral convictions, would maximize intrinsic value.[45]

Frankena recommended what he termed a *mixed deontological theory,* containing two fundamental and independent principles of ethics: (1) *beneficence,* or *utility,* a principle enjoining one to "maximize the total amount of good in the world," and (2) *justice.* One consults rules to discern the right in a particular situation, but to determine which rules one should live by requires adherence to those rules best fulfilling the combined requirements of utility and justice.

PRACTICE CONCEPTION OF RULES. John Rawls distinguished between the *summary conception* of rules and the *practice conception* of rules.[46] The summary conception means that "rules are pictured as summaries of past decisions," and serve as maxims or guides to be employed or ignored, whereas the practice conception of rules means that,

44. William K. Frankena, *Ethics* (Englewood Cliffs, N.J.: Prentice-Hall, 1963), p. 30.

45. Richard B. Brandt, "Toward a Credible Form of Utilitarianism," in *Morality and the Language of Conduct,* H. Castaneda and G. Nakhnikian, eds. (Detroit: Wayne State University Press, 1963), p. 139.

46. John Rawls, "Two Concepts of Rules," *Philosophical Review* 64 (1955), pp. 3–32.

"if one holds an office defined by a practice, then questions regarding one's actions in this office are settled by reference to the rules which define the practice." To question these rules or to change them is tantamount to assuming the role of reformer. In another paper, Rawls contended that we should not act to augment the general happiness, if our action would result in bringing misery to an individual.[47]

Critical Comment. A major criticism of act-utilitarianism is its inability to resolve the question of the precise distribution of the good. Marcus Singer attacks Bentham's greatest happiness principle on this matter, but the problem holds for all act-utilitarians. Not only is it impossible to know the results of our actions, much less predetermine them, but should the good be the point of emphasis in our actions, or should we be concerned about the greatest number sharing the good?

A more general objection to act-utilitarianism states that to make moral decisions on the basis of the general good without the help of a body of moral rules is time-consuming and impractical—one must analyze each situation as it arises.

Act-utilitarianism has been charged with leading to immoral conclusions. Criminals are punished because it is believed that this action will produce salutary consequences. Punishing an innocent man may also produce beneficial results, yet it is unquestionably unjust and immoral to do so, despite whatever desirable consequences might ensue. John Stuart Mill was aware of the conflict of act-utilitarianism with some of our most widely accepted moral ideas. He wrote in his *Utilitarianism:*

> In the case of abstinences indeed—of things which people forbear to do from moral considerations, though the consequences in the particular case might be beneficial—it would be unworthy of an intelligent agent not to be consciously aware that the action is of a kind which, if practised generally, would be generally injurious, and that this is the ground of the obligation to abstain from it.[48]

Act-utilitarianism has been indicted not only for substituting expediency for ethics, but also for failing to provide sufficient grounds for actions. A person may be excused from his obligations and promises on the basis that the consequences following from the kept promise will not be the best possible, and that another course of action will produce better results.

The problem confronting the rule-utilitarians involves more than finding a valid principle worth applying; it involves finding one ap-

47. John Rawls, "Justice as Fairness," *Philosophical Review* 67 (1958), pp. 164–194.

48. John Stuart Mill, *Utilitarianism,* vol. 3, *Dissertations and Discussions* (Boston, William V. Spencer, 1865), p. 326.

plicable to particular or peculiar situations, which becomes an impossible task if each situation is unique, as some act-utilitarians contend. Hence, the problem here is one of formulation and application. Also, a rule that generally leads to the greatest good may violate other moral rules in its distribution of the good.

5

Self-Realizationism: The Good Life as Fulfillment of Potentialities

Representatives of self-realizationism as an ethical theory span two and a half millennia and include: Plato (ca. 429–347 B.C.); Aristotle (384–322 B.C.); St. Thomas Aquinas (ca. 1225–1274); and the neo-Thomists, Søren Kierkegaard (1813–1855), Thomas Hill Green (1836–1882), Francis Herbert Bradley (1846–1924), and Brand Blanshard (1892–). (Note that in the present treatment St. Thomas Aquinas will be discussed in chapter 6 on scholasticism and neo-Thomism, and Kierkegaard will be discussed in chapter 11 in connection with the school of existentialism which he founded.) Throughout history self-realizationism has always held an appeal; currently, its fundamental premises have been adapted by psychologists and psychiatrists for a better understanding of personality theory and for psychotherapeutic purposes.

Self-Realizationism Defined. Self-realizationism in ethical theory is a perfectionist philosophy which maintains that the highest good or moral ideal for an individual consists in realizing, actualizing, or fulfilling his true nature or self, together with his many innate and varied potentialities, special capacities, or abilities.

The true self may be regarded as an ideal self requiring actualization. The individual attains moral perfection through the realization of his potentialities, so that he achieves the most complete or exhaustive development of his personality. Self-realization entails not only the process of rationally organizing the various aspects of personality into an integrated whole within the individual, but also his proper integration or relationship with others, i.e., with society.

Plato: The Realization of the Good. The most fruitful source of Plato's ethical theory is found in his *Republic,* which states that ethical knowledge is even more austere than mathematics. The principles and conceptions of ethical knowledge, subsumed under *the good,* are still more abstract than geometrical ones. "The idea of good is the highest knowledge."[1] The influence of Socrates is quite perceptible in the

1. Plato *Republic* 6.505.

Protagoras, Timaeus, and the *Laws,* wherein immorality or evil is attributed to ignorance, inasmuch as no one is voluntarily bad.

HAPPINESS AND GOOD: THE ULTIMATE MORAL MOTIVATION. For Plato, the good is identified as the philosopher's ultimate object of contemplation, for it is not only the ultimate nature of the universe, its essence, but its goal as well. The good is the purpose of the world, the form that it assumes, its power, and as its essential being, it is God. The idea of good, that is, the ideal good, is God. Furthermore, the Good, as man's highest ideal, must be pursued and brought into realization, by man's perfecting himself, i.e., by his becoming as Godlike as possible. The *idea* (good, God) is the final cause of the phenomenal world, the end for which all things strive.

The ultimate aim (*summum bonum*) of man is good or happiness, and thus it is solely on a moral basis that man's true happiness will be found, for the blessed state of human existence is the happy soul sharing in the intimacies of the divine world of ideas. Besides celestial happiness found in intimacy with the highest good, there are lesser goods of various gradations, such as sense pleasures (i.e., the pure and painless ones). Realization of the ideal good through sensuous pleasure by artistic sensuous imitation of the beautiful yields joyous results. Sensual pleasure, gratification of appetite, is of an inferior quality to the sensuous joys of beauty, and in turn the sensuous are inferior to the intellectual. "I affirmed that mind was far better and far more excellent as an element of human life, than pleasure."[2]

For Plato, to ask what a thing is is to inquire: For what good is it? What is its purpose? All of nature's activity is designed for some purpose, some end to be attained. In the case of man, his various talents, faculties, and arts function for some end, for some use, for some good. Doing what a man is good for, what he is best equipped by nature to do, cultivating and utilizing his talents, results in perfecting himself, developing his virtues, and realizing the Good. Self-perfection is the reflection of God, the fulfillment of self, and the attainment of the good life; it is in the flourishing of the good life that beauty abounds.

A life that is put to its proper use is beautiful; therefore, *the beautiful is useful, and the beautiful is good.* Thus, the true, the good, the beautiful combine in one, and are realized when man's true end unfolds as he perfects himself. The good life is one that is truly beautiful. Happiness is contingent upon moral beauty and goodness.

GOODNESS AS IDEAL. Real goodness is ideal, and the actual world is merely an approximation, resemblance, or copy of pure and timeless forms (ideals). "In nature the Good is striven for but never to be attained. . . . Of all being, [Good is] the idea which is beyond all other

2. Plato *Philebus* 66.

ideas; it is also the defining principle of being."[3] Good is prized above knowledge and truth. "The idea of the Good is elevated above other ideas."[4]

The attainment of ideal reality and ideal goodness, which is the highest and most real life, is achieved by the mind of rational persons, for physical objects give us only imperfect and shadowy reflections of the ideal or real world. The mind of man, being the only contact he has with true reality, must therefore be his finest self, that which is most significantly and truly man. Consequently, man's highest calling is intellectual in nature, a longing for knowledge, the philosophical pursuit of truth and goodness, for such is the function of the human soul. The soul is acquainted with truth, because the soul once dwelt in true or ideal reality, there face to face with reality, good, God, before coming to earth incarnate. But the acquisition of a body and sense caused the soul's knowledge to sink into the depths of memory.

Learning truth, beauty, and goodness is therefore merely reviving or recollecting what is hidden in the unconscious soul. The soul, supersensible in nature, imprisoned within a body foreign to itself with its distorting sense phenomena, must find its true life by emancipation from the senses and the imperfect phenomenal world, by ascending to the real world of the absolute, there to dwell with truth, beauty, and goodness. The soul finds its happiness in retirement from the sense world, dying, as it were, from sense existence and its imprisonment by freeing itself through knowledge and virtue. "These pleasures of knowledge, then, are unmixed with pain; and they are not the pleasures of the many but of a very few."[5]

THE NATURE OF THE GOOD LIFE. The good life, the actualization of ideal good, can be only imperfectly realized while one is on earth, owing to the interference of imperfect sense organs. Furthermore, only he who has insight into the truth, the good (that is, only the virtuous) may imitate it here on earth. However, inasmuch as virtue can be taught, the goal of education and that of moral cultivation become one, namely, the imitation of the good by realizing as much good as possible, though it be imperfect within the life of each person.

A good life is an orderly one, guided by reason; consequently, only those few endowed with philosophical wisdom can come within reach of the good. The good life is one of harmony, the harmonization of the virtues' orderly functioning, each with respect to its own capacity. Those without true knowledge, lacking in philosophical wisdom, or

3. Raphael Demos, *The Philosophy of Plato* (New York: Charles Scribner's Sons, 1939), p. 71.

4. A. H. Armstrong, ed., *The Cambridge History of Later Greek and Early Medieval Philosophy* (Cambridge: At the University Press, 1967), p. 19.

5. Plato *Philebus* 52.

those who fail to acquire virtue by birth, may do so by being educated in right opinion regarding virtue or trained in it by practice.

THE FOUR CARDINAL VIRTUES. Platonic ethical theory derives the cardinal virtues from a threefold division of the soul, the first of which is the rational division with its powers of reason, while the other two divisions are nonrational or passionate. These two are the important activity of the will, i.e., the spirited activity, and the less important activity of the sensuous appetite. The three divisions correspond to localized bodily functions of three organs, namely, the head, heart, and liver (stomach), respectively.

Plato defined virtue in terms of excellence; consequently, whoever by birth excels in one of the three aspects of the soul by possessing a preponderance of it, attains its corresponding virtue: (1) excellence in reason with its intelligence gives him the virtue of *wisdom;* (2) excellence in the activity of the will gives him the virtue of *courage;* and (3) excellence in the activity of the sensuous appetite gives him the virtue of self-control, moderation, or *temperance.* "Temperance . . . is the ordering or controlling of certain pleasures and desires."[6]

When these three virtues (wisdom, courage, and temperance) function harmoniously together and are ordered and ruled by reason, then *justice* emerges as the concomitant virtue. "One man should practise one thing only, the thing for which his nature was best adapted,—now justice is this principle. . . . Justice [is] doing one's own business."[7] Wisdom and justice in their higher aspects merge as one, wisdom. The other two virtues reflect wisdom at work, wisely ordering the activity of the soul; accordingly, they are aspects of wisdom. "Being perfect is therefore wise and valiant and temperate and just."[8]

Justice is a social virtue, realizable in interpersonal relations, in society, the state. Justice reigns when each person with the virtue most peculiar to himself makes his significant contribution to society in accordance with his particular virtue: those with wisdom contribute to culture and are rulers of the state; those with courage become warriors imbued with devotion to duty; and those possessing self-control, with their appetite in obedience to themselves (exhibiting moderation), obey men of wisdom well.

As nature is aristocratic in awarding virtue, so must the state in which justice prevails (the ideal of the perfect society) be one in which every individual is in his right place, doing that task for which he is best suited by nature. The result of this harmony is not only justice, but also happiness for the individuals within the state; otherwise, injustice, disorder, and misery result. Justice is morality actualized

6. Ibid., 6.430.
7. Ibid., 6.433.
8. Ibid., 4.427.

in the life of the state (every man where he is best suited by nature, perfectly adapted for his contribution to society).

As a personal ethic, justice is also an equitable and desirable balance and harmony within the individual, making for a wholesome adjustment.

> But in reality justice was such as we were describing, being concerned however, not with the outward man, but with the inward, which is the true self and concernment of man: for the just man does not permit the several elements within him to interfere with one another, or any of them to do the work of others,—he sets in order his own inner life, and is his own master and his own law, and at peace with himself; and when he has bound together the three principles within him, which may be compared to the higher, lower, and middle notes of the scale, and the intermediate intervals—when he has bound all these together, and is no longer man, but has become one entirely temperate and perfectly adjusted nature, then he proceeds to act, if he has to act, whether in a matter of property, or in the treatment of the body, or in some affair of politics or private business; always thinking and calling that which preserves and co-operates with this harmonious condition, just and good action, and the knowledge which presides over it, wisdom, and that which at any time impairs this condition, he will call unjust action, and the opinion which presides over it ignorance.[9]

CRITICAL EVALUATION OF PLATO'S ETHICAL THEORY. According to Lillie, the major contributions of Plato in the field of ethics are: (1) "his recognition that goodness consists in the natural and proper functioning of our human nature" and (2) "his view of society as the normal background of the moral life."[10] These contributions, however, were developed by Aristotle, and it is the Aristotelian enunciation that has been more widely discussed in textbooks and philosophical literature. Perhaps to these two observations of Lillie's should be added the central place of reason and of self-realization as two more contributions of Plato, not to mention the cardinal virtues.

On the critical side of the ledger, it has been noted that Plato has been guilty of a *biverbal definition* in his explanation of happiness. Stace commented:

> If you could conceive an absolutely just and upright man, who was yet weighed down with every possible misery and disaster, in whose life pleasure had no part, such a man would still be absolutely happy. Happiness is, therefore, in Plato, merely another name for the *summum bonum*. In saying that the *summum bonum* is happiness, Plato is not telling us anything

9. Ibid., 4.443–444.

10. William Lillie, *An Introduction to Ethics,* 3d ed. (New York: Barnes & Noble, 1961), p. 278.

> about it. He is merely giving it a new name. And we are still left to enquire: what is the *summum bonum?* what is happiness?[11]

According to Stace, Plato's ethics allowed a man to be in complete control of his appetites, and at the same time be thoroughly selfish, hence evil.[12] Stace also noted that Plato neither denounced slavery nor troubled himself to justify it because he thought it "so obviously right that it needs no justification."[13] But to the credit of Plato, he opposed the prevailing view of his time, namely, that one should do good to friends but evil to one's enemies. Plato, according to Stace, advocated that "it can never be good . . . to do evil. One should rather do good to one's enemies, and so convert them into friends. To return good for evil is no less a Platonic than a Christian maxim."[14]

Plato has also been severely attacked by Fite for his decided partisan prejudice in his advocacy of natural aristocracy.[15] Summarizing Fite's formidable objections, Levinson listed:[16]

> "Defeated . . . irreconcilable aristocrat"; advocate of expensive special privilege;[17] regarding the masses as "not worth talking about";[18] believer in government reserved for gentlemen "to whom the pretensions of the demos are a vulgar intrusion"; one to whom the murderous Critias and Charmides appeared worthy of exoneration because, after all, "they were gentlemen"; one who hoped, perhaps, that if his own political program of enlightened aristocracy were adopted by the Athenians, it would "only reinstate and justify" the old ruling class, himself and his friends;[19] treasonably pro-Spartan, admirer of Spartan narrowness and scorner of lesser breeds, despiser of the "unexampled liberality and enlightenment" of "the 'age of Pericles' " and "all of its works."[20]

Some other scholars shared Fite's views, among them being Popper[21] and Crossman.[22] Popper dismissed Plato's thought as uncompromising

11. W. T. Stace, *A Critical History of Greek Philosophy* (London: Macmillan, 1920), p. 221.
12. W. T. Stace, *The Concept of Morals* (New York: Macmillan, 1937), p. 259.
13. Stace, *A Critical History of Greek Philosophy*, p. 225.
14. Ibid.
15. Warner Fite, *The Platonic Legend* (New York: Scribner, 1934).
16. Ronald B. Levinson, *In Defense of Plato* (Cambridge, Mass.: Harvard University Press, 1953), p. 245.
17. Fite, *Platonic Legend,* pp. 135–136.
18. Ibid., p. 26.
19. Ibid., pp. 132–135, 291.
20. Ibid., pp. 142–152.
21. Karl R. Popper, *The Open Society and Its Enemies,* 5th ed. (Princeton: Princeton University Press, 1966), vol. 1.
22. R. H. S. Crossman, *Plato Today* (New York: Oxford University Press, 1939).

totalitarianism, a contempt for democracy, and a deceptive argument for his own advantage. The anti-Platonists are unreasonably extreme in their vituperations; they forget that Plato scorned Thrasymachus when the latter cynically equated justice with the interests of the ruling class.

The existentialist philosopher Karl Jaspers also criticized Plato, saying that of history Plato knew nothing, nor did he have a consciousness of the terrible, inevitable reality of evil. Furthermore, "Plato's Eros knows no *agapē,* no love of man as man, no love of my fellow man. Consequently, Plato knows no human dignity as a claim of every man on every man."[23]

One must not conclude from these caustic criticisms that the majesty of Plato's philosophy has been diminished, for his influence upon the entire history of philosophy is testimony enough to his dominant position.

Aristotle: Self-Realization and Eudaemonism. Our treatment of Aristotle will be based predominantly upon his book *Nicomachean Ethics,* owing to its completeness, clarity, and organization, and the *Eudemian* version will be referred to for interpretive purposes mainly. Even in antiquity men discussed the *Nicomachean.* Cicero intimated that Nicomachus (Aristotle's son) could well have edited the *Nicomachean Ethics,* hence its title. Few philosophers have enjoyed the reputation of Aristotle, whose influential thought still holds a decided sway today.

A PHILOSOPHY OF HAPPINESS (EUDAEMONISM). Eudaemonism, derived from the Greek *eudaemonia,* signifies a philosophy of happiness —not mere pleasure, but well-being, a happy spirit, a pleasant state of mind. "Happiness then is the best and noblest and pleasantest thing in the world."[24] Aristotle (384–322 B.C.) maintained that an individual's state of happiness resulted from a life governed by reason, moderation, and the actualization of one's potentialities.

Aristotelian philosophy is thoroughly teleological in all of its aspects; all nature—human, animal, vegetable—is made with a purpose, for the reason that "nature makes nothing in vain." The goal for which man is created is the realization of *the good;* consequently, the goal of human activity is the pursuit of good, good being defined as "an activity of the soul in accordance with virtue."[25] Aristotle's view that good, man's highest goal, not only eventuates in happiness, but is in itself a state of happiness, is comparable to the Socratic theory that virtue is happiness. "We always desire happiness for its own sake and never as a means to

23. Karl Jaspers, *The Great Philosophers: Socrates, Buddha, Confucius, Jesus, Plato, Augustine, Kant* (New York: Harcourt, Brace & World, 1962), p. 165.
24. Aristotle *Nicomachean Ethics* 1.10.
25. Ibid., 1.6.

something else. . . . We conceive happiness to be the most desirable of all things. . . . Happiness is something final and self-sufficient, being the end of all action."[26]

Socrates had claimed that knowledge is virtue, and that virtue is happiness. Aristotle agreed with Socrates to a limited extent, asserting that, although virtue produces happiness, not all virtues are of the intellectual type, since some are moral virtues and these depend upon the practical will for their exercise or development. Thus, Aristotle disagreed with Socrates about the intellective will, believing that the individual makes a choice between good and evil, for moral states are voluntary, inasmuch as it is in one's power to act as he chooses. "Virtue and vice are both alike in our own power; for where it is in our power to act, it is also in our power to refrain from acting."[27]

The intellectual virtues result in superlative happiness; however, not all happiness is of equal value or import. The quality of happiness proceeds in an ascending scale from inferior modes (through actualization of our lower natures, as in our vegetative or physical activities), to the median mode (through fulfillment of our animalistic characteristics), and finally to the pinnacle of happiness in its sublimest form (through the blossoming of our highest nature, i.e., our rational or distinctively human nature).

THE LIFE OF REASON. "Activity" is the *conditio sine qua non* of happiness: that activity which human nature requires, involving man's highest characteristic (reason), must be exercised if a person ever expects to experience the sublimest happiness. "Happiness is an activity of soul in accordance with complete or perfect virtue."[28] While activity produces happiness, perfect activity produces perfect happiness. To illustrate by an example of our own: physical activity, such as walking, swimming, or skiing, is a definite source of happiness, but is inferior to that quality of pleasure which a higher form of life can produce. The lower animals achieve a median degree of happiness when they experience pleasant emotions and feelings from the quite proper gratification of their appetites, but man achieves, through the exercise of his supreme nature, the highest degree of happiness. Man's supreme nature, not shared with the animals, is his rational nature (or "divinest part"), with his scientific abilities developed fully, his talents in music, art, and literature, his creativity, in full flower. Happiness emerges from the contemplative life. "The happy life is not one of search for truth, but one of contemplation of truth already attained."[29] In the *Eudemian*

26. Ibid., 1.5.
27. Ibid., 3.7.
28. Ibid., 1.13.
29. William D. Ross, *Aristotle,* 5th ed. (New York: Barnes & Noble, 1949), p. 234.

version, Aristotle defined the ideal as that which "will most produce the contemplation of God."[30] But the contemplative life includes (according to the *Politics*) an aesthetic appreciation of fine literature, music, plastic art, and pictorial art.[31]

In the light of the above, it becomes clear that reason is confronted with the dual task of the pursuit of knowledge and the control or guidance of the emotional and physical life of man, an animal possessing intellect. The man who is blind to reason is also impervious to happiness of the highest quality (happiness in its celestial form).

MORAL AND DIANOETIC VIRTUES. The soul's rational aspect controls desires, the realm where moral virtues are found and where choice is possible. Regular practice makes moral virtue habitual. The virtuous character of such habitual action is due to its conformity with reason. Plato defined virtue as excellence; Aristotle defined it as habitual moderation.

Of virtues, two forms are distinguishable, the ethical and the dianoetic; the ethical virtues fall under the direction of the will but are governed by the intellect—rational control—whereas the dianoetic virtues are of an intellectual nature, as exemplified in science, art, philosophy, and practical intelligence (wisdom). Dianoetic virtues are superior to the ethical virtues, since the latter pertain either to sensual enjoyment on the animal level or to social enjoyments on the human level; but dianoetic virtues pertain to the scientific or philosophical sphere of life.

Practical reason controls the moral virtues. The intellect controls the dianoetic virtues. Unlike Socrates, Aristotle contended that the will has the power to select immoral action contrary to right insight.

THE DOCTRINE OF THE MEAN. The right act, *moderation,* is flanked on either side by a vice. Moral virtue is defined as a mean between two vices, i.e., two extremes, with the vice of deficiency on one side of virtue, and the vice of excess on the opposite side. The mean is defined as what "right reason prescribes."[32] "Virtue then is a state of deliberate moral purpose consisting in a mean that is relative to ourselves, the mean being determined by reason."[33] The moderate amount varies with the individual.

To find the mean is as difficult as it is for some persons to find the center of a circle, for it consists in doing the right thing, to the right person, at the right time, in the right way, for the right purpose, and to the right extent.

> Moral virtue is a mean state; . . . it is a mean state as lying between two vices, a vice of excess on the one side and a vice of

30. Aristotle *Ethica Eudemia,* in *The Works of Aristotle* (London: Oxford University Press, 1915), 1249^b.
31. A. E. Taylor, *Aristotle* (New York: Dover, 1955), p. 99.
32. Aristotle *Nicomachean Ethics* 6.1.
33. Ibid., 2.5.

> deficiency on the other. . . . That is the reason why it is so hard to be virtuous; for it is always hard work to find the mean in anything, e.g. it is not everybody, but only a man of science, who can find the mean or centre of a circle. So too anybody can get angry—that is an easy matter—anybody can give or spend money, but to give it to the right persons, to give the right amount of it and to give it at the right time and for the right cause and in the right way, this is not what anybody can do, nor is it easy. That is the reason why it is rare and laudable and noble to do well.[34]

Either extreme is not equally evil, for some deficiencies are more vicious than certain excesses, while certain excesses are worse than their corresponding deficiencies. "Of the two extremes one is more sinful than the other. As it is difficult then to hit the mean exactly, we must take the second best course, as the saying is, and choose the lesser of two evils, and this we shall best do in the way that we have described, *i.e. by steering clear of the evil which is further from the mean.*"[35] Take for example the virtue of courage with its vicious extremes: cowardice on the side of deficiency, and foolhardiness on the side of excess. If a person's courage fails, it is preferable that he sin on the side of cowardice, in this author's opinion, since the folly of a fool more readily terminates in disaster than the actions of a coward. There is even a saying to the effect that "he who fights and runs away will live to fight another day."

The list of Aristotle's virtues, together with the accompanying vices on the deficient or excessive side, is as follows.

Vice of Deficiency	Virtue (Moderation)	Vice of Excess
1. cowardice	courage	foolhardiness
2. insensibility	temperance	licentiousness
3. stinginess or illiberality	generosity	prodigality
4. meanness or niggardliness	magnificence	vulgarity (ostentatious display of wealth)
5. humility	magnanimity, great-soulness, or high-mindedness	vanity
6. lack of ambition	no name (or a whole-some ambitiousness)	overambitiousness
7. indifference or impassivity	gentleness	irascibility
8. self-depreciation or irony	truthfulness	boastfulness or preten-tiousness

34. Ibid., 2.9.
35. Ibid.

Vice of Deficiency	Virtue (Moderation)	Vice of Excess
9. boorishness	wittiness	buffoonery
10. contentiousness, quarrelsomeness, or moroseness	friendliness	obsequiousness or flattery
(Supplementary—Not Virtues in the Strict Sense, but Emotions)		
11. shamelessness	modesty	bashfulness
12. maliciousness	righteous indignation	enviousness
	The Sum of All Virtues	
13. injustice	justice	injustice

As the supreme virtue, *justice* is the sum of all virtues, the highest, the *complete* virtue. "Justice therefore in this sense of the word, is not a part of virtue but the whole of virtue; its opposite, injustice, not a part of vice but the whole of vice."[36] Justice may refer to the whole realm of virtue (or of vice as injustice) or in a restricted sense to particular goods of fortune, such as honor, property, and the like. In addition to justice being what is lawful (universal justice), *particular justice* would refer to fairness or equality, its extremes being injustice; justice in this sense pertains to proportion. From particular justice there emerge two forms: (1) *distributive justice,* the equitable distribution of wealth and honor among the citizens; and (2) *remedial justice,* fair transactions between two individuals. Inasmuch as justice consists of a moral state (rather than actions), it is difficult to attain.

THE RIGHT ACT. Virtue per se differs from right acts in being a characteristic trait of one's personality, whereas the right act is a single or isolated instance of moderation, the performance of the right thing, to the right person, in the right way, to the right extent, for the right purpose, and so on. Virtue is a personality characteristic that results from the regular practice of the right act until it becomes a habit of the individual.

Accordingly, a person may do the right act without necessarily being virtuous, and conversely, one may be virtuous yet commit an act of vice. Aristotle asks us to consider the case of a man who is faithful to his wife, yet succumbs to the act of adultery once in an unguarded moment of capitulation. Did he commit a wrong act? Yes. Is he an adulterer? No, because the adulterer is one by disposition. A person may be an adulterer without ever having committed adultery; he can be one by natural disposition, except that he has not yet indulged in it for lack of a suitable opportunity.

MORALITY AS SOCIAL. Morality, for Aristotle, is essentially social, because it is impossible to be moral or realize oneself outside of society.

36. Ibid., 5.3.

Since man by nature is a political or social animal or being, he can realize his potentialities properly only within society. Outside of the state, in isolation, ethical virtues are incapable of normal development; consequently, perfection is attainable only within a social milieu. Politics is an aspect of ethics; it comprises social ethics or practical knowledge about men in groups.

Within the state will be found persons who by natural bent are destined to lead, think independently, and make their own decisions, and others who are incapable of autonomous thought or action but prefer to obey the commands for which others are responsible. The former are masters or leaders by nature, while the latter are slaves by nature. "The male is by nature superior, and the female inferior; and the one rules, and the other is ruled; this principle, of necessity, extends to all mankind. . . . He who participates in rational principle enough to apprehend, but not to have, such a principle, is a slave by nature."[37] Each is happiest functioning according to his given nature, the master in assuming responsibility and giving orders, and the slave in obeying them without question. Neither is complete without the other, but together they make a harmonious team; each is contented to perform his duty according to his natural bent. Aristotle did not necessarily have in mind slaves taken by force in military action, but persons who would willingly by innate constitution perform servile or subordinate tasks because of internal tendencies predisposing them to do so.

Critique of Aristotelian Ethics. Though Aristotle objected to the Socratic position of an intellective will (a will directed by one's knowledge or intellect, so that if a man knows what is right he will in turn follow through with right action in accord with his understanding), he nevertheless did in effect espouse the same notion when he thought that he was arguing for a free will. The Aristotelian position is at least quite compatible with the Socratic one, because it holds that causation or motivation is internal and not that all cause is absent. "As far as this view is concerned, a man's choice may be determined by his own beliefs, character, and desires (which, in turn, may be determined by previous causes), and yet be free and responsible."[38] As long as the cause is internal and a person is not under any compulsion from sources extraneous to himself, and provided that his action is free from ignorance of his own doing, then for Aristotle the act will be a responsible one.

The ethical theory of Aristotle has been criticized on the ground that he was merely proposing the ethical standards applied to the behavior prevailing in his time among members of the leisure or moneyed class.

37. Aristotle *Politics* 1254b.

38. William K. Frankena, *Ethics* (Englewood Cliffs, N.J.: Prentice-Hall, 1963), p. 57.

The validity of this criticism becomes obvious when one considers the virtue of magnificence, which Aristotle identified as one belonging exclusively to men of great wealth. F. H. Bradley referred to this brand of ethics as standards for performing the duties of one's station, with the result that a code of ethics for the upper class is produced that would be quite disparate from that of the lower classes. Marx and other socialists would term this kind of ethical doctrines a bourgeois morality that seeks to establish itself as the true and superior moral code.

All "happiness" philosophies are confronted with the difficult problem known as the *hedonistic paradox* (a term attributed to Butler), the argument that the direct pursuit of happiness is impossible because happiness is achieved only as a by-product, the concomitant of that which is in itself not strictly speaking happiness. In other words, there is no direct road to happiness that everyone may take; rather, happiness is a state of mind arising from activity that may be quite remote from anything that is ordinarily designated happiness. Happiness may derive from an arduous accomplishment, a successful competitive feat, rearing a family well, or a host of other activities, but it fails to appear in any direct manner and cannot be overtaken in pursuit.

Not only are hedonistic ethical theories subject to the hedonistic paradox, but these and all other naturalistic ethics that subscribe to the formula of living *according to nature* are brought into question by John Stuart Mill's piquant strictures. The advice that one should live according to nature begs the question as to what is one's nature, and if human nature comprises multifarious qualities, then which is to be given precedence and which should be allowed to atrophy? "That a feeling is bestowed on us by nature, does not necessarily legitimate all its promptings."[39] Experiencing a "natural" impulse to kill or maim another does not morally justify such acts; rather, these impulses ought to be sublimated and channeled into more constructive outlets. Furthermore, the human intellect and moral agency are as natural to man as violent emotion, but what does one do when emotion conflicts with these other human qualities? Obviously, the intelligent course of action is to discriminate wisely and justly before proceeding, rather than allowing one's natural impulses to pour forth without bridling them with suitable control. A desire may be quite natural, but it does not necessarily follow that it is therefore desirable, that is, desirable to express it blindly, indiscriminately, completely, or even at all.

What is indeed considered natural should be constantly open to doubt and revision. For example, Aristotle believed that slavery, being in fact quite natural, should be extensively practiced. His limited knowledge respecting human nature led him completely astray re-

39. John Stuart Mill, *Utilitarianism* (London: Longmans, Green, 1907), p. 62.

garding this aspect of it. Bentham, disturbed by Aristotle's views on slavery, animadverted, "Aristotle, fascinated by the prejudice of the times, divides mankind into two distinct species, that of freemen, and that of slaves. Certain men were born to be slaves, and ought to be slaves.—Why? Because they are so."[40] Mistaken beliefs concerning human nature can become entirely tyrannical when they lapse into dogmatic statements.

These negative comments, although limiting the value of Aristotle's philosophical position, do not, nevertheless, diminish its import. The Aristotelian system is one of the most impressive and influential theories offered; and it has influenced the history of ethical theory for over two and a half millennia.

Thomas Hill Green: Realization of the Human Soul. T. H. Green (1836–1882) was an Oxford professor of moral philosophy who dominated the philosophical scene at Oxford through his influence that lasted for almost half a century. His principal work, *Prolegomena to Ethics,* published posthumously in 1883, was written from a modified neo-Kantian or neo-Hegelian idealistic orientation. The book is not a system of ethics so much as it is a prolegomenon, or groundwork, for an integrated theory.

Repudiating both moral sense theories and utilitarian ethical theories for their inadequate utilization of the place of reason in ethics, and their attribution of man's motivation to naturalistic causes, Green linked motivation with rational consciousness.

SELF-REALIZATION AS THE GREATEST GOOD. Green defined *the good* as the "full realisation of the faculties of the human soul," a realization which consists of a "spiritual activity" both individual and social in nature. Self-realization of the one Divine Mind is the ultimate goal of all rational conduct, and it gradually reproduces itself in man. Man's desire for full self-realization is the only desire that can be truly satisfied, and the fulfillment of this desire is genuine happiness or pleasure, not the pleasures of the hedonists that can never achieve fulfillment. It is not hedonistic pleasure, but the divine within, the ideal of realizing one's capacities, that motivates man. Moral good is not hedonic pleasure; virtue and good are viewed as human perfection, the realization of human capacities, making the most and best of the human soul.

The ultimate good is not some form of pleasure to be pursued, but an "intrinsically desirable form of conscious life," and this intrinsically desirable life is different from pleasure; it is "the full realisation of the capacities of the human soul, of the fulfillment of man's vocation, as of that in which alone he can satisfy himself." Life's fulfillment is

40. Jeremy Bentham, *An Introduction to the Principles of Morals and Legislation* (New York: Hafner, 1948), p. 268.

achieved through actions controlled by one's own "creative energy," yet full self-realization is never final and complete.

> The will of every man is a form of one consciously self-realising principle, which at the same time is not truly or fully expressed in any man's will. . . . By 'practical reason' we mean a consciousness of a possibility of perfection to be realised in and by the subject of the consciousness. By 'will' we mean the effort of a self-conscious subject to satisfy itself. . . . In men the self-realising principle, which is the manifestation of God in the world of becoming, in the form which it takes as will at best only *tends* to reconciliation with itself in the form which it takes as reason.[41]

Thus, it is found that the moral ideal, true good, produces abiding self-satisfaction, and is obtainable only through complete self-realization or perfection, that is, through art and science, the will to know the true and the beautiful; but it is also found in virtue, or the good will, or the will to be good.

THE CRITERION OF MORALITY. The criterion of all valuation, particularly moral, is the realization of the ideal described above. "Our theory has been that the development of morality is founded on the action in man of an idea of true or absolute good, consisting in the full realisation of the capabilities of the human soul."[42] The realization of the human soul is not restricted to a philosophy of individualism, for the self is a social self, and must find its fullest realization in the common good, in social values.

Consequently, good is more than personal; it is social as well. "In saying that the human spirit can only realise itself, that the divine idea of man can only be fulfilled, in and through persons, we are not denying but affirming that the realisation and fulfilment can only take place in and through society."[43] Man's capacities, in order to be fully realized, must be exercised in civil life, or else individual life will fail to attain its reality. Man's reality is fundamentally social. In this respect, the neo-Hegelianism of T. H. Green becomes evident.

PERSONALITY AND SELF-CONSCIOUSNESS. Fundamental in Green's philosophy is the role played by self-consciousness, as this is the link connecting man with personality, morality, society, and God. To begin with, personality is defined essentially as self-consciousness: it is "the quality in a subject of being consciously an object to itself."[44] Thus, self-objectification is the essence of personality, because without self-

41. Thomas Hill Green, *Lectures on the Principles of Political Obligation* (1882) (London: Longmans, Green, 1941), pp. 20–21.
42. Thomas Hill Green, *Prolegomena to Ethics* (Oxford: Clarendon Press, 1883), p. 339.
43. Ibid., p. 218.
44. Ibid., p. 208.

consciousness, self-realization is impossible. Morality, i.e., the realization of the true good, must be in and for persons. God, that is to say, the universe, must also be conceived as personal, for he is the divine principle that is realizing himself in man. Complete self-realization is not merely individual, nor even social, but cosmic or divine. The individual self must be viewed as an aspect of the divine or universal self, because morality is the eternal mind reproduced within the individual.

Interposed between nature and divine consciousness is human consciousness. Consciousness is the ground of man's freedom, desire, and ideals. Man owes his freedom to understanding and to his capacity to will. Consciousness as *knowing,* that is, man as "a subject of intelligent experience," and in virtue of his character as knowing, is a "free cause." He owes this human consciousness to "an eternal consciousness, not existing in time but the condition of there being an order in time, not an object of experience but the condition of there being an intelligent experience, and in this sense not 'empirical' but 'intelligible'."[45] Self-consciousness is inexplicable in terms of physics or natural laws, or even as developing from the unconsciousness. Because man's self-consciousness is related to the divine consciousness, the moral ideal is a desirable state of the self. "The Ego identifies itself with some desire, and sets itself to bring into real existence the ideal object, of which the consciousness is involved in the desire. This constitutes an act of will; which is thus always free, not in the sense of being undetermined by a motive, but in the sense that the motive lies in the man himself. . . . In all willing a self-conscious subject seeks to satisfy itself."[46] The characteristic nature of the good is its ability to satisfy this desire. Moral good satisfies the desire of a moral agent; in moral good he can truly find the satisfaction of himself which he is seeking. True good, accordingly, is "an end in which the effort of a moral agent can really find rest."[47]

SELF-SACRIFICE AND THE SOCIAL CONSCIOUSNESS IN MAN. For man to achieve his ideal, a completely realized life, he must act not merely as a person who lives for himself alone, but as one who lives for others as well. Man, in fulfilling his vocation in art and science, must not neglect the moral virtues as well, which involve other persons in the realization of his personal life. Man must realize himself in a social life of self-conscious persons with a good will, that is, "the will to know what is true, to make what is beautiful, to endure pain and fear, to resist the allurements of pleasure, in the interest of some form of human society."[48] The realization of his ideal may also involve a self-

45. Ibid., p. 85.
46. Ibid., p. 115.
47. Ibid., pp. 195–196.
48. Ibid.

sacrificing will, personal sacrifice for the sake of a higher good, the good of a fuller self-realization with its promise of sublime happiness. "It is equally true that the human spirit can only realise itself, or fulfil its idea, in persons, and that it can only do so through society, since society is the condition of the development of a personality."[49]

VIRTUE AND ULTIMATE GOOD. Virtue is *common good,* a good whose basis is interest, an interest that is expressed in the developing of capacities of persons, and the idea of this good on an unconscious level is responsible for the gradual creation of social institutions. Thus, the interest referred to is an interest in persons capable of similar interest, an interest in virtue. Good will, then, is the only good that is common to all men. Virtue is an end in itself, since it is clear that good will is the true end. Ideal virtue is the "self-devoted activity to the perfection of man." Accordingly, the ethics of self-realizationism is the theory of the good as human perfection.

Ultimate good, human perfection, is a state of desirable consciousness," but "desirable" means "reasonably to be desired," not necessarily *actually* desired, as is the case with hedonism. The rational person, pursuing his moral end, seeks it as his own self-realization and the realization of others, and thereby attains perfection of man, man's ultimate good, namely, a "desirable conscious life, pleasant but not pursued as pleasure."

CRITICISM OF GREEN'S ETHICS OF PERFECTIONISM. Sidgwick raised the question: Suppose all of us are willing enough to will the good, then precisely what is that which we are all willing? The question is, what is good? and it is merely begging the question to answer that good is "the will to promote the will to be good in mankind."[50] Green claimed:

> The good has come to be conceived . . . as a spiritual activity in which all may partake, and in which all must partake, if it is to amount to a full realisation of the faculties of the human soul. Thus the ideal of virtue which our consciences acknowledge has come to be the devotion of character and life . . . to a perfecting of man.[51]

The answer has an attractive ring to it, but what is its meaning? It provides us with no direction. "The state of mind which we are directed to aim at in ourselves and others is a state which involves a fundamental unanswered question: Suppose us all willing the good, what should we all will?"[52] Accordingly, Green has provided only an empty notion. The

49. Ibid., p. 219.
50. Henry Sidgwick, *Lectures on the Ethics of T. H. Green, Mr. Herbert Spencer, and J. Martineau* (London: Macmillan, 1902), p. 73.
51. Green, *Prolegomena to Ethics,* p. 340.
52. Sidgwick, *Lectures on the Ethics of T. H. Green,* pp. 73–74.

most that Green offered by way of content to his will other than the goodness of volition in oneself and in others is "the will to know what is true, to make what is beautiful." But if the good will is simply the will to experience knowledge and beauty, are not then knowledge and beauty the true goods?

Francis Herbert Bradley: Realize Your Station and Its Duties. Considered by some the foremost ethical thinker among the British idealists, the neo-Hegelian philosopher F. H. Bradley (1846–1924) is known principally (in ethics) for his *Ethical Studies* (1876). He enjoyed his peak influence among philosophers during the period from publication of his major work on metaphysics, *Appearance and Reality,* in 1893, to the end of the first decade of this century. Confronting natural evil as a major problem, he held that evil, notwithstanding its existence, is unreal. Considering everything from the standpoint of the whole, he concluded that evil contributes to the world's harmony. Bradley's *Ethical Studies* and *Principles of Logic* (1883) were severe assaults on Mill's utilitarianism and logic.

Under the sway of T. H. Green, Bradley's ethics of self-realization calls for the realization of the true self. His ethical work is more Hegelian than his others, and though an idealist, he found Kantian ethics excessively formal and abstract. Both he and Green were actively engaged in social ethics and social reform. For Bradley, society determines a person's position and status, hence what he is. Thus morality is social, and ethics is a question of one's station and one's duties. It is a socialized self that is realized.

WHY SHOULD I BE MORAL? A basic problem of ethics confronting Bradley is: "Why should I be moral?" which is tantamount to inquiring: "What good is virtue?" or "For what good is it?" These questions imply that virtue is a means rather than an end in itself. But is virtue merely an instrumental good by which we acquire pleasure, health, wealth, and so forth? Is it good for a good, or is it good for itself? "Why should I be moral?" is a compound question which assumes that there is a good, an end in itself that is not morality, but to which morality will lead one.

Bradley asserts that morality *is* an end in itself, and that that end is self-realization, an action which brings about the actualization of that end. "For morality the end implies the act, and the act implies self-realization."[53] The end we seek or "the end we desire is the finding and possessing of ourselves as a whole."[54] Thus, you must "realize yourself" and "realize yourself as a whole." "The self is realized in a whole of ends because it is a whole, and because it is not satisfied till it has

53. F. H. Bradley, *Ethical Studies,* 2d ed. (London: Oxford University Press, 1927), pp. 55–56.
54. Ibid., p. 73.

found itself, till content be adequate to form, and that content be realized; and this is what we mean by practical self-realization."[55]

MY STATION AND ITS DUTIES. "Duty for duty's sake" is meaningless, false, and impossible, unless it signifies the realization of *the good will,* a will superior to oneself, the end of which is self-realization—not an abstract good will, but the will of living finite beings found in a moral organism, conscious of self-realization. The good will is not abstract, but a concrete universal, a moral organism conscious of self-realization of the whole body and the realization of each individual member.

> It gives me the fruition of my own personal activity, the accomplished ideal of my life which is happiness. In the realized idea which, superior to me, and yet here and now in and by me, affirms itself in a continuous process, we have found the end, we have found self-realization, duty, and happiness in one—yes, we have found ourselves, when we have found our station and its duties, our function as an organ in the social organism.[56]

The answer to the question: What is required of us to achieve self-realization? is now made evident by the reference to "our station and its duties." Man is not an isolated being, but a social one, existing in a family, a society, a state. His specific duties are determined by his station in society; particularly, the spirit of its laws and institutions indicate the life he ought to live. "Man is a social being; he is real only because he is social, and can realize himself only because it is as social that he realizes himself. The mere individual is a delusion of theory; and the attempt to realize it in practice is the starvation and mutilation of human nature, with total sterility or the production of monstrosities."[57] The moral world is a social one; otherwise, it would not be real. Ideals too are not real unless one makes them so, and "there is nothing better than my station and its duties, nor anything higher or more truly beautiful."[58]

THE SELF-CONTRADICTION OF MORALITY. Since morality is a process of realization, it is confronted with a self-contradiction, that of the ideal self, which must be actualized in the will, conflicting with the self as it is in process of striving toward the ideal, but always in a state of imperfection. The achievement of the ideal terminates all obligations; consequently, all morality vanishes.

> Morality does involve a contradiction; it does tell you to realize that which never can be realized, and which, if realized, does efface itself as such. No one ever was or could be perfectly

55. Ibid.
56. Ibid., p. 163.
57. Ibid., p. 174.
58. Ibid., p. 201.

> moral; and, if he were, he would be moral no longer. Where there is no imperfection there is no ought, where there is no ought there is no morality, where there is no self-contradiction there is no ought. The ought is a self-contradiction.[59]

Morality impels one toward the ideal goal which makes it possible, but if the ideal goal were to be fully achieved, that would leave no moral end to pursue and thus would destroy the ground or reason for morality as self-realization. Nevertheless, morality motivates us to attain its ideal.

Morality is self-contradictory also for the reason that it is an endless process; "it is a demand for what cannot be." The explanation of the self-contradiction of morality lies in the fact that man is a contradiction. He is both an ideal self and an imperfect self.

MAN'S MORAL CONSCIOUSNESS AND HIS RELIGIOUS CONSCIOUSNESS. The contradiction of morality is resolved in religion, for while morality is imperfect and implies perfection, it finds its perfection in religion. "Morality issues in religion."[60] Religion is practical, the doing of that which is moral; "it implies a realizing, and a realizing of the good self."[61]

However, morality is not identical with religion; religion is superior. For the religious consciousness, the ideal of the individual person's morality becomes a real object, not an abstract idea in the head as is the case with the moral consciousness. "For morals the ideal self was an 'ought,' an 'is to be' that is not; the object of religion is that same ideal self, but here it no longer only ought to be, but also is."[62]

What, then, is this object of religious consciousness? It cannot be finite, a thing or person in the world, nor can it exist in the world; furthermore, it cannot be the sum of all things and persons, since if any individual part is not divine, then their collective aggregation will not produce divinity either. The object of religious consciousness "is the ideal self considered as realized and real. The ideal self, which in morality is to be, is here the real ideal which truly is. . . . We find in the religious consciousness the ideal self as the complete reality."[63] Man's will is given by the object of religious consciousness in order "to realize the ideal." The moral consciousness reveals a bipolar self: myself and the ideal self, as does the religious consciousness, but in the case of the religious consciousness, the ideal self is "real and all reality."

God is the unity of the two natures, and the divine will is the religious consciousness's own true and inmost self. To make the ideal one with my own will, to unite the human-divine and make it my own will, is an

59. Ibid., p. 234.
60. Ibid., p. 314.
61. Ibid., p. 315.
62. Ibid., p. 319.
63. Ibid., pp. 319, 321–322.

exercise of faith, not faith as mere blind belief, but faith as commitment.

> You must believe that you too are one with the divine, and must act as if you believed it. . . . Faith then is the recognition of my true self in the religious object, and the identification of myself with that both by judgment and will. . . . It is the belief that only the ideal is real, the theoretical and practical assertion that only as ideal is the self real.[64]

The moral *ought* becomes a religious fact of reality. The moral ideal which ought to be becomes by faith an accomplished reality.

In conclusion, it may be said that in morality, the process of realization, the ideal end is offered as a claim to be real but only in the process of evolution, while in the faith of religious consciousness, the end is given as a fact already evolved.

CRITICAL COMMENTS ON BRADLEY'S ETHICAL THEORY. A number of the criticisms mentioned in the critique on Aristotelianism are relevant to Bradley's moral views, especially the comment that such views constitute the bourgeois ethic of the man of superior rank or class.

But there are more serious objections to Bradley, among them being his insistence in coupling ethics with religion. He is not the only philosopher who believed that "morality issues in religion";[65] however, there is growing dissatisfaction with ethics involving God, as if one were predicated necessarily on the other, or as if without God ethics would vanish because it finds its sole authority in religion. Notwithstanding the fact that the separation of ethics and religion does not lead to atheism, it is equally true that a valid system of ethics need not be implicated in theism. Many laymen query: If there is no immortality, then why be moral? Such a question assumes that morality must be rewarded in a specific manner, such as assurance of residency in heaven with its attending happiness. Yet, morality can be and often is quite rewarding by being self-rewarding. The Stoics and many other philosophers have testified that "virtue is its own reward"; Diogenes Laertius recorded Plato as saying: "Virtue is sufficient of herself for happiness."[66]

In response to the question, Why are we moral? Baier has said:

> It should be pointed out that, in ordinary contexts, this is not a question that calls for explanation. On the contrary, that people are moral is taken as "natural," as not requiring explanation. Many philosophers who have argued that it is natural to be moral have probably merely wished to assert that such behavior is not strange, odd, foolish, perverse, and therefore in need of

64. Ibid., pp. 325, 328.
65. Ibid., p. 314.
66. Diogenes Laertius *Plato* 42.

> explanation. This point is well taken. A person who is moral need not justify his behavior, or explain it. On the contrary, it is immorality that stands in need of justification and, other things being equal, of explanation.[67]

Basically, Bradley's ethics does not possess the objectivity that he fancied it did, but is essentially a relative ethics contingent on the prevailing mores. Society dictates a man's station and what is expected of him while occupying a given status. Accordingly, Bradley's position does not allow for individuality, because one who leaves the prescribed path of society has in effect strayed from or abandoned his moral duties.

Apparently, Bradley has fallen under the sway of the Hegelian influence by overemphasizing social relationships, for "my station and its duties" reduces ethics to society's prescriptions rather than norms selected autonomously by an individual.

Brand Blanshard: Goodness—The Satisfaction That Ensues upon Fulfillment. Brand Blanshard (1892–   ), an American philosopher of the Idealist school who spent his teaching years at the University of Michigan, Swarthmore College, and Yale University, developed his ethical theory in the influential work, *Reason and Goodness* (1961).

REASON AND GOODNESS: BLANSHARD'S SELF-REALIZATIONISM. One's immediate *duty* is to attempt to find the right act and execute it. Therefore, it is necessary to ascertain the right act in order to perform one's duty, rather than discharging duty for the sake of duty, as Kant advocated. The *right act* is defined as the one which produces the greatest good or at least the one that is not less than the greatest; this latter proviso is necessary in order to cover those exceptional cases in which there are rival actions capable of producing good results of equal quality.

In turn, *good* is defined as that which "fulfils those impulses or strivings of which human nature essentially consists, and in fulfiling them brings satisfaction. . . . *The* good is nothing short of what would fulfil and satisfy wholly."[68] The ends or objectives sought, which constitute the particular goods recognized, are at best provisional, since the fulfillment or satisfaction of any given desire leaves, at the same time, much to be desired, i.e., a residual desire. Consequently, the good of any individual person is constantly undergoing revision; at least the conception of it is.

THE GOOD AND THE DESIRABLE. Blanshard defined human nature as "essentially a set of activities directed toward ends" and human life

67. Kurt Baier, *The Moral Point of View* (Ithaca, N.Y.: Cornell University Press, 1958), pp. 295–296.

68. Brand Blanshard, *Reason and Goodness* (New York: Macmillan, 1961), p. 343.

as "a striving toward these ends."[69] Experiences alone may be considered directly or immediately good, and these experiences may be regarded as intrinsically good, when the following two requirements are met: (*a*) the fulfillment of an impulse, drive, or need, and (as a concomitant of fulfillment) (*b*) the experience of satisfaction or pleasure. Fulfillment and satisfaction are indispensable components; although each may vary independently of the other, yet each is necessary for the attainment of good; otherwise the achieved good is incomplete. Since fulfillment and satisfaction are provisional and incomplete, goodness is always a matter of degree. Ideal goodness would consist of that life which is wholly fulfilled and satisfied. However, no good is absolute in the sense of an actual good capable of giving us permanent contentment.

It becomes evident from what has been said in reference to goodness that it involves a theory of the constitution of the human mind, of value experiences, and of needs or impulses. From the outset in infancy, the process of human consciousness is goal-seeking, a stream of activities directed along a given course as one strives to attain one's ends. The mind initially is motivated by impulse and instinct, but not by desire in the strictest sense of Blanshard's use of the term. Impulse is understood as an urge or felt tendency directing behavior toward a certain course; and desire, although otherwise similar to an urge, involves consciousness of its end as well. It is true that animals also possess these drives, but man's distinguishing feature is his ability to think about his drives, and even elaborate upon them without necessitating the presence of a sense sign or a response from a given stimulus to awaken the idea and maintain it.

Experiences of satisfaction produce and define desires, because past satisfactions cultivate desire. The indifferent or unsatisfactory experiences cannot create or maintain desires within us. The materials of the good life are based upon the strength of instincts and impulses upon which desire is founded. Ideas of that which is truly desirable are contingent upon what man actually desires, in the same sense that desire stems from satisfaction. Consequently, what man considers important, genuinely prized, are objects of satisfaction as reflected in and developed by his desires. Whatever is incapable of being desired cannot be genuinely desirable, and the only candidates for the truly desirable, i.e., *the good,* are those that are capable of being actually desired. Although the good is not, strictly speaking, limited by past satisfactions, it is, however, discovered and ascertained by satisfactions gained through desire, whereas satisfactions are contingent upon innate interests and early successes relating to them.

69. Ibid., p. 315.

PRINCIPAL GOODS. Man's major goods are reducible to forms of impulse-desire; for example, the desire for understanding has its own distinguishable impulse, instinctive curiosity. Thus, the end of the activity of knowing is contemplation, not action, as viewed by the school of pragmatism. As to the number of distinguishable conative drives of impulse-desire in human nature, Blanshard does not hazard a guess on this controversial issue. Man's theoretic impulse drives him to understanding, resulting in knowledge as the concomitant good of its fulfillment; his aesthetic impulse seeks harmony and proportion, and its concomitant fulfillment is the good known as beauty. Each is a different kind of good, the desirable end of its own impulse-desire.

Each good, as the end of impulse-desire, is not only autonomous in its own right, but judged and governed by its own standards implicit in and peculiar to itself. To employ a foreign standard (one belonging to another good) is to do violence to each form of goodness. In this regard Dewey was mistaken in criticizing Platonic good with reference to social consequences, because Plato's objective was the vision of the true, a vision that should be judged by the canons of truth. The views of Tolstoy and Lenin in judging a poem would both be myopic, for the reason that the former would have it judged by its moral influence, and the latter by its value in its application to the class struggle. Each good or impulse-desire directs the process of its own realization toward its desired end, and each has its own purpose.

FULFILLMENT AND SATISFACTION. A genuine good, not a defective one, unites fulfillment and satisfaction; consequently, it is erroneous to assume that, because the good (in order to be good) must satisfy, its quality of goodness depends solely upon the degree of satisfaction or pleasure experienced. "Fulfilment is achieving the end that our impulse is seeking; satisfaction is the feeling that attends this fulfilment."[70] Each has an indispensable function, fulfillment being the attainment of the end that impulse-desire is seeking, and satisfaction being the resultant feeling accompanying fulfillment. Consequently, the most comprehensive fulfillment and satisfaction of impulse-desire possible is the ethical sense of the good.

Comprehensiveness transcends individual or personal impulse-desires to desires generally, desires of all men; such a comprehensive good would be supreme above all, the greatest good (*summum bonum*).

> Though this account of the good lays stress on desire, it is not so much on *de facto* desire, the want or wish of the moment, as on reflective desire, the desire that emerges after correction by thought and experience. The good is what brings fulfilment and its attendant pleasure to desire of this self-amending kind. These desires arise because we are the sort of beings we are,

70. Ibid., p. 309.

> and wisdom lies in making them more accurately and fully expressive of human nature.[71]

Blanshard modestly adds that this theory of the good is not novel, but stems from the ancient Greek philosophers.

RIGHT ACTION. Good, being defined as that experience which satisfies and fulfills, lays the base upon which to define the *right;* for right, apart from good, is meaningless. Right, then, defined in terms of good, is that which "tends to bring into being as much experience that is at once satisfying and fulfiling as any alternative action. . . . An act is right if it tends to produce *not less than* the greatest good attainable."[72]

Inasmuch as many different courses of action may lead to the greatest good, it would be erroneous to speak of *the* right act in the sense of its being the only right one. Unlike G. E. Moore, Blanshard does not claim the right act to be the one that produces the best actual consequences, but the one in which the best are intended or expected, hence the reason for his use of the expression "tends to produce."

DUTIES AND OBLIGATIONS. Blanshard's is an altruistic ethic because it places upon an individual the moral obligation (under certain circumstances) to sacrifice his own satisfactions for that of another person. As the definition of duty, Blanshard offers "the imperative laid upon us by a *summum bonum* which is prescribed by human nature itself."[73] One's duty is to attempt to locate the right act, the right act being that which is productive of the greatest good, and goodness being the fulfillment of those impulses or strivings which comprise human nature.

The right act, defined as the action tending to produce not less than the greatest satisfying and fulfilling experience, may obligate a person to use his efforts in behalf of fulfilling the impulse-desire of another individual whose potential is greater. "Goodness is no respecter of persons, only of the potentialities of persons. If my neighbor's capacities are such as to carry him further than mine toward a rich and satisfying life, his life is more significant, more important, than mine."[74] Caring for imbeciles at the expense of normal persons is a dubious moral practice, and the potential good of a Shakespeare commands us to seek dutifully the fulfillment of his good ends. The dignity of man and sacredness of human personality must be based upon what a man might become potentially, as well as what he actually is.

Implicit in what has been said above is a criterion of morality: "So act as to bring about the greatest good," and from this criterion the concept of *ought* is ascertained. "[To say] I ought to do something is

71. Ibid., p. 313.
72. Ibid., p. 321.
73. Ibid., p. 332.
74. Ibid., p. 322.

ultimately to say that if a set of ends is to be achieved, whose goodness I cannot deny without making nonsense of my own nature, then I must act in a certain way."[75] To produce the good, then, becomes one's duty. Not duty for duty's sake, but duty for the sake of the good. The *summum bonum* grants duty its imperative character. Just as thought does not aim at thinking but at truth, so duty does not aim at duty but at good. The logical ought is the desire to know, and similarly the ethical ought commands as its own end, *the* good that all men seek, and to which all desire aspires. Reason's function in the moral life is the ordering and unification of desires. The goodness of duty, then, is primarily extrinsic. Moral obligation is "the claim upon us of ends appointed by our own nature."[76]

EVIL AND PAIN. Good is defined as the fulfillment and satisfaction of impulse-desire. Intrinsic evil consists of one or a combination of the following: (1) the inability of impulse-desire to attain its end, (2) frustration of impulse-desire, and (3) obstacles confronting impulse-desire. Both fulfillment and satisfaction are necessary requisites of goodness; the failure of either one constitutes a defective or imperfect good. The euphoric idiot may experience much satisfaction yet be low in the fulfillment factor; consequently, he is not enjoying a genuine good, but a defective one.

Evils may assume the form of pain or frustration, though ultimately both are alike. Such is the case with Milton's blindness and Beethoven's deafness. Death, as the greatest of evils, is regarded as such because it is an uncompromising disruption of all one's efforts. "If good consists in fulfilment and satisfaction, their frustration will be regarded, naturally and universally, as evil."[77]

Pain, another archevil, is so regarded because satisfaction ensues from its decrease and demise, and satisfaction is concomitantly inhibited by its increase. Pain flouts both satisfaction and fulfillment; as its intensity increases, the exercise of powers diminishes, and, correspondingly, dissatisfaction grows as pleasure decreases. The blight of satisfaction is either displeasure or pain.

MAN'S NATURE AS BASICALLY GOOD. Moral evil, inverse of moral goodness, is condemnable owing to its potentiality as the "generator of all kinds of other evils." Vice becomes the disposition toward evil because it is bad. Pure malice, if such there be, is the enemy of every kind of good existing. Morally wicked persons are either abnormal or of inhuman construction.

As far as human beings are concerned, pure devils do not exist among them, inasmuch as man is structured so that he is good by nature. This is evident from the fact that human nature is framed in

75. Ibid., p. 331.
76. Ibid., p. 333.
77. Ibid., p. 339.

such a manner "as to seek, inevitably and universally, a set of great goods; his whole life is a groping after them."[78] The same holds true for the criminal, who, although motivated comparably to everyone else, is misguided in his own judgment. The criminal is striving for the same good ends that others desire, but in unapproved and mistaken ways.

> If human nature is governed, as we hold it is, by certain powerful impulse-desires whose fulfilment and satisfaction provide the meaning of good, we should expect that there would be no such thing as moral badness, if that means a settled will toward the bad because of its badness, that choices of the bad as such would seldom or never occur, and that when they did seem to occur, they would generally turn out, on examination, to be choices of evil *sub specie boni.*[79]

CRITICAL COMMENTS ON BLANSHARD'S ETHICAL THEORY. Blanshard's ethics is and has always been teleological in nature. During one period he tended to favor the ideal utilitarianism of Moore, but he abandoned it because of his dissatisfaction with its nonnatural character. True to self-realizationism, Blanshard viewed good as contingent upon fulfillment-satisfaction.

Though T. H. Green and F. H. Bradley, as well as Blanshard, were idealists, there is no social ethic and certainly no trace of Hegelianism in Blanshard, whose satisfaction-fulfillment model of self-realizationism makes no concessions so far as a thoroughgoing individualism is concerned. This characteristic, the absence of any social consciousness or any regard for a social ethic, is perhaps one of the principal inadequacies of Blanshard's position. His view seems to be that morality is "my own business," yet it is impossible to live normally and derive fulfillment or satisfaction in isolation without being in a social setting. Even for me to sit at this typewriter alone has its wide social ramifications, for it is expected that the reader, who is ever in my thoughts, creates a social milieu for what appears at first glance to be a solitary effort. My satisfaction in writing achieves its highest fulfillment when others share the ideas I have expressed by reading them. Without others, my efforts would be almost without purpose.

Blanshard's satisfaction-fulfillment model is deficient for failing to spell out the meaning, particulars, and ramifications of this theory. One is not told specifically what he personally must do to achieve fulfillment; somehow, from a general pattern, a person must fumble his way through and if sufficiently fortunate find fulfillment, not owing to Blanshard's theory but through sheer luck or accident. In other words, when a young student is advised: "Go out and fulfill yourself!" His reply would be: "How? Specifically, what shall I do?" The best that

78. Ibid., p. 342.
79. Ibid.

can be said for the satisfaction-fulfillment model of self-realization is that it may accurately report what has happened to one who has achieved satisfaction-fulfillment. But that is comparable to informing a man who has acquired a million dollars that he is fortunate or successful, without providing the guidelines for him or anyone else to find the path to success. To know what success is, is not the same as routing one's way to it.

Perhaps the most objectionable element of Blanshard's ethics is that portion enjoining one to sacrifice his own life to enrich that of his neighbor's even though his neighbor's life may be already enriched immensely above his own. It virtually suggests that we give to the rich person to make him richer, but the affront is that what is given to him must be taken from the impoverished. Blanshard advised, "If my neighbor's capacities are such as to carry him further than mine toward a rich and satisfying life, then his life is more significant, more important, than mine."[80] He felt justified in making this statement on the claim that goodness is not a "respecter of persons." Not only is this claim clearly untenable; it would be interesting to see Blanshard make a case for goodness without the introduction of persons. Good divorced from persons is meaningless.

To assert that another must be sacrificed for my goals and satisfaction-fulfillment is an affront to democracy. As this author sees the matter, another person (even though he be an idiot) has as much right as anyone else to seek and find satisfaction-fulfillment, and if the search for satisfaction-fulfillment is to be done in concert with the efforts of another, then he should have every right to expect to derive satisfaction-fulfillment for himself rather than merely being ancillary or a contributary to the satisfaction-fulfillment or good of another.

80. Ibid., p. 322.

6

Ethics of Scholasticism and Neo-Thomism: The Vision of God as Man's Highest Good

Scholasticism derives its name from the medieval philosophers who were schoolmen, professors in the universities then extant. The schools, being under the domination of the Christian church, had scholars who endorsed the dogmas of that church. The intellectual achievement of the time was climaxed in the philosophy of St. Thomas Aquinas, from whose thinking neo-Thomism is derived. Neoscholasticism and neo-Thomism, movements growing out of the mid-nineteenth century, attempt to cope with contemporary problems by an updated reapplication of the principles of Aquinas and other representatives of scholasticism.

In this section the ethical doctrines of St. Augustine (354–430) will be treated, as well as those of the scholastic St. Thomas Aquinas (ca. 1225–1274), followed by the views of the foremost contemporary neo-Thomist, Jacques Maritain (1882–). Neo-Thomism adheres essentially to the philosophy of St. Thomas, but adapts Thomistic philosophy for modern application.

Thomistic philosophy was influenced chiefly by Aristotelianism, the philosophy of Augustinianism, and Pauline thought. Through St. Augustine, St. Thomas also made use of certain ideas of Plato, principally those dealing with Plato's four virtues, utilizing them in conjunction with St. Paul's three virtues as a basis for his own discussion of the cardinal virtues. Thus, in St. Augustine's intellectual ancestry are to be found Plato and St. Paul.

By virtue of the papal encyclical of Leo XIII in 1879, Thomism has been declared the official philosophy of the Roman Catholic Church, but not all Roman Catholics adhere to Thomism, as is evidenced by members of the Franciscan order, who embrace Scotism, and members of the Augustinian order, who adhere to St. Augustine's teachings. Protestant thought has been greatly influenced by St. Augustine, particularly through Martin Luther, who was an Augustinian monk.

St. Augustine: Ethics as the Love of God. As will soon become apparent, Augustinian ethics concerns various ways that a person expresses his love for the Deity. For example, even courage (as well as other Platonic virtues) is construed in terms of love.

NATURE AS ESSENTIALLY GOOD. Augustinian ethical theory is premised on the existence of a *good* God who created both nature and man. Inasmuch as God created nature, then by virtue of that fact, it must be good. Anything natural is good. From where, then, does evil come? Obviously, there is much evil in the world. Augustine attributed human evil in the form of war, murder, and the like to man's abuse of free will, man's perverted use of natural objects and of his own personal nature. Natural evil is the privation of good, the absence of good.

EVIL AS PERVERSION OR NATURE DISORDERED. Since God, the creator of both human nature and physical nature, is good, it follows that he created all things good. Taken as a whole, the objects within this world are "very good, because their *ensemble* constitutes the universe in all its wonderful order and beauty."[1] When each thing is in its rightful place and properly regulated, then good is manifest. Evil is perversion, the misuse, abuse, of orderly regulated nature. Evil, then, is a corruption, a disruption of orderly nature.

Nature corrupted is deprived of its order, form, or measure, i.e., its good. Accordingly, evil is anything which injures or abuses that which is natural, thereby frustrating the good, namely, natural processes. A being, any being either man or physical nature, in the process of corruption, is being deprived of its good, its order, its original nature as God created it. "Every being, therefore, is a good; a great good, if it cannot be corrupted; a little good, if it can."[2]

Vice is evil because it runs contrary to human nature; it corrupts man's good nature. This corruption, vice, is contrary to the will of God inasmuch as it runs counter to nature as God created it in its purity. Nature, per se, is never contrary to God's will; but vice, the distortion of natural form, order, is. To condemn nature, including man's, is to judge God as evil; and though one must hate the sin (perversion of man's nature), it is incumbent upon one to love the sinner. The removal of sin from man's nature finds him both good and worthy of love; accordingly, it is not the man we hate, but the sin.

EVIL AS THE PRIVATION OF GOOD. Augustine maintained that evil is the privation of good, its absence. Evil, rather than being an entity, is a defect in good. When the natural object is restored to its pristine state, then evil vanishes, just as healing takes place in the case of a flesh wound or a broken leg. When the painful wound disappears, the leg reverts to its original nature and functions in an orderly manner; thus

1. St. Augustine, *The Enchiridion,* trans. J. F. Shaw (Edinburgh, 1892), chap. 10.
2. Ibid., chap. 12.

good is recovered by means of restoration to a natural state. It is not evil that is abolished (for if evil were a positive thing, then it would still exist); it simply does not exist, except as the absence of good. The absence of good health is evil or ill health, the absence of an orderly state is an evil one, the absence of any natural functioning within man is evil.

Consequently, it follows that, without good, evil cannot exist (because it is a dissolution of good) and is parasitic in character. Evil was never originally created by God, but results as a breakdown in natural order; "from what is good, then, evils arose, and except in what is good they do not exist."[3] From an incorruptible nature, evil cannot result. If nature or human nature, like God's, were incorruptible, then evil would be nonexistent. As long as a person remains true to his nature, he is good.

Whereas evil cannot exist without good, good can and does exist without evil. Although God does not create evil, yet he tolerates it; furthermore, even God's permission of evil is a good act on his part. God's will, which is invariably good, may even at times be fulfilled through man's ill will.

FREEDOM OF THE WILL. The root of all human evil rests with the will of man, his freedom to choose ill or good, to disrupt orderly nature or to promote its harmony. Although all nonnatural evil originates with the evil will of man, it cannot be said that the vitiated will of man stems from God. God gave man a free will, but for man to abuse it by choosing to pervert nature renders it evil. Even the maculate will is the privation of a good one, the good one corrupted. "For the turning from the superior to the inferior, becomes bad, not because the things whereunto it turns is bad, but because the turning is bad and perverse."[4] A man appreciating a beautiful woman does not sin unless his mind turns to lust, the will assenting to evil desire. Desires per se are not sinful, but acceding to them is.

The will can become evil, but there is no *efficient cause* making it so; it does so by means of its own free action; it is its own cause. Morality cannot exist severed from the will, for it is only by virtue of man's possessing a will that his soul and its activities can be designated good. To assert that something can cause the vitiated will is to affirm that God created evil, and, indirectly, the evil will.

As elaborated during his later career, Augustine's concept of the autonomous will with its prime position in the personality is critically emasculated, or at the very least, if it does not topple from its elevated position, it is compromised by sharing a place with the will of a pre-

3. Ibid., chap. 11.
4. St. Augustine, *The City of God,* trans. John Healey (1890), bk. 12, chap. 6.

destined puppet-form of man who is dependent upon grace for the achievement of the exquisite state of the beatified.

The first concession that the will makes to grace is the pursuit of truth through revelation, provided one desires to obtain the blessed state which issues from knowledge. Nevertheless, the will does hold a significant position, in that God's revelations are bestowed upon that individual who, owing to the goodness of his will, proves himself a person worthy of God's truth. Although revelation is derived through faith, faith entails assent (the free exercise of choice by the will) to the revealed ideas—not merely an intellectual acceptance, but a volitional act. Faith, dictated to by a good will, is prior to knowledge, even in those matters of highest import, such as salvation and revelation.

FREEDOM AND PREDESTINATION. The Augustinian antonomous will, rather than being determined by any external entities, including the motives of understanding, determines them. Augustine's attempt to reconcile this doctrine of the freedom of the will to that of his growing predestinationism assumed that the foreknowledge of God lacks causal power to determine the will because it is in a timeless state of eternity, while the uncaused will functions in the present world of time.

Progressively, however, Augustine's doctrine of freedom conceded still more to predestinationism by assuming that only the first man, Adam, had a free will, but by resorting to sin, he involved all subsequent humanity in a corrupted nature incapable of will and goodness, caused by the inheritance of Adam's original sin. Man's redemption is no longer by choice of will, but by God's grace, which elects those persons whom he chooses for salvation by inscrutable divine decree, while others are left to damnation owing to divine justice. Since all good emanates from God, only those redeemed by grace may perform good by virtue of divine revelation. Man's unaided will proves incapable, by sheer effort, of doing good. Good is the activity of the redeemed by grace; and evil is the sin of those of a corrupt nature.

The concept of the freedom of the will was never abandoned completely by Augustine, as is evidenced by his later works, the *Retractions* and *The City of God*. The problem of evil is dealt with by arguing that it is preferable for God to grant man freedom to do good than to create mere puppets incapable of sinning, because of a lack of freedom. Although original sin, caused by concupiscence, corrupts man's nature, yet freedom of will still remains a fact, supported by grace.

ETHICAL DUALISM. An ethical dualism of good and evil prevails in the history of civilization as a battle between God and the redeemed against the devil and his fallen angels, the kingdom of heaven against the world, a race of saints in an alien world against a race of corrupt men in the world quarreling for power and earthly goods. The church, a saving institution of this temporal earthly life, belongs to the kingdom of God rather than to the world. Although an omnipotent God created the world, it remains permanently divided into the realm of Satan and the realm of God's own redeemed—evil and good—each antithetical to the other, an indelible remnant of the Manichaeistic doctrine of Augustine's youth.

The earthly world is man's battleground, the warriors of God on the side of good confronting those of the world and evil. Man's stay on earth is a lasting struggle of the soul combating the forces of evil, the prize being an eternity of peace and everlasting blessedness in the knowledge and contemplation of God.

THE GREATEST VIRTUE (LOVE) AND THE GREATEST GOOD (GOD). The *summum bonum* is God, and the greatest virtue is the love of God, but the perfection which this highest good requires as a condition of its attainment is entrance into the heavenly kingdom. "If you ask us now what the city of God says, first to this question of the supreme good and evil, it will answer you at once: Eternal life is the perfection of good, and eternal death the consummation of evil; and the aim of our life must be to avoid the one, and attain the other."[5] Dods translated the foregoing passage as "Life eternal is the supreme good, death eternal the supreme evil." But, obviously, the life eternal is only the necessary precondition, for the enjoyment of the real highest good, namely, God, for Augustine unequivocally and emphatically stated in his *Concerning the Nature of Good:* "The highest good, than which there is no higher, is God, and consequently, He is unchangeable good, hence truly eternal and truly immortal. All other things are only from Him."[6]

The greatest good is attained by beholding God, divine truth, which renders man blessed. Man's will seeks after God, as this is man's search for happiness, and its satisfaction is found in being in the presence of truth, God, a state of blessed contemplation. This state is comparable to that posited by Plato and Aristotle, who viewed the state of greatest good or happiness as contemplation. In this ideal state of intellectual contemplation of divine truth, the striving of the will ceases, for it has found its peace, its goal, its God. "Thou hast made us for thyself, and our heart is restless, until it find its rest in thee."[7] God, our highest and perfect good, is also the perfection of all good things.

FOUR SPECIFIC VIRTUES. Man's chief good must therefore be not only the object of his pursuit, but also the object of his love, by which he is led to and united with God. Virtue is that which leads to the

5. Ibid., bk. 19, chap. 4.
6. St. Augustine, *Concerning the Nature of Good,* in vol. 1, *Basic Writings of Saint Augustine,* ed. Whitney J. Oates (New York: Random House, 1948), p. 431.
7. St. Augustine *Confessions,* bk. 1, chap. 1.

happy life, God; accordingly, virtue is defined as "nothing else than perfect love of God."[8] Specific individual virtues are simply aspects of the virtue *love,* and are identical with Plato's four cardinal virtues: "Temperance is love giving itself entirely to God; fortitude is love bearing everything readily for the sake of God; justice is love serving God only, and therefore ruling well all else, as subject to man; prudence is love making a distinction between what helps it towards God."[9] By means of these four virtues, by love, we are led to God and, consequently, to our reward, eternal life and knowledge of truth which is our highest good, that is, God. Accordingly, to live well is to love God.

Ancillary to the love of God is the love of self and neighbor, for this is the best path to the love of God. Love of God, then, is the sole essence of moral value, with its fourfold characteristic. From love springs faith, and from faith love flourishes to fullness; a synthesis of the two yields hope, the joyful longing of love.

St. Thomas Aquinas: The Vision of God as Perfect Happiness. The ethical theory of St. Thomas is dominated by Aristotelianism with strains of Plato and even stronger elements of St. Augustine and St. Paul. The Thomistic ethic is *eudaemonistic* in espousing the search for happiness; teleological in designating the purpose or striving of man as the search for goodness, namely, God; and intellectualistic in concluding that the final end of man is the contemplation of God.

THE SUMMUM BONUM: HAPPINESS IN THE VISION OF GOD. Like Aristotle, Aquinas believed that all nature, human and nonhuman, was so designed as to act for some end, which is its good. The purpose or end of everything is a good, namely, God. Since all things are directed to this end, it follows that all things tend to be like God; have a disposition (*synderesis*) to be like God, seek to imitate divine goodness. This natural tendency of created things to be like God stems from his being their cause; therefore he is responsible for the direction of things toward himself. Things devoid of knowledge seek their good, just as every intellectual substance (souls, human beings) does. Consequently, for the intellectual substance to reach its goal, it must fulfill its nature, attain its own good, the knowledge of God.

The goal of any intellectual substance, a human soul, is to know God. True human happiness does not consist in carnal pleasure, honors, glory, wealth, worldly power, material goods, sensuous goods, art, prudence, or even moral virtue; but, rather, it consists ultimately in the contemplation of God. The intellect was made to seek truth, and is therefore satisfied when it finds absolute truth, the vision of God.

However, man's ultimate happiness is unattainable in this life, inasmuch as the vision of God, that is, seeing God in his essence, is impos-

8. St. Augustine, *On the Morals of the Catholic Church,* trans. Richard Stothert (Edinburgh: T. and T. Clark, 1872), chap. 15.
9. Ibid.

sible in this life, because earthly creatures can know God analogically, by reason only, not face to face. Man has an innate desire which cannot be set at rest until it possesses the knowledge of God, and then he finds peace of soul. Nevertheless, the human creature cannot see God's essence with his unaided natural abilities, but requires the assistance of divine light to attain the vision of God in his essence. The created intellect, man, is limited in all that can be seen of God, and consequently, has only a degree of participation in the divine vision, some men possessing a more perfect vision of God than others. The perfect vision of God is reserved for the life to come, and those with a vision of God are made partakers of eternal life; they will not only see him forever, but their every desire will be fulfilled, complete with ultimate happiness. While he is on earth, man must be content with partial happiness, temporal good, imperfect beatitude.

THOMISTIC VIRTUE. Natural virtues, intellectual and moral, are dispositions of perfect things (things perfectly disposed according to nature) to achieve that which is best, and are defined in terms of habits. St. Thomas's definition of virtue is: "Virtue is a good habit of mind, by which we live righteously, of which no one can make bad use."[10] Thus, virtues are good habits, operative habits productive of good works, perfecting man that he may live well, consequently directing him to his ultimate end, happiness.

INTELLECTUAL VIRTUES. The intellectual virtues, consisting of understanding, science, and wisdom, are so regarded owing to their ability to perfect the speculative intellect to pursue its good, the truth. Understanding is the habit of discerning principles; science perfects the intellect for deducing conclusions; and wisdom, whose considerations entail the highest causes, sublimest knowledge, judges and orders all truth.

MORAL VIRTUES. Whereas the intellectual virtues guide the reason, the moral virtues direct the appetite toward right living. Moral virtue consists of a mean which directs man to his good by perfecting the appetitive part of man's soul and requires conformity to its governing rule or measure. Evil, conversely, is imbalance, an extreme of excess or deficiency.

Among the moral virtues are found four principal or cardinal virtues, namely the four Platonic virtues of prudence, justice, temperance, and fortitude. The latter two are virtues whereby reason controls the passions, and the former two are virtues whereby reason controls itself (prudence) or other actions besides the passions (justice).

THEOLOGICAL VIRTUES. In addition to the natural virtues discussed above, there are three theological virtues: faith, hope and love, or

10. St. Thomas Aquinas *Summa Theologica* in *The Basic Writings of Saint Thomas Aquinas,* ed. Anton C. Pegis (New York: Random House, 1945), Q. 55, Art. 4 (vol. 2, p. 416).

"charity" (a triad which St. Thomas took from St. Paul). Unlike other virtues, the theological virtues do not consist of a mean, but increase in strength as one ascends to the summit; moreover, they are infused in us by God, and become known to us by divine revelation through the Christian sacred scriptures. Therefore, they must be distinguished from both moral and intellectual virtues. Theological virtues direct man to supernatural happiness with the assistance of the divine, that is to say, they direct us to God. Consequently, the rule and measure of theological virtues is God himself, rather than mere reason, as was true in the case of natural virtues, for the measure of theological virtues requires superhuman power. Faith is rule (control of events) according to God's truth, charity is rule according to his goodness, and hope is rule according to his omnipotence and love. The theological virtues shed supernatural light upon the intellect, equipping it with supernatural principles: faith leads the way to that which is to be believed, hope directs the will to this end as attainable, and charity transforms the will into a spiritual union with that end. In this manner, man's appetite, yearning, is moved toward its natural end, that is, is directed to God, its good.

Of the theological virtues, love is supreme; of the intellectual, wisdom; and of the moral, justice. Inasmuch as the intellectual virtues perfect reason, their excellence surpasses the moral virtues, which perfect the appetite. All virtuous action has the same purpose, the direction of man to his final end, his good, which is happiness, and this is achieved by means of the conformity of action to the rule of reason, with the exception of theological virtues, whose rule is God.

THE RIGHT ACT. As its ultimate goal, the human will desires happiness, the right act being that action which is the means to the attainment of ultimate happiness. For every act of will, every deliberate act, to be moral, it must be in accord with right reason, since reason directs us to God. Accordingly, if man's lower natures, his vegetative and sensitive (physical and animal) natures, are to be aligned with morality, they must be ordered according to reason, rationally directed.

SIN. Besides being something contrary to reason, sin is that which is contrary to eternal law, God's reason. As a human act, sin is a voluntary act; it is a word, deed, or desire which is contrary to eternal law, the prime law of God which directs man to his end, i.e., good, happiness, and God. Sin, on becoming habitual, is vice, for vice consists of being ill-disposed, disposed in a manner not befitting one's nature. Vice, therefore, is contrary to virtue and to nature.

Sin stains the soul, mortal sins indelibly so. Venial sins are pardonable because reparable, whereas mortal sins are irreparable because they destroy charity and turn man away from God, hence call for eternal punishment. Punishment is meted in proportion to the severity of sin; for venial sins, the punishment is only temporal. Among the mortal sins, those which transgress the love of God are blasphemy and perjury, whereas those which transgress the love of neighbor are murder and adultery.

LAWS: ETERNAL, NATURAL, HUMAN, AND DIVINE. All laws stem from God, who ordained them for the common good as rules and measures of human acts in order to direct man to his end. Among the various kinds of law, St. Thomas distinguished four: (1) *Eternal law* is so termed because it is the law of God's regulative reason, his conception of things by supreme reason which is not temporal, not subject to time, but everlasting. (2) *Natural law* is law dependent upon man's ability, owing to his rational nature, to be able to participate in eternal law, hence his ability to discern good and evil by the divine light within him, which is the function of natural law; natural law cannot be altered, for it emanates from human nature; for example, the natural law of self-preservation cannot be changed. (3) *Human law* is law devised by human reason to arrive at particular determinations; it constitutes our body of civil laws, humanly devised laws which are derived from natural laws. (4) *Divine law* is that law which man receives by special revelations from God, such as those found in the Bible. These exceed man's ability, and complement the natural laws by providing man with laws beyond his competence to judge.

Eternal law is part of the nature of God, existing in him, and as the exemplar of divine wisdom, is the source of all law, including natural law, which is part of the nature of man. Man's inclinations express natural law, as is evidenced by the drive of sex and the drive of self-preservation. Universal dictates of right reason in their entirety constitute the natural direction to the pursuit of man's good. From reason, then, the will receives its moral dictates, its obligations, but reason does not capriciously impose them. Rather, it derives them from the object of practical reason, the good or God, which issues in happiness for the soul that attains its object. Though reason imposes obligations, nevertheless it is grounded upon human nature, a nature designed by God, with God as its object. Thus moral law is both natural and rational, a law of nature made articulate and obligatory by reason.

The precepts of natural law are arranged in a hierarchical order which corresponds to the order of natural inclination: the first natural inclination is one which man shares with every substance, self-preservation; the second is an inclination shared with animals, sex and training of offspring; the third is a natural inclination which is singularly human, because it pertains to man's rational nature, that of yearning to know truth concerning God and to live socially among men. Inasmuch as human nature does not change, neither does the natural law, and concomitantly the moral law does not either.

WILL VS. INTELLECT. It will be recalled that in discussing good and evil, St. Augustine gave the place of first importance to the will, but St. Thomas attributes greater power to the intellect. St. Augustine had assigned a place of central importance to the will despite the neo-Platonic influence that made him regard the goal of man as the contemplation of God, whereas the intellectualism of St. Thomas dominates his philosophy throughout, rendering the will subject to the intellect, with the final goal of both will and intellect being the contemplation of God, a vision of the divine essence. Reason dictates, and the will acts accordingly, yet both pursue the same end of achieving the perfect beatitude, the essence of God, which is the essence of goodness. The vision of God of which these men speak is from the beatitude of Jesus: "Blessed are the pure in heart, for they shall see God."

Jacques Maritain: Ethics of Theocentric Humanism. Maritain has developed an ethical theory based upon the scholasticism of St. Thomas Aquinas, yet with sufficient modifications to make it peculiarly his own. Strains of humanism and personalism are dominant in his theory, for which he has had various names such as *Christian humanism, true humanism, integral humanism,* and *theocentric humanism.*

ANTHROPOCENTRIC HUMANISM. The modern image of man stems chiefly from the thought of Descartes, Locke, and Rousseau, who, according to Maritain, made modern man angelic, as innocent as Adam, a Christian gentleman no longer requiring grace, miracles, or revelations, for he was the product of natural religion. Man's redemption stemmed from the fundamental goodness of his nature. The secularization process elevated nature above God and Christ, completing the philosophy of anthropocentric humanism.

Anthropocentric humanism, a product of materialism and positivism, rejecting absolute truth and values, depicted modern man as one who "knew truths—without the Truth,"[11] the truth being supratemporal, absolute, proceeding from either God or reason. Secular humanism construed man as divine, granting him dignity and basic human rights, but without God; peace and fraternity, but without Christ; brotherly love, but without the love of God. It dismissed evil as an imperfect or temporary stage in evolution which would eventually be transcended. Worshiping life as of infinite value, but denying the soul, secular man gives money, but not himself—his soul. He leads "a life in common without common good";[12] believes in liberty, but not with self-mastery, moral responsibility, or free will; believes in "equality—without justice,"[13] in enslavement to machines and the law of matter. He looks for happiness, for utility, but without a purpose; and for democracy,

11. Jacques Maritain, "Christian Humanism," *The Range of Reason* (New York: Scribner, 1952), p. 187.
12. Ibid.
13. Ibid.

but without brotherly love. Bankrupt in principles, and without values, he is left to a "universe of words, a nominalistic universe."[14]

The present outcome of secular humanism that has dismissed God for man is the position of Marxism and Nazism. Marxism, with its godless temporal salvation, is an alienation of man and forfeits his personality by dissolving his individuality into a collective man, an organization man devoid of free will, eternal destiny, and the image of God, who survives in the collective consciousness as a mere "particle of the social whole."[15] Communion is reducible to economy activity, and paradise to a human endeavor, in a fabricated "world beheaded of reason,"[16] where personality is sacrificed to the god of industry. Marxism's "intoxication with matter"[17] leads to self-degradation, over-optimism, and the "animalization of the image of man,"[18] wherein human dignity is exchanged for a species of man sprouting from the "genealogical tree of monkeys."[19] Human personality is reduced to animality, interpreting reason and freedom of will as merely illusory; spiritual men endowed with "poetic creation, human pity and devotion, religious faith, contemplative love, are only the sublimation of sexual libido or an outgrowth of matter. Man is unmasked, the countenance of the beast appears."[20] God has been abandoned by man, who has also lost track of his own soul, vainly taking refuge in masks, behind which is death.

Marx, Darwin, and Freud have contributed to this picture of modern man up to this point; they did it on the basis of eliminating God by use of reason, but Nietzsche, with his philosophy of irrationalism, despising intelligence, adds his contribution to anthropocentric humanism by proclaiming the superman, will to power, death of truth, and death of God. Rejecting optimism, morality, freedom, dignity, justice, peace, and goodness, he ushered in Nazi racism, with its mysticism of instinct, hatred of reason, perversion of language, and demonic religiosity, reducing God to a racial demon; and man, a *Volksgeist,* a political whole, finds "self-realization through violence,"[21] with not even the promise of a "decoy of happiness and liberty,"[22] but only a biological inferno with its bloody sacrifices, with "reason gone mad,"[23] and man sacrificed to the "blind god of history" with its "good tidings of Deception."[24]

14. Ibid., p. 189.
15. Ibid., p. 190.
16. Ibid.
17. Ibid., p. 191.
18. Ibid.
19. Ibid.
20. Ibid.
21. Ibid.
22. Ibid.
23. Ibid.
24. Ibid.

THEOCENTRIC HUMANISM. In opposition to this view, theocentric humanism seeks to construct a new Christendom built upon Christian values by regenerating the human community through the restoration of man's true image. It is an *integral humanism,* reconciling the temporal or secular with the eternal or divine. Personality with human rights and human dignity is restored, not in separation from God, but including him, from whom stems the dignity of man. This new God-centered humanism would integrate human and divine by introducing "a new Christian order no longer sacred but secular in its forms. . . . This new humanism, which has in it nothing in common with bourgeois humanism, but has a real and effective respect for human dignity and for the rights of human personality, I see as directed towards a socio-temporal realisation of that evangelical concern for humanity which ought not to exist only in the spiritual order, but to become incarnate; and towards the ideal of a true brotherhood among men."[25]

Theocentric humanism would introduce the divine into the temporal order, thereby sanctifying it, thus uniting God and the world. The result would be a democracy based on *Christian personalism,* an awakening of the Christian conscience, a temporal world existentially attached to Christ, with love the basis of liberty, justice, civic friendship, and social regeneration.

NATURAL, MORAL, AND ETERNAL LAW. The true image of man, according to integral humanism, unites the body of man (the result of an evolutionary process) with his immortal soul (the creation of God). Man's dignity is derived from the image of God, and human rights are derived from God-given natural laws. *Natural law* (part of man's nature), inasmuch as it issues from *eternal law* (the nature of God) and is known by practical reason as a guide for man's conduct, becomes moral law. Our moral laws, then, are natural laws; as such, they reflect eternal law, the "eternal wisdom of God and the divine essence itself,"[26] upon which natural law is founded. "The eternal law is not written upon paper, it is promulgated in the divine intellect and is known in itself solely by God and by those who see Him and His essence."[27]

CHRISTIAN HUMANISM AND THEOCENTRIC HUMANISM. Human nature and moral law are given to man by the eternal plan of the wisdom of God. Man, as the image of God, is called upon to live a divine life, and a natural one of realizing the potentialities of his God-given nature by subjugating his animal nature and the material world to the dominion of reason, with the aid of God and his own freedom.

25. Jacques Maritain, *True Humanism* (New York: Scribner, 1938), pp. xvi–xvii.

26. Jacques Maritain, "Natural Law and Moral Law," in *Moral Principles of Action,* ed. Ruth Anshen (New York: Harper & Row, 1952), p. 65.

27. Ibid., p. 68.

Reason and love will revitalize and elevate human history. God's love participates in man's love for man, vitalizing the natural virtue of friendship. Such love renders unequals equal. Knowing that death does not end all, man sacrifices for man willingly, even dies for those he loves. Imperishable man becomes a "god by participation." God is the ultimate end of man in *Christian humanism,* and man tends toward God through self-perfection, from the imperfect happiness of earthly existence to perfection of love, in a vertical movement toward the divine where self-perfection and God are united. A horizontal movement of the temporal aims of civilization is augmented by the vertical movement of eternal souls.

Theocentric humanism gives history a meaning, a direction, and a supreme ideal, namely, the institution of a brotherly city where standards of justice and friendship will be continuously perfected. The supreme ideal calls for the "inauguration of a brotherly city" with "the hope that the existential *state* of human life and the structures of civilization will draw nearer to their perfection, the standard of which is justice and friendship."[28] "The inauguration of a common life which responds to the truth of our nature, freedom to be achieved, and friendship to be set up at the core of a civilization vitalized by virtues higher than civic virtues, all these define the historical ideal for which men can be asked to work, fight, and die."[29]

Evaluation of Scholastic Ethics. The major objection lodged against the scholastics is that their philosophies are not conclusions derived from the spirit of free thought and human experience, but are foregone conclusions imposed upon these thinkers by a hierarchical church to which their conclusions must give way. The strength of this objection is readily seen in the method of scholasticism: a person accepts the dictates of church dogma (which are considered by the institution as eternal truths); then he seeks reasons to justify the church's foregone conclusions.

A more serious objection to St. Thomas's thought is that it offers virtually nothing original, but is an eclectic, or borrowed, philosophy. Nevertheless, it does contain some distinctively Thomistic or original ideas. Furthermore, a unique synthesis is a contribution in its own right.

Perhaps the objections confronting the philosophy of Aquinas are more valid in respect to Maritain, the most influential neo-Thomist of this century. Yet Maritain, despite his desire to be known as a *paleo* (old) Thomist, rather than a *neo* (new) Thomist, has also made original contributions in the form of Christian humanism, the synthesis of evolutionary theory and humanism with Christianity, the synthesis of

28. Maritain, *Range of Reason,* p. 198.
29. Ibid.

existentialism with Thomism, and the synthesis of personalism with scholasticism. The fact that he did not exercise his intellectual liberation by breaking sharply from neo-Thomism can be counteracted by his claim that it was his intellectual right and free thought that led him to neo-Thomism, as is true with some Protestant neo-Thomists, as, for example, Mortimer Adler.

More specifically, Thomism and neo-Thomism suffer from the same objections as those made to Aristotelianism. From the standpoint of democratic thinking, it is repugnant to believe that certain individuals are privileged to do the thinking for others and to direct their destinies, while other persons are obliged to follow blindly. If Thomism is true, then democracy is a mistaken notion.

The objection relating to persons becoming servile followers without questioning authority becomes even more grave when affiliated with theophanic experiences that are supposedly above question. St. Paul, for example, asserted authoritatively that all earthly power is given by God, hence must be obeyed. The inference is that reform is precluded, and that even evil leaders must be obeyed. The Thomists accept this position, because they see all law, including civil and moral law, as eventually originating from divine law.

An objection raised by Mothershead is that Thomistic ethics eliminates all hopes of progress, since "if what man is *now* defines good, all so-called progress must be evil."[30] In other words, the only option open to man is to remain at a standstill or to deteriorate by perversion. Such a thought has a stultifying effect on society; this is confirmed by the fact that the medieval period was one characterized by the lack of progress in social institutions, as indicated by references of some historians to it as the "Dark Ages."

30. John L. Mothershead, Jr., *Ethics* (New York: Henry Holt & Co., 1955), p. 301.

7

Classical Intuitionism: The Immediate Apprehension of Moral Principles

Of the classical forms of ethical intuitionism, the present chapter will treat four types: (1) the theories of two Cambridge Platonists, Ralph Cudworth and Richard Price; (2) Joseph Butler's conscience theory; (3) James Martineau's idiopsychological theory; and (4) Josiah Royce's ethics of loyalty. Kantian intuitionism, a deontological intuitionism (ethics of duty), together with later forms of intuitionism, will be discussed in chapter 8.

By ethical intuitionism is meant the theory of the immediate apprehension of right and wrong, the possession of innate conceptions of moral principles by a unique moral faculty or moral sense somewhat comparable to other human senses. Right, good, duty, and justice, are directly intuited, independently of any appeal to consequences in order to discriminate right from wrong. Moral truths are grasped immediately as self-evident truths known by means of moral intuition.

Moral right and wrong can be ascertained without resorting to the outcome or consequences of one's behavior, as is the case according to utilitarianism. Intention, motive, will, and the like are regarded as moral or immoral, whereas the consideration of ulterior consequences is irrelevant. Sidgwick explained this distinction as follows: "The fundamental assumption of intuitionism is that we have the power of seeing clearly what actions are in themselves right and reasonable. Though many actions are commonly judged to be made better or worse through the presence of certain *motives,* our common judgments of right and wrong relate, strictly speaking, to *intentions.*"[1] The only indispensable motive is the will to do right.

Unlike teleological theories of ethics, which identify the right act by reference to the *summum bonum* (greatest good), the good pursued, or the good desired, intuitionists claim to be able to comprehend the right act without reference to the end, that is, without regard for the ultimate consequences of the act. The classical intuitionist considers moral

1. Henry Sidgwick, *The Methods of Ethics,* 7th ed. (London: Macmillan & Co., 1907), p. xxviii.

obligations and moral actions intrinsically good, not merely a means to a good. Furthermore, despite the act's being good, the consequences can possibly be disastrous, and vice versa. "Let justice be done though the heavens fall" well characterizes intuitionism, especially the Kantian mode.

THE CAMBRIDGE PLATONISTS

A small group of philosophers and theologians in the seventeenth century, most of whom were connected with Cambridge University, ushered in a renaissance of Platonism in ethics and theology, coming to be known as the Cambridge Platonists. Their views were reactionary, and the form which this reaction assumed was an attack upon Thomas Hobbes—his naturalism, his empiricism, and his atheism. They found their rallying point in a metaphysical basis for moral principles grounded on Platonic idealism and Cartesian innate ideas.

Although the founder of Cambridge Platonism was Benjamin Whichcote, in the area of ethical theory its principal proponents were: Ralph Cudworth (1617–1688), Henry More (1614–1687), and Richard Cumberland (1631–1718). Perhaps the most important ethical theorist of this general type of intuitionism was the Cambridge Platonist Richard Price (1723–1791), author of *A Review of Chief Questions and Difficulties of Morals* (1757).

Cambridge Intuitionism Defined. Platonic in outlook, the Cambridge moralists argued that moral law is eternal and immutable, an absolute law issuing from the character of God, which never changes. As statutes of right and wrong, moral laws are discernible by every rational being intuitively, as is the case with Platonic ideals. Unlike the hedonists, who approve of the right inasmuch as it directs one to good (pleasure), the intuitionists approve of right for the reason that it is true, basing their contention on the fact of man's rationality. As an intelligent being, man cannot but approve of the true, else it would be folly. One chooses the right because it is real and true, for will serves rational preference, right and wrong being forms of true and false. One becomes dutiful owing to his rational character. To will what ought to be is to understand what eternally and immutably is, for right is both axiomatic and self-evident.

Richard Cudworth: Moral Principles as Eternal and Immutable. The most distinguished of these neo-Platonic Cambridge moralists is Cudworth, who, under the influence of Platonic ideas and renewed inspiration emanating from Cartesianism, undertook to establish moral principles upon an "eternal and immutable" basis.

MORAL LAWS AND ETHICAL OBJECTIVITY. Moral laws, being eternal and immutable, are independent of the will of any being, including the divine being. Just as God cannot make a circle square, he cannot alter the nature of immutable moral good. "Moral good and evil, just and unjust, honest and dishonest . . . cannot possibly be arbitrary things, made by will without nature; because it is universally true, that things are what they are not by will but by nature."[2] By "nature" is not intended physical nature, but the nature of principles, mathematical principles and moral ones. "Neither can Omnipotence itself (to speak with reverence) by mere will make a thing white or black without whiteness or blackness; that is, without such certain natures. . . . Omnipotent Will cannot make things like or equal one to another, without the natures of likeness and equality."[3] The natures are the qualities of the objects as well as their essence.

Thus good and evil possess objective ontological status and validity, are real in their own right, and are known by reason in the same manner in which principles of mathematics are apprehended. From divine reason, knowledge regarding them proceeds to the human mind, because their truth is akin to intelligible and universal essences of mathematics. Eternal truths, being part of the makeup of God, eternal and unchangeable as God himself, hold true for God as well as for man, even as the laws of geometry do. Consequently, there exists in the universe an objective sphere in which right and wrong moral principles exist, and these moral, immutable objects of good and evil, just and unjust, man's reason apprehends. Even as God had no choice as to whether he would be omniscient or omnipotent, he lacked choice as to the eternal and immutable nature of moral good and evil. "The will and power of God have no command inwardly either upon the wisdom and knowledge of God, or upon the ethical and moral disposition of his nature, which is his essential goodness."[4]

EVALUATION OF CUDWORTH'S ETHICAL THEORY. Cudworth, as one of the Cambridge Platonists, sought to accord a status to ethical principles comparable to geometrical figures, so that they would have a "constant and never-failing entity of their own." His departure from Plato consists in his relegating the eternal and immutable moral ideas to the mind of God, whence they are conveyed to man's mind. Cudworth's shortcoming is in terminating his system abruptly at this juncture, without offering a list or code of morality. But this deficiency is common to all of the classical intuitionists of Cudworth's period.

Instead of being a systematically complete ethical theory, Cudworth's is principally a polemic. He sought to attack two views, one common to Duns Scotus, Ockham, Calvin, and Descartes, and the other espoused by Hobbes. The former believed, as Descartes explained, that if God chose to do so, he could make a cube identical with a sphere, or right

2. Ralph Cudworth, *A Treatise Concerning Eternal and Immutable Morality* (London, 1731), chap. 2, sect. 1.
3. Ibid.
4. Ibid., chap. 3, sect. 8.

identical with wrong; on the other hand, Hobbes reduced morality to legality, to the will of sovereigns. Morality was relegated by Cudworth to an objective, immutable, eternal sphere, where it possesses a universal essence of its own.

Richard Price: Moral Truths as Innate. According to Price, reason discerns moral truths directly by an innate intuition that is capable of immediately apprehending right and wrong in a manner comparable to intuiting logical and mathematical principles. "We have a power immediately perceiving right and wrong; . . . this power is the Understanding."[5] The axiomatic moral principles command obligation in "virtue of natural and antecedent right," not by a will; "it is truth and reason, then that, in all cases, oblige, and not mere will." The eternal moral truths apprehended directly by reason are moral imperatives, "nothing then becoming obligatory, which was not so from eternity; that is, obeying the divine will, and just authority."[6]

Moral principles are God's will for the reason that they exist from all eternity as immutable objects. "Thus, then, is morality fixed on an immovable basis, and appears not to be, in any sense, factitious; or the arbitrary production of any power human or divine; but equally everlasting and necessary with all truth and reason."[7] No will whatever has the power to render things good or obligatory unless they possessed goodness antecedently from all eternity.

MORALITY AS IMMUTABLE AND ETERNAL. In the same sense that geometric principles are eternal and immutable, so, too, are moral axioms; and in the same sense that geometrical principles are apprehended intuitively by reason, so are moral laws also apprehended intuitively. "Morality is eternal and immutable. Right and wrong, it appears, denote what actions are. Now whatever any thing is, that it is, not by will, or decree, or power, but by nature and necessity. Whatever a triangle or circle is, that it is unchangeably and eternally. It depends upon no will or power, whether the three angles of a triangle and two right ones shall be equal. . . . Every object of the understanding has an indivisible and invariable essence; from which arise its properties, and numberless truths concerning it."[8]

Even the omnipotence of God is incapable of altering the nature of these eternal truths: moral, logical, and mathematical. These are necessary truths that cannot be destroyed by any power, human or divine, and their destruction would entail the destruction of reason and knowledge itself.

THE INDEFINABILITY OF RIGHT. To define rightness is an impos-

5. Richard Price, *A Review of the Principal Questions in Morals,* 3d ed. (London, 1787), chap. 1.

6. Ibid.

7. Ibid.

8. Ibid.

sibility, inasmuch as it is a simple notion, consequently indefinable. Its reality is indubitable, discernible through immediate apprehension by a rational being only. " 'Tis a very necessary previous observation, that our ideas of right and wrong are simple ideas, and must therefore be ascribed to some power of immediate perception in the human mind. He that doubts this, need only try to give definitions of them, which shall amount to more than synonymous expressions."[9] Note the striking resemblance between this theory of the indefinability of right and that of G. E. Moore's concept of the indefinability of good (discussed in chapter 4) and W. D. Ross's indefinability of right (discussed in chapter 8).

The confusion in ethical theory, claimed Price, arose from failure to recognize the fact of the indefinability of right. Unless right and wrong are directly perceived by a power within the rational person, capable of immediately perceiving such, then he will be forever blind to right as an axiomatic truth.

EVALUATION OF PRICE'S ETHICAL POSITION. Like Cudworth, Price is also polemical, although constructively so. Assuming a position that is interestingly related to that of Butler and Kant, Price differs from Cudworth regarding the moral criterion. Morality is, for Price, known necessarily, immediately, and intuitively, yet acquired from a contemplation of actions, whereas, for Cudworth, law or a modification of the mind is the criterion of moral judgment. While reason is the moral guide and judge, moral approval, however, entails an emotion of the heart as well as the activity of understanding.

Price, like Cudworth, has ventured into the region of the mysteries of the metaphysical, providing no specifics as to the nature of the moral emotion related to the heart, as well as being deficient in supplying other particulars. Essentially, the theory is as Price admitted, a refutation of Hutcheson's principle of "the greatest happiness for the greatest numbers" (cited in chapter 4).

BUTLER, MARTINEAU, AND ROYCE

Considered one of the most outstanding moral philosophers in the history of ethical theory, Joseph Butler is remembered best for the emphasis he placed upon conscience and for allocating to it the central position that it maintains in ethical thought. Butler's moral philosophy is found in numerous sermons delivered to students at Rolls Chapel, England. While Butler's affiliations were with Oxford University, Martineau's were in connection with Manchester New College, England, and Royce's with Harvard University.

Joseph Butler: An Ethics of Conscience. The intuitional ethics of

9. Ibid.

Joseph Butler (1692–1752), found principally in his publications *Fifteen Sermons Preached at Rolls Chapel* (1726) and *Of the Nature of Virtue* (the appendix of his *Analogy of Religion,* 1736), has been of prime importance and influence, especially among the British moral philosophers, of whom he has been regarded as the greatest figure by many scholars.

Despite his being a bishop of the Anglican Church, Butler claimed that his theory was not a theological ethic, but an empirical one free from revelation, grounded in human nature and experience. Traces of hedonism, self-realizationism, Stoicism, and Christian ethics are detectable in his system.

SYNOPSIS OF BUTLER'S INTUITIONISM. Man has a given nature that calls for a specified and appropriate course of action. The fundamental ethical issue is, as with Aristotle, the purpose of man. As the constitution of the watch is "adapted to measure time," so man's constitution is "adapted to virtue." Not all human activity is suitable, but only that which corresponds to his true nature. "The correspondence of actions to the nature of the agent renders them natural,"[10] and that which is discordant with human nature is unnatural and evil. Not all natural propensities or springs of action are of *equal* moral significance, nor is the strongest drive necessarily the best, nor of the greatest moral worth. Certain natural inclinations, or principles, as Butler preferred to term them, are morally superior to others, those actions corresponding to the higher motives being the more desirable morally.

Agreeing with Hobbes that self-love is important for man's welfare, Butler nevertheless objected to Hobbesian egoism by arguing for the important role played by the principle of benevolence, a principle shared with Bentham.

> Reasonable self-love and conscience are the chief or superior principles in the nature of man, because an action may be suitable to this nature, though all other principles be violated; but becomes unsuitable, if either of those are. Conscience and self-love, if we understand our true happiness, always lead us the same way. Duty and interest are perfectly coincident; for the most part in this world, but entirely, and in every instance, if we take in the future, and the whole; this being implied in the notion of a good and perfect administration of things. Thus, they who have been so wise in their generation, as to regard only their own supposed interest, at the expense and to the injury of others, shall at last find that he who has given up all the advantages of the present world, rather than violate his conscience and the relations of life, has infinitely better provided for himself, and secured his own interest and happiness.[11]

10. Joseph Butler, *Sermons* (London, 1726), Sermon 3.
11. Ibid.

Accordingly, an inviolate conscience is one unharassed by tormenting pangs, or, to word it positively, one that expresses pleasure and satisfaction regarding the activity and behavior of the person in possession of that particular conscience.

Man's moral motivation springs from four major sources in human nature: (1) *self-love* or desires, the rational pursuit of which yields personal or individual happiness; (2) *benevolence,* whose rational pursuit leads to collective or social happiness, (3) *appetites,* passions, and affections, which encompass certain instinctive motives such as the maternal, hunger, sex, and other drives whose fulfillment produces happiness; (4) *conscience,* sovereign over the preceding three sources in authority, priority, control, and judgment, which produces actions that achieve man's greatest good. Speaking of the "moral faculty; whether called conscience, moral reason, moral sense, or divine reason; whether considered as a sentiment of the understanding, or as a perception of the heart," Butler asserted that it is not "at all doubtful in the general, what course of action this faculty, or practical discerning power within us, approves and what it disapproves."[12] Conscience, the guide of moral action, the moral ability to be able to discriminate between right and wrong conduct, is a "principle of reflection," a unique, moral form of introspection.

THE HEDONISTIC PARADOX. Butler's decisive attack upon hedonism has been conclusive. It consists of what is termed the "hedonistic paradox," the belief that happiness is not attainable as the object of direct pursuit, but issues as a concomitant of that which is in itself not necessarily regarded as happiness. No object exists that can be labeled happiness; there is no "royal road" to happiness, for the reason that it results as a by-product of that which is not deemed happiness per se, but, nevertheless, the attainment of which is accompanied by happiness.

To pursue pleasure for its own sake solely cannot be considered the usual behavior of man; on the contrary, man pursues other goals as the most desirable manner of achieving happiness. Egoistic hedonism is not only self-defeating, but it fails to consider that man's behavior is designed to benefit others as well as self.

Actually, men rarely chase after pleasure (happiness) as an intrinsic good, i.e., as an end in itself. Rather they seek a neutral goal which in itself is devoid of happiness; yet its acquisition is attended by happiness, such pleasure issuing as a by-product of, or the accompaniment of, the neutral objective. If a person desires happiness, then he must seek it in other avenues, the finest road to it being the fulfillment of human nature, achieved under the guidance of introspective reflection (conscience), which is man's unique moral faculty for the direct discernment of ethical behavior.

12. Joseph Butler, "Of the Nature of Virtue," *The Analogy of Religion* (London, 1736), dissertation 2.

Conscience: The Criterion of Morality. Conscience is the sovereign determiner of moral conduct, and holds veto power over the lower principles, which occupy a secondary status to it. Conscience is *the* criterion of right and wrong, a moral faculty that makes man a "law unto himself." "It is by this faculty, natural to man, that he is a moral agent."[13] Conscience is more than a mere feeling; it is *reflection* construed as *introspection,* whereby a person intuitively discerns moral and immoral behavior even antecedent to its actual occurrence.

For behavior to be designated moral, it must come under the scrutiny, discretion, and value judgment of conscience. Consequently, a natural impulse, instinct, or principle may conceivably be prohibited by conscience, but a good moral life is perfectly coordinated in all of its natural propensities in accord with conscience. While the authority of conscience is final, nevertheless the good life will have all of its natural drives coincide in perfect harmony, though under the rule of conscience.

Vice as the Violation of Human Nature. It should now be apparent that if the moral or virtuous life is one comporting with human nature, the fulfillment of innate propensities, then vice as its opposite must be a departure from or violation of human nature. "Vice is contrary to the nature and reason of things; . . . it is a violation or breaking in upon our own nature."[14] Respecting the nature of man, "virtue consists in following, and vice in deviating from it."[15] Inasmuch as the moral life is rational and in accord with conscience and reflection, the implication is that vice must be irrational behavior contrary to conscience and reason. While the former leads a person in the direction of happiness, the latter yields misery.

Virtue, rather than being an arduous task, is relatively quite easy because it consists in merely following human nature. Man is born to virtue, not vice, which is thoroughly foreign to man's nature. Man is adapted to virtue, but vice is a maladjustment, the distortion of the innate constitution.

Unlike other beings, animate or inanimate, the human possesses moral agency, control over his conduct.

> Our nature, *i.e.,* constitution, is adapted to virtue, as from the idea of a watch it appears, that its nature, *i.e.,* constitution or system, is adapted to measure time. What in fact or event commonly happens is nothing to this question. Every work of art is apt to be out of order: but this is so far from being according to its system, that let the disorder increase, and it will totally destroy it. This is merely by way of explanation, what an economy, system, or constitution is. And thus far the cases are

13. Butler, *Sermons,* Sermon 3.
14. Ibid., preface.
15. Ibid.

> perfectly parallel. If we go further, there is indeed a difference, nothing to the present purpose, but too important a one ever to be omitted. A machine is inanimate and passive: but we are agents. Our constitution is put in our own power. We are charged with it; and therefore are accountable for any disorder or violation of it.
>
> Thus nothing can possibly be more contrary to nature than vice; meaning by nature not only the *several parts* of our internal frame, but also the *constitution* of it. Poverty and disgrace, tortures and death, are not so contrary to it. Misery and injustice are indeed equally contrary to some different parts of our nature taken singly: but injustice is moreover contrary to the whole constitution of the nature.[16]

HUMAN BEINGS VS. ANIMALS. Whereas vice is the disruption of nature, virtue consists in following nature, a human nature or constitution comprised of diverse instincts or innate propulsions, of which some are shared by man with the animal kingdom. While some of these propensities lead to individual happiness, others lead to the general welfare of the community, social happiness. But singularly unlike the lower animals, man possesses a conscience, that is, reflection, by which he directly discriminates among his various options or choices of action, permitting him to approve of some and repudiate other forms of behavior. Butler concisely stated his position: "Mankind has various instincts and principles of action, as brute creatures have; some leading most directly and immediately to the good of the community, and some more directly to private good. Man has several which brutes have not; particularly reflection or conscience, an approbation of some principles or actions, and disapprobation of others."[17] Animals respond instinctively to their natures by law and by environmental factors, and so does man, but the human being's motivation supersedes self-love, sensual appetites, love of power, and even friendship or compassion. Man's conscience, or reflection, provides absolute direction, assuming supreme authority over the rest of his nature as well as his overt behavior.

A life ruled by conscience (man's decisive moral faculty) leads not only to virtue, but to self-interest, public interest, and happiness. Conscience, self-interest, benevolence, and virtue do not contradict one another, but coincide harmoniously in support of each other.

CRITIQUE OF BUTLER'S CONSCIENCE THEORY OF ETHICS. Butler assumed that everyone is fully cognizant as to the nature of virtue and that the only task of ethics is to demonstrate that it is a course of action harmonizing with man's nature. When queried as to the matter, he simply refers to veracity, justice, and the common good

16. Ibid.
17. Ibid.

as our ethical goals. His assumption that the common good or virtue is invariably compatible with human nature does not seem to be the case among the multitude of criminals, whose conviction and incarceration testify otherwise.

Furthermore, Butler's ethical criterion, *conscience,* not only lacks a content; it remains undeveloped, failing to provide a table of actual duties. One is not provided with a course of action which conscience would approve. Moreover, his reference to conscience is ambiguous; at times it is perilously close to common usage, and at other times it signifies the principle of reflection or the principle of approbation (that is, reason), in which case it would be based upon concern about the propensities to action, or motivation.

Conscience, as most persons are familiar with the term, is a feeble criterion of moral behavior, for the reason that many inveterate criminals not only never suffer from its dictates, but in some instances exhibit a flexible conscience which may even applaud their crimimal actions when cleverly executed to escape detection.

Still worse, many individuals with an oversensitive conscience are misled, some even to the point of confessing to crimes that they never committed. Some helpless neurotics, at the mercy of their tyrannical consciences, actually feel better when some adverse circumstance befalls them, as if atoning for their sins and experiencing the concomitant acquiescence of conscience. Even Butler's disciple, Martineau, asserted, "The blessings of a satisfied conscience are least experienced where they are most deserved."

In psychoanalytic language, these conscience-ridden persons are *ego-alien,* functioning with a conscience that seems to belong to another and to negate the dictates of their own intelligence (or principle of reflection). Their conscience instead of being their own natural endowment is conditioned in them by external sources, such as parents, teachers, church indoctrination, and society at large. The ideal situation would be the cultivation of a state of maturity wherein a person's conscience is in perfect harmony with his moral values as he appreciates them in the light of his own understanding, and responds to them naturally and spontaneously.

James Martineau: Ethics as a Psychological Disposition. Butler's most distinguished follower, James Martineau (1805–1900), founded his ethical intuitionism on moral consciousness as a reality in its own right.

IDIOPSYCHOLOGICAL ETHICS DEFINED. A term of Martineau's coinage chosen to designate his particular ethical theory, *idiopsychological,* implies morals to be a personal matter of an individual's peculiar psychological or spiritual personality characteristics. Moral right and wrong are intuited by a moral consciousness or faculty, independent of external consequences. Morality is essentially a person's good intentions, dispositions, motives, rather than specific overt actions. Moral consciousness contains: merit, demerit, praise, blame, temptation, compunction, duty, virtue, obligation, authority, right, wrong, and other moral sentiments together with their divine source.

PERSONALISTIC INTUITIONISM. The intuitional ethic of Martineau is postulated upon the premise that morality has significance for persons alone. Right and wrong exist in and for persons; only persons, not things, are moral. It is not the performance of the *act* that is in itself moral, but the person who initiated it. That is to say, persons, not actions, are moral. Actions themselves are neutral until a person comes into contact with them, and at that point they become moral issues.

The essence of morality is not a matter of doing, but of being. One does not *do* morality, one *is* moral. "What we judge is always the *inner spring* of an action, as distinguished from its outward operation."[18] Morality is inner, existing in and for persons alone. In sympathy with Leslie Stephen, Martineau quoted him: "It may be briefly expressed in the phrase that *morality is internal.* The moral law, we may say, has to be expressed in the form, *'Be this,'* not in the form 'Do this.' "[19] Unless a rule is capable of being expressed in precisely this manner, it lacks a distinctively moral character.

An *ethics of motive* relates to moral law, whereas an *ethics of action* pertains to legal and other rules. F. H. Bradley and T. H. Green phrased the matter well: the former in asserting that "morality has not to do immediately with the outer results of the Will: acts, so far as they spring from the good will, are good: what issues from a moral character must likewise be morally good";[20] and the latter in writing that "it is not by the outward form that we know what moral action is. We know it, so to speak, on the inner side."[21]

The preceding discussion obviously implies that the realm of morality is restricted to persons and inner personality, not external objects, nor even the actions that particular individuals perform. The reason for this conclusion is that persons, not things, are praised or blamed; moral judgment is directed solely toward persons. "Self-evidently, it is *persons* exclusively, and not *things,* that we approve or condemn."[22] On those occasions when epithets of praise are applicable to impersonal or physical objects, it is always with the implication that they are the expressions of some mind, human or divine. To applaud an object of art is to refer to the personal being responsible for it.

18. James Martineau, *Types of Ethical Theory,* 3d ed. (Oxford: Clarendon Press, 1891), bk. 1, chap. 1, sect. 1.
19. Ibid.
20. Ibid.
21. Ibid.
22. Ibid.

> What else means the memorable parody of Comte on the Hebrew hymn, "The heavens declare the glory of God,"—viz. that the only glory they declare is *that of Newton and Laplace? i.e.* the heavens themselves, as a physical splendour and infinitude, have nothing glorious to say to us: first when brought into contact with *some mind,* have they significance to move us; and if they represent to us *no prior and inner mind* whose eternal thoughts they hang aloft, they must wait for the genius of some *outward observer and interpreter* ere they can mean anything sublime.[23]

The same holds true respecting the actions or consequences of human behavior; unless one can relate a good or evil outcome to some particular person or persons, then praise or blame is meaningless.

> The approbation or disapprobation which we feel towards human actions is directed upon them as personal phenomena; and if this condition failed, would disappear, though they might still, as natural causes, be instrumental in producing much good or ill. Their moral character goes forward with them out of the person; and is not reflected back upon them from their effects. Benefit and mischief are in themselves wholly characterless; and we neither applaud the gold mine, nor blame the destructive storm.[24]

CRITERION OF THE RIGHT ACT. On the premise that morality is inner, within the person exclusively, it follows that the right act refers to inner motivation, will, intention. An action is right when prompted by a moral disposition, and in the case of conflicting dispositions, then the morally praiseworthy motivation ought to prevail.

A person may be predisposed to act from a number of promptings; however, the right act consists in permitting the higher one to displace the lower. For example, love is an inclination superior to fear; consequently, if an individual is confronted with a situation in which either one of these may incite him, then it would become obligatory upon that person to elect the higher motivation, love. But if it should be the case that fear and fear alone is the sole motivating factor, then to be so stimulated is not immoral. Only when fear supersedes a more elevated disposition is it immoral to act owing to its inducement.

The criterion of the right act is defined as: *"Every action is RIGHT, which, in presence of a lower principle, follows a higher: every action is WRONG, which, in presence of a higher principle, follows a lower."*[25] The subordinate incentive is invariably wrong, with the possible exception of those cases when it is impossible to be motivated by

23. Ibid.
24. Ibid.
25. Ibid., chap. 6, sect. 15.

any other incentive. Reverence, the highest possible motive, is categorically right for all actions.

The various moral stimuli motivating men are ordered according to their relative positions of superiority in ascending order in the following Table of Springs of Action, as Martineau termed it:[26]

LOWEST

1. Secondary Passions;—Censoriousness, Vindictiveness, Suspiciousness.
2. Secondary Organic Propensions;—Love of Ease and Sensual Pleasure.
3. Primary Organic Propensions;—Appetites.
4. Primary Animal Propension;—Spontaneous Activity (unselective).
5. Love of Gain (reflective derivative from Appetite).
6. Secondary Affections (sentimental indulgence of sympathetic feelings).
7. Primary Passions;—Antipathy, Fear, Resentment.
8. Causal Energy;—Love of Power, or Ambition; Love of Liberty.
9. Secondary Sentiments;—Love of Culture.
10. Primary Sentiments of Wonder and Admiration.
11. Primary Affections, Parental and Social;—with (approximately) Generosity and Gratitude.
12. Primary Affection of Compassion.
13. Primary Sentiment of Reverence.

HIGHEST

CRITIQUE OF MARTINEAU'S ETHICAL THEORY. Classical intuitionism climaxed with Martineau's rendition of it. Since that time, ethical thinking of this mode assumed the form of deontology, a refined or sophisticated form of intuitionism. Despite Martineau's effective presentation of classical intuitionism, his theory contains many areas of weakness.

In approving censoriousness as a moral motivation only if no other motivation is present, Martineau is granting moral permission to the reprobate on the bottom of the moral heap to respond in a manner that no one else is entitled to do. What is worse, he is making the most moral of persons immoral, when that individual can respond with reverence, but responds instead with compassion. Compassion is not only a noble expression of feeling, but at times is also probably more holy or salubrious than reverence itself.

Another complication of this system is reflected in the case of the persons who may express their reverence for unsalutary objects or persons, as, for example, the many individuals who revered Hitler. On the other hand, rather than being immoral, it appears to be quite

26. Ibid., sect. 13.

right to express censoriousness against the Nazis' behavior in the concentration camps.

Reviewing the table of thirteen springs of action leaves one pondering why the scale is arranged as it is; e.g., what criterion places love of liberty beneath love of culture, since a number of people regard a culture without liberty as an inferior one indeed? Furthermore, one queries why many other propensities are omitted from the table, such as: a sense of achievement, a desire for understanding, aesthetic responsiveness, or a wholesome sense of humor.

One of the strongest strictures confronting Martineau would come from Kantians, who would refuse to allow feeling to contain moral value on the grounds that one's feelings are not subject to the will of the individual. According to Kant, unless love is construed as good will, it falls outside the bounds of morality, inasmuch as a person can command good will toward others, including those he has never yet met, but love cannot be so dictated by one's will.

Finally, Martineau made morality an inner matter, not one of consequences, notwithstanding that the only way that he can support the moral value of his thirteen springs of action is by reference to the consequences that normally proceed from a given disposition. Unless consequences are conjoined with predispositions, it would be virtually impossible to make a case for the moral value of a feeling and its relative position in an ascending scale.

Josiah Royce: The Ethics of Loyalty. Regarded as America's foremost idealist, Josiah Royce (1855–1916) taught at Harvard University with his famous pragmatist colleague, William James, during the "golden years" of Harvard's philosophy department. Normally, Royce is not classified with the classical intuitionists, but his insistence that morality is based upon an inner spirit of loyalty makes it possible to include him in this category.

THE CENTRAL POSITION OF LOYALTY. Loyalty is the central idea in the ethics of Royce; virtue is defined in terms of loyalty, as are duty, the right act, and the greatest good. "If loyalty is a supreme good, the mutually destructive conflict of loyalties is in general a supreme evil."[27] Only loyalty is of moral worth, other qualities acquiring their moral value from loyalty. "Loyalty to universal loyalty is indeed the fulfilment of the whole law."[28] It is not the object to which one is loyal that is of moral significance, but loyalty, the spirit of loyalty, the inner experience itself; hence the intuitionism of Royce.

LOYALTY AS THE SUPREME GOOD. Loyalty *itself* is good, not the cause to which one's loyalty is sworn. Loyalty is the supreme moral value, so great that it is the supreme good. "Loyalty is, for the loyal

27. Josiah Royce, *The Philosophy of Loyalty* (New York: Macmillan, 1908), p. 116.
28. Ibid., p. 146.

individual himself, a supreme good, whatever be, for the world in general, the worth of his cause."[29] A person's *devotion* to a cause, then, and not the cause itself is of highest moral worth.

True, it would be preferable for a person to be loyal to a cause worthy of his loyal devotion, but the moral quality of a person is his loyal spirit, not the cause per se to which he has subscribed. The selection of a cause is a matter of intelligent enlightenment, and not a question of morality, but loyalty's splendor is enhanced when it is devoted to a cause worthy of it. No one is infallible, and therefore anyone is liable to choose a cause that does not deserve loyal adherence, but everyone is capable of loyalty, of making a decision, selecting a cause, and being decisively and faithfully loyal to it. "In choosing and in serving the cause to which you are to be loyal, be, in any case, loyal to loyalty."[30]

LOYALTY TO LOYALTY. It is true that loyalties often conflict, one man's with another's, or one man may experience conflicting causes within himself. When this is the case, then one must be *loyal to loyalty,* loyal to the spirit of loyalty. "And so, a cause is good, not only for me, but for mankind, in so far as it is essentially a *loyalty to loyalty,* that is, is an aid and a furtherance of loyalty in my fellows."[31] The spirit of loyalty itself is holy; therefore, it is a sin to destroy a person's loyal feelings to any cause whatever, good or bad. To do so would be disloyal to loyalty. "And of all things that thus have warred with loyalty, the bitterest woe of humanity has been that so often it is the loyal themselves who have thus blindly and eagerly gone about to wound and to slay the loyalty of their brethren. . . . For such a sin is precisely what any wanton conflict of loyalty means."[32]

The criterion of a good cause is whether it promotes or reduces the spirit of loyalty in us and others. Loyalty is our *summum bonum,* and although particular loyalties change, the spirit of loyalty must remain. The individual virtues, such as justice, truth, and benevolence, are simply aspects or phases of loyalty, for any one of the virtues without loyalty loses its moral merit. For example, justice devoid of loyalty is diminished to vicious formalism, and benevolence lacking loyalty is reduced to dangerous sentimentalism.

In his *Sources of Religious Insight* (1912), Royce developed a religion of loyalty, essentially moral in character, wherein he cited the fundamental dual principle of loyalty:

> The first is: *Be loyal.* The second is: *So be loyal, that is, so seek, so accept, so serve your cause that thereby the loyalty of all your*

29. Ibid., p. 101.
30. Ibid., p. 121.
31. Royce, *Philosophy of Loyalty,* p. 118.
32. Ibid., pp. 116–117.

> *brethren throughout all the world, through your example, through your influence, through your own love of loyalty wherever you find it, as well as through the sort of loyalty which you exemplify in your deeds, shall be aided, furthered, increased so far as in you lies.*[33]

A person, by being loyal to his own cause, in so doing serves to advance the cause of universal loyalty.

Royce defined loyalty as *"the willing and practical and thoroughgoing devotion of a person to a cause,"*[34] loyalty calling for choice willingly executed, complete devotion, and its practical expression. It also calls for self-control, self-sacrifice, altruism, social concern, and a cause possessing personal worth. "My thesis is that *all those duties which we have learned to recognize as the fundamental duties of the civilized man, the duties that every man owes to every man, are to be rightly interpreted as special instances of loyalty to loyalty.* In other words, all the recognized virtues can be defined in terms of our concept of loyalty. And this is why I assert that, when rightly interpreted, loyalty is the whole duty of man."[35]

Criticism of Royce's Philosophy of Loyalty. It is quite admirable for a person to be loyal and foster loyalty in others, but Royce's ethics of loyalty is a gross oversimplification of the matter. A person may be intensely loyal yet commit the most heinous crimes, as was true of the Nazis who chauvinistically followed Hitler. But if loyalty possesses the moral worth ascribed to it by Royce, then either it is critically deficient as a moral value or it requires something else to render it morally effective. Loyalty is blind without suitable direction, either from the intellect or from a code of ethics by which it may be governed.

The most that can be said for Royce's ethics of loyalty is that he has emphasized a much neglected moral value, his error being its overemphasis to the complete disregard of other vital moral values. Furthermore, the qualities that Royce claimed for loyalty could virtually be claimed for many moral values, including justice and goodness.

33. Josiah Royce, *The Sources of Religious Insight* (New York: Scribner, 1912), p. 202.
34. Royce, *Philosophy of Loyalty*, pp. 16–17.
35. Ibid., pp. 139–140.

8

Deontological Intuitionism: The Immediate Apprehension of Duty

The present treatment of deontological intuitionism will include Kant (1724–1804) and the four most influential of the following six contemporary deontologists: Horace William Brindley Joseph (1867–1943), Harold Arthur Prichard (1871–1947), William David Ross (1877–1940), Charlie Dunbar Broad (1887–), Alfred Cyril Ewing (1899–), and E. F. Carritt (1876–1964). With the exception of Kant, the German philosopher at the University of Königsberg, and the Cantabrigians C. D. Broad and A. C. Ewing, the entire group are Oxford University men.

Deontology, the ethics of duty, consists of a theory of duty and moral obligation. The term finds its etymology in the Greek *deon,* meaning obligation, or that which is necessary, hence, moral necessity. In contemporary ethics, intuitionism is dominated by deontological theorists, philosophers who accept the validity of the experience of obligation and seek to explain it. Deontologists hold that knowledge of the supreme good is unnecessary in deriving knowledge of moral obligation, for the latter is a derivative of intuition.

KANTIAN INTUITIONISM: REVERENCE FOR DUTY

Kant's system calls for a reverence for moral law, universal in character. The moral law binds us absolutely to moral obligation.

The Good Will. Kantian ethical theory is founded upon the concept of a *good will,* and whatever is extraneous to will falls outside the domain of morality. "Nothing can possibly be conceived in the world, or even outside of it, which can be called good without qualification, except a Good Will."[1] Moral obligation can be only that which a man can effect by will; what lies beyond one's will falls outside the domain

1. Immanuel Kant, "Fundamental Principles of the Metaphysic of Morals," in *Kant's Critique of Practical Reason and Other Works on the Theory of Ethics,* trans. Thomas Kingsmill Abbott, 3d ed. (London: Longmans, Green, & Co., 1883), p. 9.

of moral responsibility. If we cannot, by the sheer act of willing it, become happy, intelligent, healthy, and so on, then those things cannot be moral obligations, hence they lack moral significance. If they can be effected by the right employment of intelligence, knowledge, and effort, but not by the sole command of will, then the acts that produce them are acts of prudence, not moral actions.

Man is not morally responsible for the results of his actions, or for any consequences whatever; his duty is to moral law, an unempirical, nonfactual principle which must freely be obeyed by the rational will as his sole responsibility. *"Duty is the necessity of acting from respect for the law,"* that is, *moral* law; accordingly, one's motivation is duty. As for the consequences of one's actions, with which the utilitarians were so deeply concerned, Kant would say, "Let justice be done though the heavens fall." The moral law must be obeyed without consideration of ensuing consequences, that is, consequences must be viewed in the light of the moral law, and the law is not obeyed because of consequences. Consequences belong to the physical or natural universe of empirical data, but moral obligation pertains to the moral law, a nonempirical supersensible reality of a supersensible or transcendent world. Happiness, love, pleasure, and other natural inclinations cannot be moral concerns, since they pertain to the empirical world of fact and cannot be commanded by an act of free will (practical reason); therefore, they are not moral duties.

> It is in this manner, undoubtedly, that we are to understand those passages of Scripture also in which we are commanded to love our neighbour, even our enemy. For love, as an affection, cannot be commanded, but beneficence for duty's sake may; even though we are not impelled to it by any inclination—nay, are even repelled by a natural and unconquerable aversion. This is *practical* love, and not *pathological*—a love which is seated in the will, and not in the propensions of sense—in principles of action and not of tender sympathy; and it is this love alone which can be commanded.[2]

Duty, then, is an act of will, a free and autonomous will, one which is not coerced by extraneous forces, but is self-legislated, commanding itself. What the rational moral law commands, the good will chooses. Duty responds to practical reason, will, and not to inclination.

Man, as a rational being, possesses an autonomous will.

> Morality then is the relation of actions to the autonomy of the will. . . . A will whose maxims necessarily coincide with the law of autonomy is a *holy* will, good absolutely. The dependence of a will not absolutely good on the principle of autonomy (moral necessitation) is obligation. This then cannot be applied

2. Ibid., pp. 15–16.

> to a holy being. The objective necessity of actions from obligation is called *duty*.[3]

Duty pertains to motive, intention, will; otherwise the action is one of mere rote, overt behavior morally void, a mere exercise, or what Kant termed *legality*. To perform an action which people would ordinarily regard as moral, and not be prompted out of a sense of duty or reverence for moral law, is devoid of moral content, moral value. Therefore, heaven and hell are not suitable forms of moral motivation; to refrain from evil because of fear of being consigned by God to hell is not to behave as a moral personality, but to adhere "legally" to codes of behavior as an automaton. Heavenly promises or hellish threats reduce man from a moral personality to an amoral entity, an animal.

To tell the truth when you are forced to do so is not a moral action, but extramoral, amoral. For an act to be moral it must be prompted by the autonomous will, not by forces extraneous to it. The mere routine overt behavior of a person who appears as if he is acting out of morality is amoral. "The mere agreement or disagreement of an action with the law, without regard to the motive from which the action springs, is called *legality;* but when the idea of duty arising from the law is also the motive of the action, the agreement is called the *morality* of the action."[4] Consequently, to act according to morality, but not out of it (i.e., not from good will), is not of moral significance. Interpreting Kant, this would mean that to donate blood to the blood bank willingly, by choice, is to do a moral act, but to do so when coerced or shamed into it is to do a morally neutral act. The inverse is also true; to do an evil act when forced, but not to do it willingly, is not immoral, but to do an evil act willingly (even though at the same time forced to do so) is immoral.

THE CATEGORICAL IMPERATIVE. The categorical imperative, the imperative of morality, is a moral command which is binding upon a person under any and all situations, as an end in itself, and is not subject to the hypothetical conditions seeking some particular desired end. Extenuating circumstances do not alter obligation to the moral law, for a categorical imperative is absolute and unconditional. Right is right and must be done independent of circumstances, for duty is performed for duty's sake, not for the sake of some outcome which suits our desires.

Hypothetical imperatives, of the form "If you want this, do that," on the other hand, are means to a good (rather than a good in itself, an intrinsic value), while actions stemming from them are good for some purpose. Precepts of prudence are hypothetical. A modern

3. Ibid., p. 58.
4. Kant, "Metaphysic of Morals," *Critique of Practical Reason,* p. 275.

example might be: If you want to prevent a Hitler from murdering millions of innocent persons, then execute him.[5] But to transform this conditional imperative into the categorical imperative, the supreme principle of morality or the Kantian criterion of moral right and wrong, enjoins a person to extract the objective principle of the action under consideration and to universalize it. The principle of the action being *killing,* he must, in order to formulate the categorical imperative, query: Can I will that all persons kill at their own discretion or whim? Can I will that killing be a universal law to which every person is entitled if he so desires? Only a negative answer can be given to this, because if I answered *yes* to it, then contradiction would result, the destruction of mankind, for I should be granting others the privilege of killing me; therefore, I am obliged to deny myself the right to *will* to kill even a Hitler or a Nero, regardless of the circumstances.

The categorical imperative stated by Kant is: *"Act only on that maxim whereby thou canst at the same time will that it should become a universal law."*[6] Only that is a duty which can be universally applied and generalized into a law. The categorical imperative implies that what is right for one person is right for all, and what is wrong for one is wrong for all. The moral law is binding on all rational beings alike, and it is man's duty to respect the moral law. If you cannot universalize your action so that it becomes right for all persons to do it (regardless of your particular situation), then it is wrong for you also. The moral law relates not to external circumstances or consequences, but to internal will and obligation, as Kant argued:

> I am never to act otherwise than so *that I could also will that my maxim should become a universal law*. . . . Let the question be, for example: May I when in distress make a promise with the intention not to keep it? I readily distinguish here between the two significations which the question may have: Whether it is prudent, or whether it is right, to make a false promise. The former may undoubtedly often be the case. . . . Now it is a wholly different thing to be truthful from duty, and to be so from apprehension of injurious consequences. In the first case, the very notion of the action already implies a law for me; in the second case, I must first look about elsewhere to see what results may be combined with it which would affect myself. For to deviate from the principle of duty is beyond all doubt wicked; but to be unfaithful to my maxim of prudence may often be very advantageous to me, although to abide by it is certainly safer. The shortest way, however, and an unerring one, to discover the

5. See Brendan E. A. Liddell, *Kant on the Foundation of Morality: A Modern Version of the Grundlegung* (Bloomington, Ind.: Indiana University Press, 1970), p. 113.

6. Kant, "Fundamental Principles," p. 38.

> answer to this question where a lying promise is consistent with duty, is to ask myself, Should I be content that my maxim (to extricate myself from difficulty by a false promise) should hold good as a universal law, for myself as well as for others? and should I be able to say to myself, "everyone may make a deceitful promise when he finds himself in a difficulty from which he cannot otherwise extricate himself"? Then I presently become aware that while I can will the lie, I can by no means will that lying should be a universal law. For with such a law there would be no promises at all, since it would be in vain to allege my intention in regard to my future actions to those who would not believe this allegation, or if they overhastily did so would pay me back in my own coin. Hence my maxim, so soon as it should be made a universal law, would necessarily destroy itself.[7]

Note that moral decisions are made without regard to consequences, but only with the highest respect for duty, an internal activity involving a rational person, free to obey no other person or thing but his own will under the direction of reason as the moral law dictates. The categorical imperative of duty, then, is: *"Act as if the maxim of thy action were to become by thy will a Universal Law of Nature."*[8]

MAN'S DIGNITY AND THE KINGDOM OF ENDS. Man, by virtue of his being a citizen of a moral kingdom, a moral world order, possesses infinite intrinsic value, *dignity*.

Man's autonomous will is self-governed, self-legislated, without any cause external to itself, accordingly free to obey only reason as it presents the moral law to the will. Forcing a person to obey you is not to be construed as his obeying you willingly. An armed thief (to cite a hypothetical case that is not Kant's) may force you to hand your money over to him, but he cannot force you to do it willingly. The will obeys only its possessor, and yields to no external coercion, only rational persuasion. "A rational being belongs as a *member* to the kingdom of ends. . . . He belongs to it *as sovereign,* when while giving laws he is not subject to the will of any other."[9] Those beings possessing a rational good will belong to a kingdom of ends by virtue of their ability to establish their own moral ends by self-imposed objective moral laws.

"Rational nature exists as an end in itself." Since man, as a moral being, is an end in himself, he possesses absolute worth, *dignity*. Things have relative value because their value is always utilitarian, and once having lost their utility, they become valueless. But man must be treated as an end in himself, never merely as means, owing to his dignity, his infinite intrinsic value, and his ability to participate in a

7. Ibid., pp. 18–19.
8. Ibid., p. 39.
9. Ibid., p. 52.

kingdom of ends as a moral legislator establishing moral laws or ends to pursue. The practical imperative relating to men is: *"So act as to treat humanity, whether in thine own person or in that of any other, in every case as an end withal, never as means only."*[10] The application of this rule (according to this author) would allow us to discard objects when they are no longer serviceable to us. But when a man has lost his usefulness to us, we must still be concerned for him as a person, and treat him with due respect and proper concern. Reverence for the worth of man is the basis of morality, and a person is dutiful, not for material gain, pleasure, and the like, but for *reverence for himself* as a person, a moral agent. Reverence for the moral law is self-respect, and vice versa. Action for duty's sake is action stemming from reverent respect for moral law. "The moral law is holy (inviolable). Man is indeed unholy enough, but he must regard *humanity* in his own person as holy."[11]

In the kingdom of ends, objects possess either value or dignity: dignity if they are irreplaceable, value if they can be replaced by an equal value. Persons are priceless, of infinite intrinsic value, hence enjoy dignity. Marketable objects of utilitarian value are priced according to their use value, but man is above all price.

> In the kingdom of ends everything has either Value or Dignity. Whatever has a value can be replaced by something else which is *equivalent:* whatever, on the other hand, is above all value, and therefore admits of no equivalent, has a dignity. Whatever has reference to the general inclinations and wants of mankind has a market value; . . . but that which constitutes the condition under which alone anything can be an end in itself, this has not merely a relative worth, *i.e.,* value, but an intrinsic worth, that is, *dignity.*[12]

THE *Summum Bonum,* VIRTUE, AND HAPPINESS. The Kantian concept of virtue is comparable to fortitude. Fortitude, which consists of the resolute purpose to resist an unjust strong opponent, becomes virtue when it resists influences opposing moral character within a person. "Virtue is the strength of the man's maxim in his obedience to duty";[13] it is the moral strength of the will, its potency in obedience to duty. Despite Aristotelianism to the contrary, virtue is not a habit, unless that habit consists of the action of the rational will as it implements the idea of moral law. Unless there is freedom, that is, unless habits, feelings, emotions, and so on are at the command of a person's will, they cannot qualify as moral obligations. Kant

10. Ibid., p. 47.
11. Kant, *Critique of Practical Reason,* p. 180.
12. Kant, "Fundamental Principles," p. 53.
13. Kant, "Preface to the Metaphysical Elements of Ethics," in *Critique of Practical Reason,* p. 305.

regarded habits, feelings, emotions, and the like as "pathological" states, and accordingly were extraneous to the will.

The greatest moral perfection is attained through performance of one's duty. Thus, man is duty-bound to *perfect* himself, but since man cannot will for other persons, then it is not his duty to see to the perfection of others. The complement of virtue is happiness (understood as the complete satisfaction of one's needs and inclinations). Happiness, being defined as "the condition of a rational being in the world with whom everything goes according to his wish and will,"[14] entails the cooperation of the world of nature harmonizing with the will of man, but since man cannot will this, it is not obligatory to be happy. Inasmuch as man can contribute to the happiness of others, a person is bound by duty to advance the felicity of others. It is permissible to pursue happiness for oneself, but it is an ill will that does not seek the joy of others. Accordingly, the duty of man is twofold: (*a*) the greatest moral *perfection of himself,* and (*b*) the promotion of the *happiness of others.*

Man's inclination, his *sensuous will,* seeks happiness as its objective, but his *moral will* has virtue as its goal; when the two are united, the *summum bonum* results. The *summum bonum,* then, consists of two elements; "virtue and happiness together constitute the possession of the *summum bonum* in a person."[15] The supreme condition of happiness is virtue, for virtue is the worthiness to be happy. Inasmuch as it is an a priori moral necessity to produce the *summum bonum* by freedom of will, and inasmuch as it is an impossibility to achieve it in an earthly existence, therefore it becomes a moral necessity, a postulate of practical reason, to conclude that the soul must be immortal if the *summum bonum* is to be realized. Otherwise, the obligation to perfect our moral personality loses significance. Life would be a cheat if immortality were not a reality, because immortality of the soul is a necessary presupposition of the *summum bonum* (virtue accompanied by happiness commensurate with the degree of a person's virtue). Perfect happiness, the result of holiness, ought to issue from "the perfect accordance of the will with moral law." But perfection in the present world is an impossible task; therefore, there must be a future world in which we can perfect ourselves, and, as a concomitant, possess happiness because we are worthy of it, the two together (virtue and happiness in combination) being the realization of the *summum bonum.* All of this is the great and marvelous plan of the "Author" of the moral world order, consequently the added necessity of postulating the existence of God.

PHILOSOPHY OF RELIGION. Religion, too, rests upon moral founda-

14. Kant, *Critique of Practical Reason,* p. 221.
15. Ibid., p. 206.

tions, for Kantian theology consists of moral laws as divine commands. Here, the nature of man, being dual, presents a problem. The sensuous nature of man is inclined toward evil, while his moral nature strives for perfection and the subordination of natural impulses. Man's bent toward evil indicates that he is conscious of moral law, but deviates therefrom. Thus, the so-called depravity of human nature is not intrinsic evil, but perverseness, in the sense of human frailty. On the other hand, to say that man is created good means that man is created capable of doing good, and "the original *constitution* of man is good. . . . The original good is *holiness of maxims* in following one's duty."[16] Since the moral law so commands, it inevitably follows that we can become better persons; the road to virtue and perfection is prompted by duty, supported by divine power and redeeming love, effecting in man a change of heart, a new spiritual birth, a new creation. We then become members of the moral kingdom of God, the true Church, comprising the ethical community of the redeemed. Our earthly task, social ethics, is the moral development of the whole, which in the infinite future will eventuate in perpetual peace among all peoples by the establishment of right, law, and constitutional governments.[17]

CRITICISM OF THE KANTIAN ETHIC. The most common criticism of Kantian ethics is directed against its formalism, which does not allow for teleological elements. More than duty for duty's sake is required; it needs to be supplemented by some utilitarian values such as those elaborated in Sidgwick's theories. Ewing[18] argued that the utilitarian complement is necessary in order to choose between conflicting imperatives. Paulsen also recommended teleological supplementation to strengthen the Kantian ethic; he pointed out that lying is not repugnant because of its self-destructiveness, but because it "destroys an essential good, namely, the confidence that is the fundamental condition of all social life."[19] Schilpp claimed that Kant was aware of his extreme formalism and the need to consider consequences of an act as the basis for teleological balance.

> On the one hand, he saw that a moral obligation taking no note of the facts of human life and experience is an absurd and useless abstraction, and on the other, he realized that a "moral" obligation which did not obligate unconditionally—one which

16. Kant, "Philosophical Theory of Religion," *Critique of Practical Reason,* pp. 352, 354.

17. See Immanuel Kant, *Perpetual Peace* (New York: Liberal Arts Press, 1957).

18. A. C. Ewing, *Ethics* (London: English Universities Press, 1953), p. 63.

19. Friedrich Paulsen, *Immanuel Kant: His Life and Doctrine* (New York: Frederick Ungar, 1963), p. 328.

> was merely a means or instrument to some already established or accepted Good—is no genuine moral obligation at all, however beneficial it may be in a "practical" way.[20]

Jeffrie G. Murphy has defended the Kantian ethic, rejecting the popular interpretation of Kant as holding that actions are devoid of moral value unless performed from reverence for duty.[21] He believes that it was Kant's intention to treat legality as a subhead of morals. But, as Murphy himself admitted, no less a Kantian scholar than H. J. Paton sided with the prevailing interpretation. Scheler too was apparently unhappy with Kant's formalism, for he developed an ethics of material values, thus adding specific content to form, in his *Formalistic Principle in Ethics and the Material Ethic of Value,* published in 1916.

A number of scholars have attacked the categorical imperative, including several British philosophers, who contend that Kant's supreme principle of morality is a categorical imperative for only some persons, those whose psychological natures have been so conditioned. C. D. Broad[22] believes that imperatives which currently possess the strength of being categorical for some individuals were once merely hypothetical, and with time and the successful employment of them, they gradually acquired the strength of being categorical for certain persons and for society. Concurring with this interpretation, A. J. Ayer asserts that moral precepts hold the strength of categorical commands for some persons because their moral motivation stems from fear of God's displeasure, or concern for the enmity of society.[23] Such arguments (critical of Kant) are basically Freudian, attributing conscience to a social development of the superego, that aspect of man's personality containing his moral, ideal, and cultural nature.

Similar to Broad's objection is one that contests all of Kant's categorical imperatives as merely hypothetical imperatives. There are no moral laws; there are only empirically derived ones. The conditional command based on the hypothetical statement, "If anyone lies, then he will incur injury," leads to the categorical imperative, "Lying is wrong," or "Thou shalt not lie." "If you do not want to be killed, then do not kill" leads to the categorical command, "Do not kill." In this regard,

20. Paul A. Schilpp, *Kant's Pre-Critical Ethics* (Evanston, Ill.: Northwestern University Press, 1938), p. 173.

21. Jeffrie G. Murphy, "Kant's Concept of a Right Action," *Kant Studies Today,* ed. Lewis W. Beck (LaSalle, Ill.: Open Court, 1969), pp. 471–495.

22. C. D. Broad, *Five Types of Ethical Theory* (Paterson, N.J.: Littlefield, Adams, 1959), pp. 123–124.

23. A. J. Ayer, *Language, Truth and Logic,* 2d ed. (London: Victor Gollancz, 1946), pp. 112–113.

some philosophers see nothing wrong with all commands being hypothetical provided they are universally applied; for example, "If I am hungry and there is no other way for me to survive, then I ought to steal bread from one who has an abundant supply" is an imperative that anyone may employ provided he is in precisely similar circumstances. Such a command can be willed to be universally applied. Another rule would be, "Kill in self-defense." W. D. Ross supported such reasoning when he wrote:

> The only safe way of applying Kant's test of universalizability is to envisage the act in its whole concrete particularity, and then as "Could I wish that everyone, when in exactly similar circumstances, should tell a lie exactly similar to that which I am thinking of telling?"[24]

Baier[25] considers an action to be right when it fulfills the condition of reversibility, when the person at the giving end may be interchanged with the one at the receiving side. It would be tantamount to being allowed to break a promise if the person to whom the promise was made is receptive to the idea. According to Kant, this is not permissible because one cannot borrow money and later decide that he does not have to pay it back, for a contract has been established that cannot be broken. But Kant is mistaken, for contracts are readily changed when both parties agree to the alteration or dissolution. Basically, Kant's universality of moral principles (categorical imperative) is established on the basis of reversibility, since, according to Kant, the reason that I denounce the breaking of promises is that I do not want to be on the side of having a promise broken that is made to me. Nevertheless, if there were no objection on my part, why could not the promise made to me be broken?

This entire line of reasoning raises another objection, comparable to the criticisms by Ayer and Broad. Hospers contends that the psychology of certain persons is such that they could will what to the rest of us would be objectionable according to the categorical imperative.[26] A normal person could not will sadistic acts, but a sadomasochistic person could do so without moral qualms, for he would enjoy both committing sadistic acts and being the recipient of them as a masochist.

Wheelright also scores the psychological factor, asserting that the universal is "relative to the manner in which concepts are employed and terms defined. Is the inheritance of property a species of steal-

24. William David Ross, *Kant's Ethical Theory* (New York: Oxford University Press, 1958), p. 34.

25. Kurt Baier, *The Moral Point of View* (Ithaca, N.Y.: Cornell University Press, 1958), p. 202.

26. John Hospers, *Human Conduct: An Introduction to the Problems of Ethics* (New York: Harcourt, Brace & World, 1961), p. 282.

ing?"[27] Thus, to a communist, capitalistic profiteering is thievery, yet even Kant himself invested money without disturbing his conscience.

Paulsen and others have shown that the categorical imperative can issue immoral commands, as in the case of a Moslem who believes that he is morally commanded to place a sabre in an infidel's back if he refuses to embrace Islam. A Moslem would not object if someone did the same thing to him in order to save his soul.

Instances can even be cited wherein the categorical imperative would command one to do two opposite and contradictory actions. For example, Kant referred to the principle of celibacy, the universalization of which would produce the termination of mankind. But the same imperative that impels us to repudiate celibacy would also defend it on the ground that today if everyone continues to have offspring without limitation or at the current pace, the consequences will be human misery and death through starvation. Perhaps the Aristotelian mean would in this case be a preferable criterion to Kant's categorical imperative. Titus and Keeton point out that Kant does not adequately account for conflicting duties; that is, one is not instructed how to decide in cases where two duties collide.[28] There seems to be merit in the view of Titus and Keeton; thus, a physician is confronted with a dilemma when he must choose between telling a patient the truth, which might cause emotional upset or even death, and concealing the truth by means of deliberately lying to the patient.

Classical philosophers such as Aristotle and modern philosophers such as Ralph Barton Perry and John Dewey would object to Kant's declaration that actions motivated by inclination are of no moral value. They would urge the contrary view that the finest moral actions are those which a person has so cultivated in his personality that they have become natural for him, have come to express a characteristic personality trait.

THE OXFORD DEONTOLOGISTS

The two deontological intuitionists among the Oxford moralists discussed in this chapter are H. A. Prichard and W. D. Ross, both of whom were inspired by the influential teaching and tradition of Cook Wilson of Oxford. One principal point distinguishing contemporary deontologists from classical intuitionists (including Kantian intuitionists) is the theory of the deontologists that right and wrong are intuited primarily in *actions,* rather than in moral principles. Moral laws are not absolute, but are rules which tend toward rightness.

27. Philip Wheelright, *A Critical Introduction to Ethics,* 3d ed. (New York: Odyssey Press, 1959), p. 126.

28. Harold H. Titus and Morris Keeton, *Ethics for Today,* 4th ed. New York: American Book Co., 1966), p. 146.

Obligatory intentions occupy a secondary status to *obligatory acts.* Owing to this distinction, these men may be differentiated both from Kantian deontology and from classical intuitionism by labeling them *neodeontologists,* or *neointuitionists.*

H. A. Prichard: Obligations as Self-Evident, and the Right Act as Directly Apprehended. Prichard's chief contribution to deontological intuitionism has been the theory that it is a mistake to try to prove the facts of obligation, because the facts of obligation (right acts) must be explained as intuitively apprehended. "The sense of moral obligation to do, or of the rightness of, an action of a particular kind is absolutely underivative or immediate."[29] The rightness of an act is indefinable in terms of the goodness it produces, and, as a simple notion and non-natural property, it is distinguishable from all else including goodness, for it is *sui generis* (unique).

ETHICS AS GROUNDED ON AN ERROR. Prichard's classic paper on ethical theory, "Does Moral Philosophy Rest on a Mistake?" raises what he considered the fundamental problem confronting contemporary moral philosophy. He answers the query in the affirmative, and he finds a parallel relation to this problem in epistemological theory, as well as a corresponding solution to the matter in mathematics. The reason moral philosophy rests on a mistake is that it attempts to answer an improper question. Epistemological theory seeks to answer the pseudoquestion "Is what we have hitherto thought knowledge really knowledge?" Such a question permits of no answer whatever, because there cannot be any. "There can be no answer to an illegitimate question, except that the question is illegitimate."[30] The same holds true for moral questions; they rest on the mistake of seeking answers to illegitimate questions.

THE BASIS OF OBLIGATION. Moral questions have been treated in two basic ways by philosophers: "*Either* they state that we ought to do so and so, because, as we see when we fully apprehend the facts, doing so will be for our good, *i.e.,* really, as I would rather say, for our advantage, or, better still, for our happiness; *or* they state that we ought to do so and so, because something realized either in or by the action is good. In other words, the reason 'why' is stated in terms either of the agent's happiness or of the goodness of something involved in the action."[31]

Plato, Butler, Hutcheson, Paley, and Mill are among those who accepted the former view, contending that we ought to do the right

29. H. A. Prichard, *Moral Obligation* (New York: Oxford University Press, 1949), p. 7.

30. H. A. Prichard, "Does Moral Philosophy Rest on a Mistake?" *Mind,* 21 (1912):35; also in *Moral Obligation* (Oxford: Clarendon Press, 1949). Pagination in this section is from the article in *Mind.*

31. Ibid., p. 22.

thing because it will issue in happiness, benefit, profit, or advantage to us. The latter view bases obligation on the goodness of the act itself or the goodness to which it leads. The former view of moral motivation fails to command our sense of obligation because it appeals to desire, yet desires lack moral force. In this respect, the latter view has a special advantage over the former and is preferable, for it commands our moral consciousness to do the act because "the act is good in itself and . . . its intrinsic goodness is the reason why it ought to be done." The goodness of the action itself is more directly related to the obligation than are the consequences of the act.

However, both views are untenable, the second for the reason "that while to base the rightness of an act upon its intrinsic goodness implies that the goodness in question is that of the motive, in reality the rightness or wrongness of an act has nothing to do with any question of motives at all."[32]

Actions, although prompted by different motivation under diverse circumstances, must be distinguished from their motives. To ask, "Ought I to pay my bills?" is to inquire whether I should bring about conditions which result in the fulfillment of prior promises. The question really means: "Ought I to bring about my tradesmen's possession of what by my previous acts I explicitly or implicitly promised them?"[33] As to the motive, there can be no doubt that it exists, if I am effecting conditions which obviously imply it. However, when the entire matter of paying bills is taken under consideration as an obligation, the act itself is considered abstracted from the motive. Even being fully cognizant of our motives for performing the act, we are not brought any closer to the answer to our question. We are under obligation to pay the bills regardless of the motive which prompts us, even if the motivation is fear of legal prosecution, for "we shall still have done *what* we ought, even though we shall not have done it *as* we ought."[34] To introduce the question of motives involves the error of assuming that "we can will to will," that is, "be moved towards being moved."[35] To will or to be motivated is to be moved toward an action in a particular manner—in the present case, to be moved toward paying the bills.

THE SENSE OF OBLIGATION OR RIGHTNESS. Obligatory actions are not reasoned out as are scientific ones, nor can they be generalized as are scientific laws. The rightness of actions consists in their originating certain kinds of things in given situations, depending on how they are related to the agent and to others. Both the situation and its relations must be considered by the agent, the initiator of the act. For example,

32. Ibid., p. 26.
33. Ibid., p. 27.
34. Ibid.
35. Ibid.

you may not have any sense of obligation to give a particular person a present until you realize that he has graciously accorded you certain acts of kindness. Obtaining the data regarding his kindly deeds is not moral thinking, but the realization that returning the kindness by a gift will originate a certain relationship and situation is; "then we appreciate the obligation immediately or directly, the appreciation being an activity of *moral* thinking."[36] We feel or become aware that we *ought* to do this act, i.e., present the gift in return for services rendered.

> This apprehension is immediate, in precisely the sense in which a mathematical apprehension is immediate, *e.g.*, the apprehension that this three-sided figure, in virtue of its being three-sided, must have three angles. Both apprehensions are immediate in the sense that in both insight into the nature of the subject directly leads us to recognize its possession of the predicate; and it is only stating this fact from the other side to say in both cases the fact apprehended is self-evident.[37]

The error of thinking that obligations are not self-evident but require proof may be traced to the fact that those actions referred to as obligations are incompletely stated, what Prichard termed "the preliminaries to appreciating the obligation being incomplete." Consider the example of the aforementioned gift; if it were not mentioned that the gift was in return for acts of kindness, then it would be perfectly legitimate to inquire: Why do it? But when the complete details of the act are stated, then it is unnecessary to offer proof or supply reasons, because the rightness of the act is immediately intuited, is self-evident. We understand obligations by moral thinking, and cannot appreciate them by argument, nor is our sense of the rightness of an act the effect of its goodness.

RIGHT AS INDEPENDENT OF GOOD. Right is independent of good, not its derivative, nor is it the case that an act is good because it is right in the Kantian sense, which reduces the goodness of actions to their motives merely.

> The rightness of a right action lies solely in the origination in which the act consists, whereas the intrinsic goodness of an action lies solely in its motive; and this implies that a morally good action is morally good not simply because it is a right action but because it is a right action done because it is right, *i.e.*, from a sense of obligation.[38]

MORALITY AS INTUITED. The conclusion of the matter is that "the sense that we ought to do certain things arises in our unreflective consciousness, being an activity of moral thinking occasioned by various

36. Ibid., p. 28.
37. Ibid.
38. Ibid., p. 30.

situations in which we find ourselves."[39] Morality, like mathematics, is apprehended directly, intuited; as in mathematics, when you doubt your conclusion that $7 + 7 = 14$, the "only remedy is to do the sum again,"[40] not to attempt proof of any other form, because the matter is self-evident. All attempts to do otherwise "are doomed to failure because they rest on a mistake, the mistake of supposing the possibility of proving what can only be apprehended directly by an act of moral thinking."[41] The process of discerning obligations is not through the usual forms of reasoning or proof, but by a direct appreciation of the obligation.

W. D. Ross: The Indefinability of 'Right'. The deontological intuitionism of William David Ross occupies a mediate position between Kant and Mill. Ross's position rests heavily upon that of Prichard and Moore, the former for his concept of obligation and right, and the latter for the view concerning the indefinability of good. A third source of influence is C. D. Broad's definition of right as meaning: "suitable, in a unique and indefinable way, to a situation."[42] Ross also borrows from Perry's interest theory of value.

While Prichard held that duty is contingent upon one's beliefs concerning facts, Ross maintained that duty depends on the facts themselves. Ross's deontology is in direct antithesis to ideal utilitarianism by holding to prima facie duties as inexplicable in terms of resulting good consequences. "It seems, on reflection, self-evident that a promise, simply as such, is something that *prima facie* ought to be kept."[43]

AUTHORITY OF MORAL RULES. Ross treats ethics as a normative science, a study which ascertains the norms of right behavior. Defined as such, ethics is in a sense false and pretentious, because the "plain man" often knows what he ought to do despite his ignorance of philosophy.

Furthermore, the authority of moral rules breaks down on occasion in practice, first, when one of my personal principles conflicts with another, or, secondly, when those of my society conflict with those of another social code.

The first conflict can be resolved if a person regards moral rules not as absolute principles "guaranteeing the rightness" of actions coming under their jurisdiction, but as rules guaranteeing the rightness of an act coming under its domain provided another aspect of the act does

39. Ibid., p. 36.
40. Ibid.
41. Ibid.
42. William David Ross, *Foundations of Ethics* (Oxford: Oxford University Press, 1939), p. viii.
43. William David Ross, *The Right and the Good* (New York: Oxford University Press, 1930), p. 40.

not fall under the judgment of another rule. In such cases of conflict the more dominant rule supersedes the other.

The second conflict is resolved by ordering rules according to a four-stage ascending level of authority. Rules commanding the highest priority are those self-evidently true, such as the one commanding us to do as much good as we possibly can. The next two classes of rules, which derive their authority from the primary ones, comprise those deduced from the first and applicable to the conditions of human nature universally, and those derived from the first but applicable to the conditions of a particular society, rather than humanity in general. The fourth class comprises rules which were once feasible and applicable to the conditions of a particular society, but have ceased to be of value, hence have been discarded.

MORAL RIGHTNESS AND PRIMA FACIE DUTIES. The *right act* is defined as that which, under a given set of circumstances, will produce the greatest good possible, and, secondly, in terms of *moral suitability,* as the act which in the light of its whole character is suitable morally, the one which under a given set of circumstances offers the greatest amount of suitability. For example, a person caught in a predicament in which the consequence of honoring one promise involves the breaking of a second is expected to act on the more suitable of the two under the circumstances, and the breaking of the other is not countenanced as right, but regarded as right only in a certain respect.

The first aspect of the definition of right is self-evident; a confrontation with a moral situation presents us with prima facie obligations, responsibilities, claims, component suitabilities which command action of us, the resultant suitability of which is better than that of any other course of action that could have been taken under those circumstances. Prima facie duties are like Kant's absolute or unconditional imperatives in cases where they do not conflict with other prima facie duties. Prima facie duties include fidelity, reparation, gratitude, justice, beneficence, self-improvement, and refraining from injuring others. When prima facie obligations conflict, then "that act is one's duty which is in accord with the more stringent *prima facie* obligation" or "that act is one's duty which has the greatest balance of *prima facie* rightness over *prima facie* wrongness."

INDEFINABILITY OF MORAL RIGHTNESS. As for the nature of moral rightness, it is *indefinable.* "Moral rightness is an indefinable characteristic, and even if it be a species of a wider relation, such as suitability, its differentia cannot be stated except by repeating the phrase 'morally right' or a synonym"[44] comparable to the color *red,* which one distinguishes from other colors merely by asserting that it is red.

MORAL RIGHT AND OBLIGATION. *Moral right* is a term which

44. Ross, *Foundations of Ethics,* p. 316.

cannot be reduced to nonethical terms, and refers primarily to actions; accordingly, actions have as their most important predicate, *right*. Right, interpreted as *moral suitability,* encompasses (to a certain extent) a person's motives as well as the consequences of his actions in the sense that results of actions issue in the maximum possible fulfillment of those moral claims which obligate a person. Nevertheless, immediate motives are not obligatory, because actions, not motives, are chosen in a moral situation. Furthermore, since motives do not fall within the sphere of our obligation, what does is the obligation to *exert* ourselves to perform a morally suitable *act*. To reiterate, duty is not the act per se, such as paying debts owed, but the activity of *setting oneself* to pay them; the resulting receipt acknowledging payment, and other consequences, are not of our choosing, hence are not obligatory. Obligations, then, are *exertions,* the setting of oneself to perform actions which are on the whole the most *suitable* to the production of maximum good.

RULES FOR THE DETERMINATION OF RELATIVE PRIORITY OF PRIMA FACIE OBLIGATIONS. Rules for determining priority among prima facie obligations are: (*a*) the greater obligation lies with the action which produces the greater good over the lesser one; (*b*) the greater obligation rests with the action deliberately and explicitly made rather than with the one made casually or cursorily; (*c*) the majority opinion of "conscientious men" should prevail in cases of uncertainty.

TWO PRINCIPAL SENSES OF GOOD. The two main meanings of *good* are: (*a*) good as a worthy object of admiration and (*b*) good as a worthy object of interest. While both are applicable to virtuous activity and intellectual activity, only the latter is applicable to pleasure—certain pleasures which benefit others becoming our obligations. Usually, those activities relating to *will* are moral activities, qualifying as morally good, just as actions, emotions, desires, and so forth may be designated morally good under certain conditions, when they pertain to interests. As such they are interests, and interests acquire their goodness from the thing in which the interest is vested.

INTENSITY AND GENERALITY OF INTERESTS. Whereas interest in personal pleasure is morally neutral, that taken in the happiness of others is of moral worth, provided it leads to a good activity. A bad activity, such as the infliction of pain on others, is an immoral interest. Respecting interests, they may be rated as to their moral worth according to their *generality* and *intensity*. The wider the scope of altruistic activity, the better the interest; the deeper the intensity of altruism, the better; and vice versa in both rules. Furthermore, actions performed with a conscientious sense of duty are of higher moral value than those lacking it; although motive is a factor rendering an action good or bad, it is definitely not the sole one. For example, willingness to sacrifice enhances moral worth.

THE CAMBRIDGE DEONTOLOGISTS

As we have seen, deontologists share the view that the validity of moral obligations is not contingent upon the consequences issuing from such obligations, and that consequently some actions are right independent of their outcome.

C. D. Broad: Moral Truths as Axiomatically Intuited. Trained at Trinity College, Cambridge, and having spent practically his entire professional career there until his retirement in 1953, C. D. Broad approached ethical theory from the problems orientation. He rejected traditional solutions based upon subjective feelings as well as those based upon objective analysis which predicated properties of a subject.

RIGHT-MAKING AND GOOD-MAKING CHARACTERISTICS: RIGHT-TENDING AND WRONG-TENDING. Moral characteristics depend upon properties which are in themselves neutral, nonmoral. These nonmoral ones, inasmuch as they confer rightness or wrongness on moral characteristics, may be called *right-making* and *wrong-making characteristics.* The same can be said of good-making and bad-making characteristics. However, since it is impossible to discover a single fundamental right-making characteristic, such as "Every lie is wrong," it becomes necessary to speak of *right-tending* or *wrong-tending* characteristics, in place of right-making and wrong-making ones. For example, deception tends to be wrong.

Acts, in the form of either statements or behavior, may conflict. Under such circumstances, the right act is the one making the "best compromise between the various moral claims on the agent, after allowing due weight to the relative urgency of each claim."[45] Careful evaluation of the claims of both right-tending and wrong-tending characteristics, each group imposing its *component obligation* upon the agent with its own degree of urgency, produces a *resultant obligation,* which is to make the best compromise possible among the various component obligations.

TELEOLOGICAL AND NONTELEOLOGICAL OBLIGATIONS. Right-tending and wrong-tending characteristics can be divided into two groups: *teleological* and *nonteleological.* The former tend to make an act right, by producing the best consequences, or wrong, by producing evil consequences. The right-tending characteristics of the teleological type have the property of being *optimific* (producing good results) and are classed as teleological because their goodness refers to the good end or result, the good consequences which the act effects. The latter, the nonteleological, are independent of consequences; "the mere fact of being

45. C. D. Broad, "Some of the Main Problems of Ethics," *Philosophy* 21 (1946), pp. 99–117.

asked a question or having made a promise imposes on one an urgent component obligation to answer truly or to perform what one has promised, quite independently of whether the consequences will be good or bad. Accordingly, these right-tending characteristics are overtly or ostensibly nonteleological."[46]

INTENTION AND RIGHTNESS. An act is designated intentional when its features and expected consequences are known to its agent. The rightness of an act must be viewed from two standpoints, namely, the position of the patient (the person affected by the agent's action) and that of the agent. From the viewpoint of the patient, an act is right when it meets and fulfills the claims which the patient has on the agent, regardless of the agent's intentions. Viewed from the standpoint of the agent's responsibility, "an act is right if and only if it is done with the intention of fulfilling the patient's claim and giving him his rights in the matter."[47]

An act may be termed: (*a*) *materially right* when it actually fulfills those claims the patient has on the agent, notwithstanding the agent's intention respecting the consequential outcome of his act; (*b*) *formally right* when the act corresponds to the agent's intention to fulfill the patient's claim upon him regardless of the ensuing consequences, good or bad; and (*c*) *perfectly right* when the act is both formally and materially right. As to the first two, material rightness has primacy, because the patient's rights are more important than the agent's intentions.

MOTIVES AND THEIR ETHICAL FUNCTION. As he notes the characteristics and consequences of an act, the agent will be attracted by some, repelled by others, and indifferent to still others. An individual's *total motive* is derived by taking into consideration his *expectation* of ensuing consequences coupled to his *belief* regarding the action itself; this comprises the first or *cognitive* aspect of a motive. The second, the *conative-emotional aspect,* is a disposition on the part of the agent to be *attracted* to or *repelled* by doing the act excited by, or arising out of, his belief. Right or wrong predicated of acts must be in reference to those which are dependent upon an individual's *volition,* not his motives, because a person has the power of choosing one of many alternative actions available to him, but he cannot pick the specific motive which will attract or repel him in performing a given act.

The psychological hedonist has erroneously concluded that pleasantness is the only object of desire in moral considerations, but there exist other feelings of obligation which may be classified as desires and aversions possessing moral significance, and they may be referred to as the *"Desire to do what is Right as such."* Among specifically moral

46. Ibid.
47. Ibid.

emotions, some are reflexive (emotions directed toward the self) and others nonreflexive (emotions directed toward others). The former consist of guilt-feelings, remorse, and self-approval, whereas the latter are those feelings of moral approval or disapproval directed toward another person's act. Right and wrong in the light of this analysis of emotional attitudes consists in being "the object of moral approval or disapproval."[48]

C. D. BROAD'S DEONTOLOGY. By accepting ethical characteristics as sui generis, Broad repudiated ethical naturalism as false. Ethical terms, such as *right, ought, good,* and *duty,* being sui generis, are not derived empirically, but a priori, even though experience provides reason with suitable occasions (including emotional ones of approval and disapproval) for the formation of these moral characteristic concepts.

Although there are no self-evident propositions about total rightness (universal propositions of the Kantian type), we can find self-evident propositions regarding specifics taking the form: "Such and such a type of intention or emotion would necessarily be fitting (or unfitting) to such and such a kind of situation."[49] It is self-evident that it is fitting to experience gratitude toward one's benefactor, and unfitting to enjoy another's undeserved suffering. "Reason needs to meet with concrete instances of fitting or unfitting intentions and emotions before it can rise, by Intuitive Induction, to the insight that *any* such intention or emotion would necessarily be fitting (or unfitting) to *any* such situation."[50]

A single nonethical characteristic common to all intrinsic goods cannot be found, nor can a single supreme principle of ethics be found among all self-evident ones.

Right and wrong are specific and unanalyzable terms; the most that can be asserted of them is appropriateness or inappropriateness; that is to say, when an act is right, then it has a factor *fittingly* related to a wider total situation, and it is wrong when inappropriately or unfittingly suited to the entire situation.

Right and good are indefinable; however, it may well be that "X is good" is definable "as meaning that X is such that it would be a fitting object of desire to any mind which had an adequate idea of its non-ethical characteristics."[51]

On introspection and analysis of one's experiences, one will find a standing desire to do what is believed right as such, and conversely, to avoid what is believed wrong as such, whether or not this particular

48. Ibid.
49. C. D. Broad, *Five Types of Ethical Theory* (Paterson, N.J.: Littlefield, Adams, 1959), p. 282.
50. Ibid.
51. Ibid.

desire is stronger or weaker than other desires or conative tendencies. The presence of the basic desire would still be recognizable, and it would assist in right action, while making wrongdoing more difficult.

A. C. Ewing: The Indefinability of 'Ought'. Like many other contemporary British philosophers treating the subject of ethics, A. C. Ewing assumed the view that *common-sense* propositions are true, and all that remains for the philosopher is to analyze them. The task which he assigned to himself is the analysis or definition of *good, moral obligation,* and *fittingness* (three fundamental ethical concepts), in addition to criticizing and stemming the tide of ethical subjectivism with its ally, ethical naturalism. Subjectivism and naturalism, by depriving moral obligation of its rational basis, seriously weaken the sense of moral obligation. Ewing synthesized the ideal utilitarianism of G. E. Moore with the deontological intuitionism of W. D. Ross and H. A. Prichard.

MORAL TERMS AS NONNATURAL PROPERTIES. Ewing stood resolute on the contention that moral terms, such as *good, ought,* and *right* are nonnatural concepts which cannot be analyzed naturalistically, cannot be reduced to the premises of naturalism or ethical subjectivism.

One defect of *naturalism,* the philosophy which reduces all ethical characteristics to the facts of some science, is that it either cannot explain *ought* or eliminates it, hence ruling out all authority for our obligations. Ethics, then, is a study of its own, underived from and irreducible to any other. The moral predicates *good, right,* and *obligation* are sui generis, nonnatural concepts existing in their own right.

UNIQUENESS OF THE "OUGHT EXPERIENCE." The uniqueness of the "ought experience" renders acts moral. Consequently, all ethical discussion must begin with the concept *ought,* or at least must be based upon it; yet, if this is the case, then *ought* is an ultimate term used to explain all other ethical terms, and the term itself is *indefinable.*

Moore considered *good* indefinable, but good can be defined; it is analyzable in terms of *ought, ought* becoming the simple or ultimate term, the fundamental concept by which all other ethical ones are explained. At least one concept must be unanalyzable, and that concept must be the fundamental one to which all others are ultimately reduced, namely, *ought.*

GOODNESS, FITTINGNESS, AND MORAL OBLIGATION. Analysis of moral experience yields three fundamental concepts: goodness, fittingness, and moral obligation. All three are explicable in terms of *ought.* Fittingness is a relation between an act and its environment, moral obligation is an imperative on the agent, and good is the "fitting object of a pro attitude."[52]

Although claiming that he developed his ethical theory independently, Ewing's ideas markedly resemble those of Ross, but he dis-

52. A. C. Ewing, *The Definition of Good* (New York: Macmillan, 1947), pp. 152, 166, 178.

agreed with Ross's view that "what ought to be done" is never morally good. To act in a fitting manner is morally good. But *ought* requires of us more than the mere act; it necessitates a certain state of mind, a given direction of attention.

Goodness is not synonymous with fittingness, but must be defined as "what ought to be the object of a pro attitude." The intrinsically good is not merely desired, but desirable, worth having for its own sake, that is, it ought to be desired. More than what ought to be chosen, good means what ought to be admired. To predicate good of anything is to claim that it is worthy of bringing into existence—that it is fitting to be brought into existence, that it ought to exist. Good is what "ought to be the object of a pro attitude."[53] Accordingly, Ewing has defined good in terms of *ought.*

As for fittingness, it holds a place of primacy over moral obligation, for the "concept of moral obligation presupposes the concept of fittingness and not vice versa";[54] consequently, fittingness is the fundamental moral characteristic of ethics. Fittingness must not be understood as an effective means, that which produces a desired end, but as worthy for its own sake, an end-in-itself. Otherwise, it would not possess the power of moral obligation. What we ought to do is not a derivative from the good, but contrariwise, *fittingness is good,* and is chosen for itself, not for a good. Both my moral obligation and the good are determined by fittingness: my moral duty becomes the most fitting act in a given set of circumstances, and the good is the fitting object of my pro attitude. Thus, *ought* understood primarily as *fittingness* becomes the basic ethical term or characteristic.

CRITIQUE OF THE OXFORD AND CAMBRIDGE DEONTOLOGISTS

Deontologists have been widely accused of advancing prima facie duties that are ethnocentric, but this objection has been rebutted, especially by Ross, by demonstrating (as has been done by some anthropologists) that the duties cited are valid cross-culturally, and that these moral values have universal worth.

Criticism of the Ethical Formalism of W. D. Ross. According to Richard Brandt,[55] Ross's theory "can never be completely perfected," nor can a complete formalist system be "put on paper . . . in black and white." The incompleteness of Ross's system is due to the impossibility of determining one's duty in a particular circumstance from the principles laid down, with the exception of those instances where prima facie obligations do not conflict. Brandt also doubted whether

53. Ibid., p. 178.
54. Ibid., p. 185.
55. Richard Brandt, *Ethical Theory* (Englewood Cliffs, N.J.: Prentice-Hall, 1959), pp. 393–395.

Ross's "statement of the basic prima facie obligations includes all the qualifications and exceptions that ought to be included" and "whether there are not more prima facie obligations in addition to those he has described."[56] But Brandt is well aware that such strictures do not repudiate Ross's system because such objections are true of most ethical systems, nor is it necessary to be complete, for one need only establish the fundamental principles of his system and examples of its execution.

There are nevertheless valid objections to Ross's deontology, such as the criticism that he does not inform us about relative stringencies when prima facie obligations conflict. Moreover, Ross does not believe that simple generalizations are possible in this connection, despite the fact that we can often know which are the more stringent obligations and can agree upon a few rough generalizations, such as the statement that the obligation to refrain from injuring others is more stringent than the obligation to do good.

Objections to Prichard's Theory. Deontologists fail to inform us what moral goodness is, or the obligatory nature of an action, except to declare that such qualities are indefinable and sui generis (a peculiar or uniquely singular class). Prichard has offered no explanation why that which he designated right is indeed right, except to lead us to believe that since it is sui generis, it is inexplicable and indefinable, consequently must be intuited. To assert that one recognizes moral facts intuitively allows no room for ethical discussion, except to say that they are indefinable and sui generis.

But if moral predicates represent moral properties, then ethical information is conveyed. How then does one verify the truth of such pieces of information? Moreover, why should these facts have a bearing on my moral choices, since my duty is intuitively discerned? There must be reasons for my obligations, and moral judgments contain information, but the deontological intuitionists do not enlighten us on these issues.

Criticisms of Ewing's Theory. An objection to Ewing's concept of good as a pro attitude has been correctly anticipated by him, but he has not coped with it adequately. He predicts that "it will be objected against me that it is only fitting to approve, or have a pro attitude towards, what is good because we first know or believe it to be good, and that if we did not believe it to be good, there would be no ground for such an attitude, so that the attitude would not be fitting."[57] Yet, he thinks that the answer rests in certain factual characteristics of those things which one designates as good. It must be concluded, then, that it is necessary to discover what is good, and then to acquire a fitting attitude (pro attitude) toward it.

56. Ibid., p. 394.

57. A. C. Ewing, *The Definition of Good* (New York: The Macmillan Co., 1947), p. 172.

Furthermore, fitting attitudes are not always necessitated by the objective situation. For example, the average person would say that the suffering of his own child requires a greater obligation on his part than the suffering of a stranger's child in the remote part of the Arctic Circle or darkest Africa, yet the stranger's child may be experiencing more intense suffering. The objective moral situation would seemingly call for a greater concern for the stranger's child, but the sense of obligation of most persons would favor their own children.

Criticism of Deontologists as a Group. Blanshard disparagingly asserted that the deontologists are saying "that promise-keeping is our duty though in fact there is no good in it at all."[58] Continuing, he added, "we are being told that state of things A may be definitely and admittedly *worse* than B, and that it may still be our duty to bring A into being."[59]

According to Warnock,[60] deontologists fail to cast light on any of the ethical problems, for they answer none of the ethical questions. The issue is dismissed by denying that there is anything to be said, and in this respect deontologists are misleading. The single contribution of these men lies in their insistence that "moral judgments . . . cannot be identified with, 'reduced to,' or analysed in terms of, any of these other things; they are *different* from these things."[61] In a very important way, moral judgments differ from empirical or factual statements, aesthetic ones, or even commands and expressions of taste.

Kai Nielsen maintains that deontologists have failed to provide suitable criteria for determining the acceptability of worthy laws, practices, institutions, and rules. In this respect, his thinking favors the quasi-utilitarian reasoning characterizing the "good-reasons approach."

Criticizing Broad, Frankena argues that he "seems to be giving as his own an account of what happens in a first-hand deontic judgment which cannot be accepted by an intuitionist, but only by one who holds what he calls an 'Emotional Reaction' theory. Thus he seems at last to have parted company with the non-naturalists altogether."[62] Rebutting Frankena, Broad merely parries the issue with the reply, "I have no decided opinion."[63]

58. Brand Blanshard, *Reason and Goodness* (London: George Allen & Unwin, 1961), p. 149.

59. Ibid., p. 150.

60. G. J. Warnock, *Contemporary Moral Philosophy* (London: Macmillan, 1967), pp. 12–13.

61. Ibid., p. 13.

62. William K. Frankena, "Broad's Analysis of Ethical Terms," *The Philosophy of C. D. Broad,* ed. Paul Arthur Schilpp (New York: Tudor, 1959), p. 555.

63. C. D. Broad, "A Reply to My Critics," *The Philosophy of C. D. Broad,* p. 813.

9

Ethical Naturalism: A Scientific Explanation of Ethics

While ethical subjectivism reduced morals to a state of mind, ethical naturalism regards morals as an epiphenomenon of the body, a by-product of bodily function, with the result that it reduces morals to a physical state of the human body.

Four leading representatives of this school have been selected for examination, one from the early period of modern philosophy and three from the contemporary scene: Thomas Hobbes (1588–1679), British empiricist; Moritz Schlick (1882–1936), logical positivist; Ralph Barton Perry (1876–1957), American behaviorist; and John Dewey (1859–1952), American pragmatist or instrumentalist.

Most of the contemporary adherents to ethical naturalism base their thinking on the psychology of *behaviorism,* a view based on the premise that only the physical body and its behavior are ultimately real, and that all else (consciousness, value, mind, immaterial or spiritual object), inasmuch as it is nonobservable, is merely a concomitant of bodily activity.

Ethical naturalism treats morals as an empirical study, a branch of natural or social science, comparable to biology or sociology. Rather than evaluating moral values, the naturalist in ethics believes that he is simply describing natural phenomena, behavioral experiences which we ordinarily call moral. Supernatural phenomena or nonnatural qualities, the conclusions of ethical intuitionism, especially deontological intuitionism, are repudiated as fables. In other words, metaphysical moral values do not exist; only natural objects, observable and measurable, do.

One chief bias of naturalism is the doctrine of *scientism,* the theory that scientific laws alone sufficiently account for all phenomena, including moral phenomena. It will be observed that ethical theories based on the philosophy of naturalism trace morality to natural desires, interests, instincts, or other behavioral factors.

Thomas Hobbes: Natural Might Makes Right. Hobbes's ethical philosophy as it is set forth in his most outstanding work, *Leviathan*

(1651), is premised on the egoistic nature of man, tracing selfishness to the instinct of self-preservation, which (in his opinion) is capable of explaining the entire volitional life, and therefore the moral life, of man.

PRIMARY LAW OF NATURE: SELF-PRESERVATION. The first law of nature is self-preservation, which drives man to seek peace in order to preserve his own life. The drive of self-preservation, the most fundamental aspect of human nature, renders man egoistic, for self-preservation is the impulse to save *my own* life, not the life of another. I possess no instinct to save others.

MAN'S NATURAL STATE AS ONE OF EGOISM. Thus, Hobbesianism is a theory of egoism, a "selfish system" as his critics later termed it. Man, he found, is born selfish, egoistic, belligerent, untrustworthy, all owing to this instinct to preserve one's own life at the cost of others—all others.

In this primitive natural state, man is without the benefit of civil law or moral law. As for moral law, none exists; good, evil, right, wrong are merely legal codes, ideas agreed upon to avoid being destroyed, a social contract in which men have engaged. Where there is no moral law, the right of nature holds, the law of the jungle, the law of "tooth and claw." Such is man's natural state, a condition in which "might makes right"; actually, there is no right or wrong, but a natural state of surviving at all costs. In a condition of this nature, man is at war—if not one of physical violence, then at least an inherent covert struggle of being at odds with others. "To this way of every man, this also is consequent; that nothing can be unjust. The notions of right and wrong, justice and injustice have there no place. Where there is no common power, there is no law, where no law, no injustice."[1]

MORAL PRINCIPLES AS LEGALITY OR SOCIAL CONTRACTS. Moral principles that are observed by men in society are merely legal agreements, social contracts to which men bind themselves for the common interest, agreements prompted by the fundamental law of nature, "Seek peace and follow it." The social contract engaged in by all parties is a relinquishing of the right of nature, the surrendering of the principle of might makes right. All this is done for the sake of self-preservation, based on the equality of men when they are considered as members of groups rather than as individuals. Alone, even the strong man cannot stand, for eventually he can be destroyed by someone else—if not by a stronger individual, then by a weaker one in ambush, or by a group of weak men banded together for the common defense against him.

The social contract is a means of giving up the rights of nature in

1. Thomas Hobbes, *Leviathan* (London, 1651), part 1, chap. 13. To facilitate reading, the archaic spelling and English of Hobbes has been updated in some instances.

order to obtain in exchange protection by law. It binds you and me to surrender, equally, some natural rights. For example, I will not kill you, for the promise that you will not destroy me; I will not steal from you if you will reciprocate; or, as Hobbes phrased it: *"That a man be willing, when others are so too, as far as for peace and defence of himself he shall think it necessary, to lay dawn his right to all things: and be content with so much liberty against other men, as he would allow other men against himself."*[2] This rule Hobbes conceived as the Golden Rule (negatively stated): Do not do to others what you do not want them to do to you. Unless this contract is agreed to, then man remains in his original state of nature, a condition of war. But if man does accept this social contract, then moral rules follow (or, for Hobbes, laws are enacted), among which are to be found: justice, gratitude, compliance, pardon, and equity.

Nevertheless, Hobbes, fully convinced of man's egoistic inclinations, did not expect man to obey the laws established by the social contract because of an altruistic will, but because of force and under penalty of law, that is, under threat of punishment by the power of law enforcement, either the monarchal power of a potent ruler or the power established by a commonwealth of people in a state.

CRITICISM OF HOBBES. Sorley asserted that Hobbes deduced morality from society, basing it on the "fiction of an 'original contract.' "[3] Later, Hobbesian naturalism was singled out for rebuke by an ethical naturalist, Schlick, who was repulsed by the egoism found in Hobbes; he did not believe that the laws of a social contract were sufficiently impelling to motivate the ordinary man ethically. He claimed, moreover, that Hobbes's entire chain of reasoning is predicated on a "fictional human nature," and that the "most important ties that naturally bind men to their environment are here left out of account."[4] The Hobbesian system raises the question "Is the evil man natural, and the good man a deviation, an anomaly, or abnormality?"

The egoism of Hobbes is sharply attacked by Wheelright, who saw the success of this system in the half-truths espoused, such as: (1) all motives are fundamentally egoistic; (2) two men desiring the same thing automatically become lethal enemies; (3) every man is an enemy of every other man.[5] If such were the case, then a social contract would be impossible, and morality could not be created by such a document, nor would evil men regard the contract as binding, but

2. Ibid., pt. 1, chap. 14.

3. William Ritchie Sorley, *The Ethics of Naturalism* (1904) (Freeport, N.Y.: Books for Libraries, 1969), p. 139.

4. Moritz Schlick, *Problems of Ethics* (New York: Prentice-Hall, 1939), p. 164.

5. Philip Wheelright, *A Critical Introduction to Ethics,* 3d ed. (New York: Odyssey, 1959), pp. 201–203.

rather would view it as a piece of military strategy and find devious means of circumventing it. Unless obligations are inwardly acknowledged, duties become meaningless, since external conditions are incapable of creating them.

Moritz Schlick: Ethics as the Capacity for Happiness. Moritz Schlick developed an ethical naturalism based on the concept that altruistic desires expressed through the activity of kindness eventuate in happiness.

SCIENTIFIC STATUS OF ETHICS. For Schlick there are no moral principles or an empty sense of duty, since values are relative to personal desire and capacity for happiness; the nonnatural *ought* can be, and is, explained by the empirical or factual *is* of ethical naturalism.

Thus, ethics is a factual science. It may seem strange for a logical positivist to allocate any scientific standing at all to ethics. But, unlike other logical positivists such as A. J. Ayer, whose positivism led him to emotivism or value nihilism, Schlick did claim the status of real propositions for value judgments, scientific ones belonging to the science of psychology.

VALUATIONS AS FACTS. Valuations are not normative, but factual, for ethics deals with the *actual,* not the normative or the *ought.* "Only where the theory of norms ends does ethical explanation begin."[6] Then Schlick adds, " 'Value,' 'the good,' are mere abstractions, but valuation, approbation, are actual psychic occurrences, and separate acts of this sort are quite capable of explanation."[7] "The moral valuations of modes of behavior and characters are nothing but the emotional reactions with which human society responds to the pleasant and sorrowful consequences that, according to the average experience, proceed from those modes of behavior and characters."[8]

Ethics is concerned not with moral laws, but with motives, inquiring into the causes of conduct, determining their order and regularity with the goal of arriving at the "causal explanation of moral behavior." Ethics, in this respect, is a branch of psychology seeking descriptive propositions, not normative or absolute laws. Values are relative, existing only with respect to the individual. "The value of an object consists in the fact that this object, or the idea of it, produces a feeling of pleasure or pain in some feeling subject."[9] A world devoid of pleasure and pain would be a world without values. Although values relate to the subject, the subject does not impute or will value to objects capriciously. The disvalue experience of pain cannot be dismissed at will.

Freedom of the will Schlick considers a pseudoproblem, since willing

6. Schlick, *Problems of Ethics,* p. 23.
7. Ibid., p. 24.
8. Ibid., p. 78.
9. Ibid., p. 24.

is simply a matter of motivation. Often there are many motivations brought to bear upon the will, and when this is the case, the dominant motive is termed an act of will, for the ascendant motive constitutes a person's preference. A person's value choices are based on the "pleasure value" of a motive. Psychological hedonism becomes the law of motivation; the most pleasant stimulus is our strongest motivation.

MORAL VALUE AS ALTRUISTIC DESIRE. Unlike Hobbes, Schlick is a strong proponent of *altruism,* a philosophy of sympathy inspired by Schopenhauer, and he reserved some of his most vehement denunciations for philosophies of egoism and "Hobbes's fiction." Egoism, even under the guise of self-preservation, is immoral, and is at best inconsiderateness, not the willing of pleasure. True pleasure or happiness is always a moral concern, and morality leads to it. Not egoistic desires, but social and altruistic ones lead to happiness and pleasure. The "same dispositions which lead to the greatest possibilities of pleasure are identical with those from which, for the most part, virtuous conduct springs; this means that virtue and happiness have the same causes, that they must go hand in hand."[10] Kindness, an altruistic disposition, always leads to happiness, for the overt expressions of happiness and altruism are the same: "Man smiles when he is gay, and also he feels sympathy; kindness and happiness have the same facial expression; the friendly man is also the happy man, and vice versa."[11] Altruistic inclinations and moral behavior are identical; the former lead to the latter, and, in turn, to happiness.

MORALITY DEFINED. From what has been said, we are able to formulate the principle of morality: "At all times be fit for happiness," or "Be ready for happiness."[12] Thus, the moral principle defines morality as "that behavior by means of which an individual furthers his capacity for happiness."[13] This definition of morality is warranted on the grounds that it can bring into realization what man in fact most highly prizes or values. The capacity for happiness is, then, the essence of ethics.

This idea is comparable to the Kantian concept of the good man being *worthy* of happiness, but the interpretation here of the Kantian theory is that he who is capable of happiness is in fact worthy of happiness, for he is the individual who is enabled to "appropriate the value of valuable things" by deriving intense feelings—feelings of joy —through their right use.

THE VALUE OF ALTRUISM. Worthiness to be happy necessitates the appropriate psychological disposition, a moral one, namely,

10. Ibid., p. 192.
11. Ibid., p. 194.
12. Ibid., p. 197.
13. Ibid.

altruism. The essential characteristic of altruism is considerateness toward others, expressed in friendly understanding of their needs and providing suitable accommodations for their fulfillment. Considerateness entails the inhibition of egoistic impulses, and this is the task not of the individual solely, but of society in its historical progress through time. With the subjugation of nonaltruistic impulses, higher or nobler impulses are developed, enabling the good to be performed willingly, as Kant would also have it. But the task, which is a lengthy and arduous one, not attained completely by anyone yet, for we are "all-too-human" (as Nietzsche contends), remains the ceaseless moral activity of civilization.

KINDNESS AND PERSONALITY DEFINED. Schlick defined *kindness* as "the totality of altruistic impulses," and *personality* as the "firm interconnection of all impulses."[14] With the understanding of personality and kindness in this light, it becomes obvious that they are "the basic conditions of a valuable existence."[15] The moral man enjoys morality, for being good comes naturally. "Man is noble because he *enjoys* such behavior; the moral values rank so high because they signify the highest joys; the values do not stand above him but reside within him; it is *natural* for him to be good."[16] The ethics of kindness is superior to the ethics of duty; the good person wants to live the most valuable life and, in all probability, does so. With the good person, morality is performed with ease; it becomes his nature so to act. Human perfection is a pleasurable endeavor.

EVALUATION OF SCHLICK'S ETHICAL THEORY. The system developed by Schlick strikes one as being superficial, with an overemphasis on kindness. To be sure, kindness is a moral quality; it is nevertheless incapable of explaining many of our moral predicaments satisfactorily. Many mothers, out of a deep sense of kindness, have committed actions resulting in misery for their children, such as the mother who, in seeking a desirable suitor for her daughter, causes her only embarrassment and disgrace. Although kindness is a wholesome and desirable motivation, it requires rational direction.

Schlick is in the logically delicate position of holding a person responsible for his actions, while at the same time denying freedom of the will. A person's motivation is due to causal psychological laws; thus, one is without freedom. If man is devoid of freedom, why then should one engage in moral reform? It would be an impossibility. But according to Schlick, once a person gains an awareness of his actions, he is by virtue of that fact responsible for his behavior because he is consciously knowledgeable of his desires. If this is true, then our most superior moral giants would be those professionals who are cognizant

14. Ibid., p. 205.
15. Ibid.
16. Ibid.

of the nature of desires and of human behavior (e.g., psychologists and psychiatrists), for these persons have the advantage of pursuing the highest ethical goals and achieving the finest values, owing to their expertise regarding motivation and human behavior.

Schlick's denial of the freedom of will also fails the pragmatic test, for in our daily lives, each of us is held responsible for his actions, because we believe that a person's choices can be deliberate, that is, that they are free, or within his powers to pursue or avoid.

An overly optimistic climate engulfs Schlick's philosophy. He assumed that those moral actions conducive to individual happiness also contribute to collective happiness or societal good. Yet, according to notable psychiatrists, especially Freud, this assumption is contrary to clinical findings. Freud traced the cause of neurosis to a frustration of the fulfillment of the needs and pleasures of the individual in direct conflict with social demands, the resulting conflict raging between one's superego and id in disharmony.

Ralph Barton Perry: The Interest Theory of Value. The line of ethical naturalism continues in the philosophy of Ralph Barton Perry, and its evolution can readily be traced. Hobbes initiated the thinking postulated on the basic nature of man as egoistic and amoral, while Schlick, contradicting Hobbesian egoism, replaced it with the hypothesis that man is fundamentally moral and altruistic by nature. In both cases human desires are under consideration, but for the one they are narcissistic, and for the other, altruistic. Pursuing the same problem, Ralph Barton Perry translated desire into *interest.*

VALUE DEFINED AS OBJECT OF INTEREST. Value is dependent upon interest; whatever is the object of a person's interest becomes an object of value. Interest confers value on objects; "that which is an object of interest is *eo ipso* invested with value. Any object, whatever it be, acquires value when any interest, whatever it be, is taken in it; just as anything whatsoever becomes a target when anyone whosoever aims at it."[17] The deeper the interest, then the more valuable the object; and the greater the number of individuals expressing an interest in the object, the greater its value. Objects increase in value concomitantly as interest is shown in them, and lose value as interest diminishes.

Perry defines *good* as *"the relation of an object to a valuing subject."*[18] Yet Perry noticed an element of circularity in his definition of value, for to state that an object is good is to assert it to be an object of interest, but what happens in the case of an addict's interest in drugs which are deleterious? For a thing to be good, does it require a *good* interest? If so, then good is defined in terms of good, resulting in complete circularity. This objection is met by claiming the interest

17. Ralph Barton Perry, *General Theory of Value* (Cambridge, Mass.: Harvard University Press, 1926), p. 115.
18. Perry, *General Theory of Value,* p. 122.

per se as good, not the object per se which can be either of positive or negative worth, helpful or destructive.

CALCULUS OF VALUE: CRITERIA OF RIGHT. When interests conflict and must be evaluated against one another, then the *calculus of value* Perry devised is employed. The calculus consists of four criteria: *correctness, intensity, preference,* and *inclusiveness.* Strictly speaking, correctness is the only criterion, whereas the remaining three are measures of value, and serve in the twofold capacity of qualifying interest and identifying its generic character or genuineness. To illustrate: "An object, wine, is better than an object, water: (1) if the interest in the wine is more intense than the interest in the water; (2) if the wine is preferred to the water; and (3) if the interest in the wine is more inclusive than the interest in the water."[19] The criterion of correctness identifies a value as genuine. The standards of intensity may be recognized as one in Bentham's hedonistic calculus, while the standard of preference is Mill's criterion for determining qualitative pleasure or value. The fourth, the standard of inclusiveness, is recognizable as a utilitarian principle of Mill and Bentham: "the greatest good for the greatest number." When a number of persons take an interest in an object, its value is augmented so that the object of interest of a single individual (all things being equal) is not as valuable as that of a community, and that of a community not as great as that of humanity. Consequently, a universal interest would be of greatest worth, our *summum bonum,* which would displace conflict with harmony.

REALMS OF VALUE. With the introduction of the *summum bonum,* the greatest good, as *all-inclusiveness of interests,* one encounters the question of realms of value. As noted earlier, the more interest taken in an object, the greater its value, and the more individuals who share that interest, the greater still that value, so that the interest in collecting stamps, which we may cite as an example, is not as great as the interest in music, for more individuals have an interest in music (and an interest greater in intensity as well); accordingly, music is of greater value than philately, the hobby of stamp collecting. Nevertheless, music and philately are both realms of value because people share an interest in each of them.

Or, to illustrate the matter in another way, since institutions, such as those in education, religion, health, and banking, hold an interest for the majority of us, they become realms of value, *shared* values. These shared values, then, are of greater worth, owing to their inclusiveness, and their harmonizing or unifying effect on other interests. They best meet the requirements of the calculus of value.

THE *Summum Bonum:* UNIVERSAL INTEREST. To obtain the

19. Ibid., p. 616.

greatest good, the *summum bonum,* would be to find that interest which is most inclusive and harmonious, for such will be the ideal. This object, this all-harmonious, all-benevolent, and enlightened unanimity, Perry identified as *universal love,* an attitude or disposition of loving-kindness toward all mankind, an "attitude of general kindly interest or amiability"—that is to say, a good will toward one's fellow man.

Perry would have the Kantian categorical imperative revised to read: "Cultivate that kind of will that is qualified to bring harmony through its universal adoption."[20] Man's highest interest, an all-benevolent will, love, will do more for the harmony and benefit of man than any other interest; consequently, this all-benevolent will is man's highest interest or greatest good, and through this, universal happiness will emerge.

CRITICISM OF PERRY'S ETHICAL NATURALISM. One of the severest critics of Perry's naturalism, Brand Blanshard, contended that Perry has gone awry by identifying goodness with interest, because interest does not necessarily transmit goodness to an object; in many cases it merely "reveals how blind we are." The most that can be ascribed to interest is that it is merely one of the conditions of goodness. As William James commented, the art displayed on the Vatican walls is valuable though it holds no interest for stray dogs (and for that matter, one may add, for unappreciative human beings). Granted that the feeling of interest is important, it is not of sufficient import to be equated with goodness per se.

It is possible for a person to develop an interest in something bad, and though the interest as such may be good, the object remains bad and unworthy of devotion. On the other hand, a good object worthy of a particular person's interest may not command his interest at all. This condition is often true of children who cannot appreciate certain objects of art, poetry, and worthwhile experiences until they have reached a certain stage of maturity. In other words, there are instances in which goodness may be present, and even when a person is aware of the fact, he still may not experience any interest. For example, reading nonfiction may be a good habit, with the individual involved so acknowledging it, yet he may not feel any interest in doing so.

It seems virtually needless to point out that Perry's definition is subject to G. E. Moore's "naturalistic fallacy." But it is much less noticeable that in Perry's system, since there can be no bad or evil interest, it follows that all interests are good. Although it could be argued that the ability to become interested (as a human experience) is good, it cannot be proved that all interests or all objects in which a person invests his interests are good.

20. Ibid., p. 682.

John Dewey: Ethical Theory of Instrumentalism. The fourth system of ethical naturalism under consideration is offered by one of the most original American thinkers in ethics, John Dewey. He was a founder of the school of *pragmatism,* or as he preferred to identify his philosophical position, *instrumentalism,* a school that considers ideas as instruments for effective action, a means for regulating environment for the satisfaction of human desires and needs.

INSTRUMENTAL THEORY OF VALUES. Dewey, dissatisfied with Perry's definition of value as any object of interest (because, as he contended, it justifies an interest in burglary), offered his own value theory by defining value as connected with liking, prizing, appraising, enjoying, and the like, yet "not with *every* liking but only with those that judgment has approved, after examination of the relation upon which the object liked depends."[21] The distinction between liking something casually and liking something that our reflective judgment has approved is that the former is accidental, without our knowledge of its nature or knowledge of its cause-and-effect relationships. The former is a mere desire, the latter is desir*able.* Enjoyments possessing value do so owing to our knowledge of conditions and consequences "and hence [have] a claim upon our attitude and conduct."[22]

Simply to state that one does in fact desire a given object is to beg the question of its desirability; the simple assertion that one wants something does not make it worth having. "There is no value except where there is satisfaction, but there have to be certain conditions fulfilled to transform a satisfaction into a value."[23] In valuation, there is a judgment, a prediction, an estimate, an appraisal. To "declare something satis*factory*" is to summon an attitude, elicit a striving to secure it, to perpetuate it. It is a logical judgment that the thing "will do," hence that it is something to be prized, to be cherished, to be enjoyed. A judgment of value "about what is *to be* desired and enjoyed is . . . a claim on future action; it possesses *de jure* and not merely *de facto* quality."[24] It is an evaluation, sanctioning the act, granting it authority, asserting its validity. Thus, the fundamental proposition is: *"Judgments about values are judgments about the conditions and the results of experienced objects; judgments about that which should regulate the formation of our desires, affections, and enjoyments."*[25]

Dewey refused to sever instrumental from intrinsic values, for he treated *means-ends* (or means-consequences) as continuous and interactive, applying the term "appraising" to things as means, and the term

21. John Dewey, *The Quest for Certainty* (New York: G. P. Putnam, 1929), p. 264.
22. Ibid.
23. Ibid., p. 268.
24. Ibid., p. 263.
25. Ibid. p., 265.

"prizing" to things as ends. But with any end-in-view, there is a union of prizing and appraising, just as ends and means are wedded. Where desires exist, ends-in-view are found. *"Propositions in which things (acts and materials) are appraised as means enter necessarily into desires and interests that determine end-values."*[26]

MORALITY AS GROWTH. With his usual aversion for the static and stagnant, Dewey offered an ethical theory with the emphasis on growth, improvement, progress. Emphatically stating this concept of morality in his *Reconstruction in Philosophy,* he unequivocally asserted, "The bad man is the man who no matter how good he *has* been is beginning to deteriorate, to grow less good. The good man is the man who no matter how morally unworthy he *has* been is moving to become better. . . . Growth itself is the only moral 'end.' "[27]

Moral growth could imply a *summum bonum,* but Dewey stood adamant in his denial of any, because human nature is altering constantly, and when its direction of movement is progressive, when there is upward growth, then the individual is said to be moral. A *summum bonum* suggests an absolute, and such fixed finalities were repugnant to Dewey, for they would terminate moral advancement, stagnating conduct by inserting it into fixed molds. There are no absolutes; a value is final only in the sense that it concludes the analytic process of resolving conflict conditions. While no absolute right exists, a right choice does, being that which resolves the confronting conflicting situation, restoring harmony. Inasmuch as when one conflicting situation is resolved, others arise which must be similarly treated, then ultimates, such as absolute good and absolute right, do not exist. Absolute good health as a fixed standard does not exist, but improvement in health does; hence, health is an end and good is a continual process, as is any other value or moral goal of man. Moral values are "directions of change in the quality of experience,"[28] as moral growth implies.

Fixed moral standards are not pragmatically feasible, due to the uniqueness of each moral situation, each with its own "irreplaceable good." Moral responsibility must be determined by intelligent choice, not by appeals to absolute moral laws, for each case is a special one calling for methods which pertain to it specifically. Moral laws are general and abstract, whereas action is specific and concrete.

Any science is moral science that contributes to the solution or alleviation of man's problems. Moreover, the natural sciences must be humanized, must contribute to moral issues, must improve man's lot, must eliminate human woe, must be socialized by contributing to the

26. John Dewey, *Theory of Valuation* (Chicago: University of Chicago Press, 1939), p. 35.

27. John Dewey, *Reconstruction in Philosophy* (New York: New American Library, 1950), p. 141.

28. Ibid.

enhancement of social progress. Evil is an instrumental problem—not a metaphysical one, but a practical one of alleviating human ills. Neither pessimism nor optimism is indicated, but *meliorism,* a happy, encouraging, and confident belief that man by an intelligent course of action will improve, progress, advance, and remedy his problems. As all things are progressive, so is happiness—not a fixed attainment, but found in succeeding, i.e., advancing in life.

MORALITY AS SOCIAL. Morality is more than a scientific and personal matter, it is a social affair: "Morality is social,"[29] socially conditioned, with value judgments and moral responsibility arising out of the social milieu. Individual actions have social consequences. Valuation as social is based on the shared experience of a community with common values used in the reconstruction of society.

CRITICISM OF DEWEY'S ETHICAL THEORY. The perennial problem of ethical naturalists of every period and description has been to reduce moral value terms to factual ones subject to empirical verification by sense observation. But each attempt to do so apparently misses "their distinctive, dynamic, and guiding function in the stream of life."[30]

Attending to Dewey's ethical theory specifically, Mothershead has two salient objections, one striking at the heart of Dewey's criterion. First, since Dewey regarded the desirable, the object of reflective thought, as compatible with social harmony, then "it appears that a want does not count as a truly post-reflective one unless it is harmonious with the want of others. We seem to have here a vicious circle, which could be broken only by frankly admitting that social harmony is being used as an objective moral standard."[31] Yet Dewey denies the existence or validity of any such absolute standard. Second, regarding post-reflective desires as moral values as Dewey did, then the question arises: "What does one do with desires that consensus deems perverse and harmful?" The implication obviously is that perversity, cruelty, suffering, and pain are moral values, provided that they are postreflective desires.

Both Morton G. White and C. L. Stevenson object to Dewey's attempt to distinguish between *de jure* and *de facto* statements. White asserted:

> In connecting the desirable (value) with the desired he must connect them in such a way as to show clearly that whereas the statement "a is desired now" is merely a statement of fact, the statement "a is desirable" is a factual statement which also has

29. John Dewey, *Human Nature and Conduct* (New York: Henry Holt, 1922), p. 316.

30. Kai Nielsen, "Ethics, History of," in *The Encyclopedia of Philosophy* (New York: Macmillan & Free Press, 1967), 3:105.

31. John L. Mothershead, *Ethics* (New York: Henry Holt, 1955), pp. 153–154.

> a *"de jure* quality." The problem, then, is to give an analysis of *"a* is desirable" when it is construed as meaning *a ought to be desired,* which will render it an empirical statement, a statement which conveys empirical knowledge.[32]

It is not that this is impossible, according to White, but that Dewey failed to accomplish the task, for Dewey construed *desirable* and *value* as "disposition-predicates," with the resultant belief that he reduced *desirable* to an empirical level. In reducing *"a* is desirable" to an empirical statement, Dewey construed "the property of being desirable as a disposition by analogy with objective characteristics like red as distinct from phenomenal appearance of red,"[33] but in so doing he neither clarifies nor defines *desirable* as meaning "ought to be desired."

The ambiguity of interpretation rests with Dewey's writing, according to Stevenson, who understood Dewey's de jure statements as predictions "selected and used in an effort to guide attitudes."[34] Otherwise, to contend that all de jure value statements are predictive would encounter the problem of predicting rain as evaluative.

32. Morton G. White, "Value and Obligation in Dewey and Lewis," in *Philosophical Review* 58 (1949): 322.

33. Ibid., p. 329.

34. Charles L. Stevenson, *Ethics and Language* (New Haven: Yale University Press, 1944), p. 256.

10

Evolutionary Naturalism: Ethics as the Product of Evolution

Each of the philosophers of evolutionary naturalism envisaged a higher man, a more developed being of greater moral significance. Nietzsche referred to that superior being as *superman* (overman), while Bergson, another exponent of evolutionary philosophy, regarded the world as a "machine for the making of gods." Specific representatives of the ethics of evolutionary naturalism selected for discussion in this chapter are: Charles Darwin (1809–1882), Herbert Spencer (1820–1903), Friedrich Wilhelm Nietzsche (1844–1900), and Thomas Henry Huxley (1825–1895).

Charles Darwin: Social Instincts as the Prime Principle of Man's Moral Sense (Conscience). The ethical theory of Charles Darwin is a derivative of his theory of evolution; it is a theory founded upon man's moral sense, conscience, as the product of social instincts. Darwin's is a biological evolution; consequently, he sought to establish an explanation of moral principles, moral consciousness, on the basis of man's physical nature, explained in terms of mechanistic laws. Man and his behavior are explained in line with his animal ancestry, from which he differs in great degree, but not in kind.

MORAL SENSE AND CONSCIENCE. Darwin recognized the "moral sense," or conscience, as the most important distinction between man and lower animals. The influence of classical intuitionism upon Darwin is notable.

Darwin repudiated the contention of the utilitarians, who sought to explain man's moral behavior on the basis of "the greatest happiness principle," because "man seems often to act impulsively, that is from instinct or long habit, without any consciousness of pleasure."[1] A man will endure fire and extreme peril to rescue a fellow creature, and even will die for another person; such behavior cannot be properly regarded as aimed at pleasure without doing violence to language. Man's motivation is not pleasure, but impulsive power, instinctive behavior, a deeply implanted social instinct. According to the doctrine of natural

1. Charles Darwin, *The Descent of Man* (London 1871), chap. 4.

selection, social instincts have "been developed for the general good rather than for the general happiness of the species."[2] By the general good is meant "rearing of the greatest number of individuals in full vigour and health, with all their faculties perfect,"[3] under prevailing conditions.

THE ACQUISITION OF VIRTUES. The virtues which prompt man to noble actions have probably been acquired through natural selection, as have the social instincts. The more enduring social instincts dominate the less persistent ones, and it is for this reason that a person will sense an obligation to obey one instinctive desire rather than another, or sense bitter regret at yielding to the temptation of self-preservation by not risking his own life to save another person, or even feel regret for having stolen food to prevent starvation. "Man in this respect differs profoundly from the lower animals."[4]

A conscience-stricken man is the victim of his social instincts, which cause a sense of regret for having antisocially expressed his desire for self-preservation, lust, vengeance, and the like.

> At the moment of action, man will no doubt be apt to follow the stronger impulse; and though this may occasionally prompt him to the noblest deeds, it will more commonly lead him to gratify his own desires at the expense of other men. But after their gratification when past and weaker impressions are judged by the ever-enduring social instinct, and by his deep regard for the good opinion of his fellows, retribution will surely come. He will then feel remorse, repentence, regret, or shame. . . . He will consequently resolve more or less firmly to act differently for the future; and this is conscience; for conscience looks backwards, and serves as a guide for the future.[5]

Compare the striking similarity of this explanation of guilt and conscience with that of Freud, who replaced the social instincts with the superego, and the egoistic instincts with the id. The above deliberations transpire through man's higher mental processes, his ability to reflect, to reason (the Freudian ego). Note also the probability that, although the egoistic instincts are stronger, the social ones will eventually conquer.

According to this very optimistic account of human development, good virtues or altruistic instincts will someday decisively dominate the egoistic ones. Man's higher moral principles, founded on social instincts relating to the welfare of others, are enhanced by social approbation and further supported by reason, which regards them as the better course of action. Sympathy, the sharing of painful experiences

2. Ibid.
3. Ibid.
4. Ibid.
5. Ibid.

of others by the remembrance of those which one previously has himself experienced, becomes the virtue and quality that Darwin termed *humanity;* by it, the human being sorrows even for the lower animals.

Furthermore, moral tendencies are relayed by heredity to one's offspring by what Darwin believed was "the principle of transmission of moral tendencies."[6] Both Darwin and Spencer believed in the Lamarckian theory of *inherited acquired characteristics,* and applied it to moral inheritance. Virtuous tendencies, once practiced until imbedded in the personality as habit, transmitted from one generation to succeeding ones, eventually emerge as innate virtues in a subsequent generation. "Looking to future generations, there is no cause to fear that the social instincts will grow weaker, and we may expect that virtuous habits will grow stronger, becoming perhaps fixed by inheritance. In this case the struggle between our higher and lower impulses will be less severe, and virtue will be triumphant."[7]

NATURAL SELECTION AND MORALITY. It may be well to add a word of qualification. The high level of morality developed in present civilizations is not believed by Darwin to be explained simply by reference to social instinct and natural selection, for other causes play a part. Furthermore, Darwin encountered logical difficulty in attempting to account for loyalty and sympathy as desirable for evolutionary progress, especially when they lead to the preservation of the unfit of society, the mentally, socially, and physically ill who become an unnecessary burden to the species, which might well benefit if they were done away with by euthanasia instead of being supported as parasites. Reason and natural selection would dictate euthanasia, but sympathy and human morality that Darwin called "the noblest part of our nature" would be betrayed. The question remains unresolved, though it seems probable that Darwin would be loyal to the "noblest part of our nature."

CRITICAL COMMENTS ON DARWIN'S ETHICAL THEORY. According to Darwin's theory of survival of the fittest, natural selection via power makes for progress. Essentially, this becomes a philosophy of "might makes right," condemned by Huxley in his evolutionary theory of ethics. It is difficult to see why conscience, social instincts, and sympathy should be the products of evolution's highest achievement during the course of natural selection.

The ethical question is not whether man obeys his impulses, but which impulse he should allow to have expression and which impulse should be repressed to a state of atrophy. Darwin seemed to think that this process is a natural one and will be cared for naturally, but Huxley disagreed and rightly contended that man must take the initiative to

6. Ibid.
7. Ibid.

discriminate as to which aspect of his moral nature should take precedence and be allowed to develop.

An assumption of evolutionary theory is that the process of evolution is one of progress, that the evolved are preferable to their evolutionary predecessors. The questions raised in regard to this point are: Are all the results of the evolutionary process good? And is every step of the process a move toward perfection? Is biological advancement necessarily moral advancement? These questions must be so resolved as to buttress the theory of evolution before its proponents can expect endorsement. But even evolutionary thinkers are in disagreement regarding them.

Herbert Spencer: Ethics of Evolutional Utilitarianism. The ethics of survival proposed by Spencer is one in which all mankind lives both a longer and a fuller life by finding suitable ways of adjusting to the social, physical, and biological environment.

THE SUPREME GOOD: LIFE'S ELONGATION. Life is of fundamental value, and the elongation of life is the supreme good, but a life extended both in length and in breadth, in quantity and quality, in longevity of days as well as in fullness or richness. Actually, the better life, one that is well adjusted to suitable ends, will inevitably have as its accompaniment the longer span of life. "Along with this greater elaboration of life produced by the pursuit of more numerous ends, there goes that increased duration of life which constitutes the supreme end."[8]

ADJUSTMENT AS MORALITY. Adjustment to life, or actions conducive to living, are those designated moral, and behavior harmful to life is immoral; life is defined as "the continuous adjustment of internal relations to external relations."[9] Having understood life in the light of adjustment, Spencer holds that the better adjusted one's life, the more moral it is. "Conduct is right or wrong according as its special acts, well or ill adjusted to special ends, do or do not further the general end of self-preservation."[10]

MORAL GOOD AS THE MORE EVOLVED CONDUCT. Implicit in what has been said is the idea that good conduct is advanced conduct, i.e., of a higher type, as far as development, progress, and evolution are concerned. Stated according to Spencer's dictum: "The conduct to which we apply the name good, is the relatively more evolved conduct; and bad is the name we apply to conduct which is relatively less evolved."[11] Evolved conduct strives toward self-preservation, reaching its apex

8. Herbert Spencer, *The Data of Ethics* (London, 1879), chap. 2, sect. 4; also found as Part I of his *The Principles of Ethics* (London, 1892). The former work was incorporated into the latter.

9. Ibid., chap. 2, sect. 7.

10. Ibid., chap. 3, sect. 8.

11. Ibid.

when individual life attains its maximum length and breadth; accordingly, "we regard as good the conduct furthering self-preservation, and as bad the conduct tending to self-destruction."[12]

MELIORISM. To assert that right conduct is that which is conducive to or enhances life implies that life is worth living, but is this assumption warranted? Does this philosophy imply optimism? Spencer's answer is neither optimism nor pessimism, but *meliorism,* or what he termed *qualified optimism,* the view that the world tends to become better. Consequently, our task is more than mere survival; it is the enrichment of life with its pleasurable bounties: good humor, good music, and so forth, and those things which are the source of man's enjoyment are defined as intrinsic goods.

Enjoyable experiences and their objects are conducive to life, and they augment it lengthwise and breadthwise. "If we call good considered intrinsically, each act adjusted to its end such as to further self-preservation and that surplus of enjoyment which makes self-preservation desirable—if we call good every kind of conduct which aids the lives of others, and do this under the belief that life brings more happiness than misery; then it becomes undeniable that, taking into account immediate and remote effects on all persons, the good is universally the pleasurable."[13] Conduct conducive to life is also conduct which elevates one's happiness.

SPENCERIAN UTILITARIANISM. The strong strain of utilitarianism in Spencer's ethical theory does not mean that he accepted the position of Bentham or Mill, for he found nature aristocratic, not democratic. Bentham's "greatest happiness principle" and his dictum "each is to count for one, nobody for more than one" are unsatisfactory inasmuch as they permit the thief as much right to his vicious activity as the good man's right to his altruistic deeds. Spencer's ethic is not so egoistic as Bentham's or Hobbes's, but a synthesis in which egoism and altruism are united. While it is true that a person must seek his own pleasure and preserve his own life, yet this is often accomplished by aiding others, and one's own welfare is jeopardized by failing to be altruistic. A compromise is indicated: we must live for others as well as for ourselves. The two are not contradictory, for in a measure self-happiness is gained by furthering another's happiness, and general happiness is furthered by promoting self-happiness. "Our conclusion must be that general happiness is to be achieved mainly through the adequate pursuit of their own happiness by individuals; while, reciprocally, the happiness of individuals is to be achieved in part by their pursuit of the general happiness."[14]

A rule of right conduct would then be one which to the advantage of

12. Ibid.
13. Ibid., chap. 3, sect. 10.
14. Ibid., chap. 13, sect. 91.

all can be adopted by everyone; and "good conduct . . . always proves, when analyzed, to be the conception of a conduct which produces a surplus of pleasure";[15] conversely, bad conduct results in a surplus of pain. From this it follows that the "absolutely good, the absolutely right, in conduct, can be that only which produces pure pleasure—pleasure unalloyed with pain anywhere."[16] In perfect conduct, pain is absent, for insofar as pain is inflicted, evil has been suffered. Evil is totally absent in the presence of absolute good.

Absolute and Relative Ethics. Absolute good brings us to the question of absolute and relative ethics, the ideal and the actual, the highest point of evolved conduct and conduct as it is evolving in a state of transition, the perfectly right and the least of the evils. When the perfectly or absolutely right cannot be realized, then one commits the least of the evils, that is, the relatively right.

The absolute right yields perfect enjoyment for all, a high state of evolutionary development in which altruism dominates motivation, and equal pleasure is experienced in either giving or receiving. Through *sympathy* man develops an "altruistic sentiment of Justice" that awakens in him a concern for the rights of others. Altruism, then, becomes a natural state of existence, and ideal conduct one with ideal humanity, the highest state of evolution—man's ultimate goal.

Comments on Spencerian Ethics. Spencer sought to harmonize his evolutionary ethics with utilitarianism by claiming a life of longevity and breadth to be one of happiness as well. However, though his theory depended on it, he failed to synthesize them with adequate proof; instead, he simply assumed that evolution has a tendency toward man's happiness.

Furthermore, he failed to draw a clear distinction "between the historical process explained by the law of evolution and the ground of its authority for conduct,"[17] a deficiency of all exponents of evolutionary ethics subsequent to Spencer's time.

Provided that the Lamarckian theory of inherited acquired characteristics is true, Spencer's evolutionary ethics has a base upon which to build, but Lamarck's theory is not widely supported among scientists today, and it is an extravagant assumption without which Spencerian ethics falls devastatingly.

According to Hill, Spencer erred in equating right with increasing complexity and integration, that is, with higher forms of evolution, because once intelligence and social organization appeared, then destructive forces in the form of disintegrating and ravaging wars en-

15. Ibid., chap. 15, sect. 101.
16. Ibid.
17. W. R. Sorley, *A History of British Philosophy to 1900* (Cambridge: At the University Press, 1965), p. 271.

sued.[18] Human development and progress depend upon human morality, not vice versa. Perhaps Spencer missed this point owing to his living in an era of relative peace. But in an era such as the contemporary scene in which a reprobate could possibly end humanity and its progress, one doubts seriously whether evolutionary forces can harness man's bent toward devastation.

Friedrich Nietzsche: An Ethics of Power. One clear indication of Darwinism in Nietzsche's ethical theory is found in his search for the *superman* (overman) which is a concomitant of the drive for superiority. The Nietzschean will to power calls for the demoralization or amoralization of culture, i.e., stripping culture of its Judeo-Christian moral content by returning to a concept of moral good as the "transvaluation of all values," the restoration of human dignity founded upon an individualistic ethic. The glorification of strength, of the will to power, became the essence of his ethics.

This premise of the drive or *will to power* (not biological strength, the will to survive merely) Nietzsche unapologetically promoted. In *The Antichrist* he wrote:

> What is good?—Whatever augments the feeling of power, the will to power, power itself, in man.
>
> What is evil?—Whatever springs from weakness.
>
> What is happiness?—The feeling that power *increases*—that resistance is overcome.
>
> Not contentment, but more power; *not* peace at any price, but war; *not* virtue, but efficiency (virtue in the Renaissance sense, *virtu,* virtue free of moral acid).
>
> The weak and the botched shall perish: first principle of *our* charity. And one should help them to it.
>
> What is more harmful than any vice?—Practical sympathy for the botched and the weak—Christianity.[19]

Neitzsche rejected the altruistic feelings, such as sympathy, stemming from the social instinct, replacing them with an egoistic expression of instincts, particularly the will to power. Although he attacked Darwin, here his assault is more especially directed against Schopenhauer and Christianity.

THE WILL TO POWER. Man does not seek happiness, but happiness results from the creative exercise of power. Venting a scathing denunciation of British utilitarian hedonism, Nietzsche snorted, "Man does not aspire to happiness: only the Englishman does that."[20]

18. Thomas E. Hill, *Ethics in Theory and Practice* (New York: Crowell, 1956), pp. 109–111.
19. F. W. Nietzsche, *The Antichrist* (New York: Knopf, 1918), pp. 42–43.
20. Friedrich Nietzsche, "The Twilight of the Idols: Or, How to Philosophise with the Hammer," in *Complete Works of Friedrich Nietzsche,* ed. Oscar Levy (New York: Russell & Russell, 1964), p. 2, maxim no. 12.

> My theory would be:—that the will to power is the primitive form of affect, that all other affects are only developments of it;
>
> that it is notably enlightening to posit *power* in place of individual "happiness" (after which every living thing is supposed to be striving): "there is a striving for power, for an increase of power";—pleasure is only a symptom of the feeling of power attained, a consciousness of a difference (—there is not striving for pleasure: but pleasure supervenes when that which is being striven for is attained: pleasure is an accompaniment, pleasure is not the motive—);
>
> that all driving force is will to power, that there is no other physical, dynamic, or psychic force except this.[21]

Power becomes the only criterion of right; an ethics of power is not bound by moral principles, but by its own strength only. Moral right is the exertion of power, while its opposite, weakness, is bad.

MASTER MORALITY AND SLAVE MORALITY. Two codes of ethics exist for Nietzsche: the ethics of the powerful, a master morality, and the ethics of the weak, a slave morality. In history, clear examples of these two types of valuations can be found in the morality of the Romans vs. that of the Jews, the former masters and the latter slaves. Note Nietzsche's characterization of *master morality:*

> The noble type of man experiences *itself* as determining values; it does not need approval; it judges, "what is harmful to me is harmful in itself"; it knows itself to be that which first accords honor to things; it is *value-creating*. Everything it knows as part of itself it honors: such a morality is self-glorification. In the foreground there is the feeling of fullness, of power that seeks to overflow, the happiness of high tension, the consciousness of wealth that would give and bestow: the noble human being, too, helps the unfortunate, but not, or almost not, from pity, but prompted more by an urge begotten by excess of power.[22]

The valuation of the master race is *good/bad* or the "noble/contemptible" dichotomy, whereas the moral valuation of the slave race is *good/evil,* good representing moral, and evil immoral. The aristocrats, the masters, have no morality, being a law unto themselves, because power determines their superior right, while the slaves must devise a system of morality, carefully calculated to subjugate the strong, their masters. The morality of the ruling group holds to the principle of performing duties only toward one's peers, the lower rank being alien to

21. Friedrich Nietzsche, *The Will to Power* (New York: Random House, 1967), p. 366.

22. Friedrich Nietzsche, *"Beyond Good and Evil: Prelude to a Philosophy of the Future,"* in *Basic Writings of Nietzsche,* ed. Walter Kaufmann (New York: Modern Library, 1966), p. 395.

them. "One may behave as one pleases or 'as the heart desires,' and in any case 'beyond good and evil.' "[23]

Citing the characteristics of slave morality, Nietzsche stated:

> Suppose the violated, oppressed, suffering, unfree, who are uncertain of themselves and weary, moralize: what will their moral valuations have in common? Probably, a pessimistic suspicion about the whole condition of man will find expression, perhaps a condemnation of man along with his condition. The slave's eye is not favorable to the virtues of the powerful: he is skeptical and suspicious, *subtly* suspicious, of all the "good" that is honored there—he would like to persuade himself that even their happiness is not genuine. Conversely, those qualities are brought out and flooded with light which serve to ease existence for those who suffer: here pity, the complaisant and obliging hand, the warm heart, patience, industry, humility, and friendliness are honored—for here these are the most useful qualities and almost the only means for enduring the pressure of existence. Slave morality is essentially a morality of utility.[24]

RESSENTIMENT. Consequently, the weak have brought about an inversion of right by a slave ethic which issues out of a deep-seated feeling of *ressentiment,* that is, a repressed resentment caused by inhibiting one's enraged feelings, one's "bottled-up" aggressions, because of an inability to direct their expression toward one's superior (who incited such feelings initially) lest this superior harm one by virtue of his superior might. "The man of resentment . . . is neither sincere, nor naïve, neither honest nor straightforward against himself. His soul *squints;* his mind loves hiding-places, alleys and back-doors; everything hidden appeals to him as *his* world, *his* shelter, *his* comfort; he is master in the art of keeping silence, of forgetting nothing, of waiting, of provisional self-diminution, of self-humiliation."[25]

Masters are free from *ressentiment* since their aggressions are given vent, expressed in fighting out differences; hence, they need not forgive each other because they harbor no ill will. "The resentment of superior man, when it appears in him, acts and exhausts itself in the reaction which follows at once, and hence it does not *poison.*"[26] The weak harbor intense ill will, inasmuch as they dare not give it free vent in open combat against their superiors.

DEMOCRATIC MORALITY AND JUDEO-CHRISTIAN ETHICS. Out of *ressentiment,* an entire system of morals is developed by the weak, one

23. Ibid., p. 396.
24. Ibid., p. 397.
25. Friedrich Nietzsche, *Genealogy of Morals* (New York: Doubleday, 1956), p. 38.
26. Ibid.

which replaces the genuinely natural ethic that stems from the will to power. It is a morality which takes every life-giving instinct and denatures it, construing sex, aggressiveness, and power as immoral, inverting them by substituting chastity, humility, and obedience, in order that the weak may subvert the strong, the slave conquer his master, the inferior race subdue the superior. Weakness is "transmuted into merit," as those who cannot retaliate transmute impotence into kindness, pusillanimity into humility, and submission into the virtue of obedience.

The time has come for a *revaluation of all values,* for the annihilation of morals (slave morality), that inversion of values which dominates our culture, the Christian culture. We must supplant slave morality with a new set of values, a new culture, a new civilization, a new man, the superman with his revaluation of all values.

THE SUPERMAN OR OVERMAN. Nietzsche proposes the concept of the ideal man, the superman, who is to usher in a civilization with a superior set of values, life-affirming values, through his revaluation of all values, disposing of the traditional values of Judeo-Christian culture, because those emanating from a rugged individualism exemplify a higher type within the human race.

Darwin claimed that herd animals were weaker than those struggling through a solitary existence, and on this postulation Nietzsche concluded that the superman must be an *individual,* a free spirit, independent of and towering above the common herd. As an individualist, the superman soars high, ascending over slave morality that is grounded in *ressentiment,* and even scales above master morality, inasmuch as master morality is also a class morality, and not that of a free spirit, of an individual who is a law unto himself, divorced from the herd.

ALL-TOO-HUMAN. Regarding his superman at times as a present realization and at other times as a being that the future will produce, Nietzsche believed that superman is he who, over the centuries, has risen out of the common herd that he alluded to as the "far-too-many." Actually, the common herd exists exclusively for the purpose that through it at some rare moment the superman will rise, as did Jesus, Caesar, Goethe, and others of comparable esteemed status. Nietzsche referred to his ideal as "the Roman Caesar with Christ's soul."

But in retrospect he reserved the superman for a future race, because by being caught in the far-too-many, we are *all-too-human.* However, Nietzsche remained indecisive as to whether superman emerges as the product of historical or Darwinian evolution, and failed to answer the question, Is he the ideal of the philosophers of German romanticism who saw the genius as a human being elevated by present conditions assisted through philosophical development, or will he evolve as a type higher than that of the human race?

CRITIQUE OF NIETZSCHE'S ETHICS. A philosopher who is neither particularly favorable nor negative toward Nietzsche, Bertrand Russell, maintained that Nietzsche's condemnation of Christian love emanates from the projection of his own fear and hatred. What he fails to realize, argued Russell, is the possibility that man may genuinely feel universal love, whereas Nietzsche himself "feels almost universal hatred and fear." Nietzsche's "noble" man is merely the man of his daydreams, a compensation for his own weaknesses.

Kaufmann asserted that Nietzsche's influence has been "frequently harmful,"[27] and that he was addicted to hyperbole, but he believes that Nietzsche's unsalutary influence is due to misconstruing what Nietzsche truly meant. Kaufmann is undoubtedly right: Nietzsche indulged extravagantly in hyperbole. He isolated certain facts to support his own position without regard for contravening ones, a fallacy known as "special pleading." For example, he embraced the essential goodness of instincts as life-affirming, but accepted only egoistic ones, while denying status to social urges that were considered genuine instincts by Darwin and contemporary psychologists. Whereas a person has a drive for superiority (power) and sex, he also has a fundamental need for love, a need to be wanted, and other humanistic social drives.

Although Nietzsche was an individualist, groups have adopted his philosophy with disastrous results for humanity. It may be argued that these groups, such as the Nazis, misinterpreted him, but even if they did, it is what Nietzsche meant to them. Correct interpretation or misconstrual notwithstanding, Nietzsche has promulgated an ethics of power that has had the effect on certain persons of reducing their behavior to that of the beasts of the jungle, destroying each other with an ostentatious display of power.

That will to power is man's basic drive is highly debatable, and has been challenged by able scientists, including Viktor Frankl, who argued that man is basically motivated by a meaningful existence (a will to meaning);[28] others, such as Max Weber[29] and David McClelland[30] postulated the basic drive to be the "achievement motive," while Abraham Maslow[31] and Kurt Goldstein[32] identified it as "self-realization." Even the most powerful man in the world would not be satisfied (as Nietzsche believed he would be) if deprived of fundamental basic

27. Walter Kaufmann, "Nietzsche," in Frank Thilly and Ledger Wood, *A History of Philosophy* (New York: Henry Holt, 1957), pp. 506–507.

28. Viktor E. Frankl, *The Will to Meaning* (New York: World, 1969), pp. 34–35.

29. Max Weber, *The Protestant Ethic and the Spirit of Capitalism* (New York, Scribner, 1958), pp. 35–61.

30. David C. McClelland, *The Achieving Society* (Princeton: Van Nostrand, 1961), pp. 36–62.

31. Abraham H. Maslow, *Motivation and Personality,* 2d ed. (New York: Harper & Row, 1970).

32. Kurt Goldstein, *The Organism* (Boston: Beacon, 1963), pp. 197–198.

needs such as respect, friendship, love, and a meaningful and self-realized life.

Concerning the character of the superman and Nietzsche's definition of values, Hill wrote:

> The difficulty is, rather, that the modes of conduct that he recommends are often so antithetical to what is intended by such terms as "morally good" and "right" that whatever commendatory terms may correctly apply to these modes of conduct cannot possibly mean the same as "morally good" or "right."
>
> The meaning of "right," whatever it is, is scarcely such as to commend either general indifference to truth or the ruthless suppression of the weak by the strong. Nietzsche's Superman is at best an inhuman self-defeating monster who, having crushed his victims, is in the end frustrated: and the terms in which he is praised are not only not those of ethical discourse, but also at many points plainly incompatible with ethical discourse.[33]

Nevertheless, to cite some of Nietzsche's significant contributions, one would have to include among others: (1) his moral giant, superman or overman; (2) his theory of *ressentiment,* which was later appropriated by Freud; (3) his belief that if a person has a reason for living, he will be able to overcome any of life's vicissitudes.

Thomas Henry Huxley: Ethics as Morally Worthy of Survival. Repudiating Nietzschean narcissistic self-assertion, Huxley resumed the trend of the evolutionary line of Darwin and Spencer, yet modifying all previous positions with the contention that the truly superior man is the one who is morally outstanding. For Huxley, moral superiority means running counter to cosmic evolution in favor of human evolution understood in terms of ethical progress.

Nietzsche sought a superman who exploited his drive of superiority as the normal concomitant of a universal and natural will to power, but such naive individualism was rejected by Huxley on the grounds that man lives as a social being because that is precisely what he is, and through the benefits of society his upward progress is much more readily assured than by going it alone. "Morality commenced with society."[34]

DUAL PROCESS OF EVOLUTION: COSMIC AND ETHICAL. Recognizing the principle that those persons who are *morally worthy should by right be the ones to survive,* Huxley saw in nature a dual process being worked out, the *cosmic process* and the *ethical process.* The two processes are in conflict, the cosmic an evil one, and the ethical a good one. The lower, the cosmic process, is based on the principle of the

33. Thomas E. Hill, *Ethics in Theory and Practice* (New York: Crowell, 1956), p. 117.

34. T. H. Huxley, *Collected Essays* (New York: D. Appleton, 1898), 5:52.

survival of the fittest, a nonmoral process; the ethical process, the higher, rejects the notion that the fittest is necessarily the best (in the sense of good), consequently worthy of survival. For if the latter were the case, then if the hemispheric temperature should cool down drastically, the *fittest* (those capable of survival) would be lichens, diatoms, and microscopic organisms. Morality must be premised not upon selfish instincts or survival of the fittest, but upon the high moral ideals of men.

As by intuition one discriminates the beautiful from the ugly, in the same manner one distinguishes between good and evil; the course of evolution merely relates the story of their emergence without evaluating what is moral, good, or preferable. The morally desirable remains the province of man. Under the direction of human intelligence, egoistic instincts, an element of the cosmic process, must be stayed, and the ethical process must supersede the cosmic. As a moral being, man does not adhere to the principle of survival of the fittest, but only to the canon of *fitting all mankind, if possible, to survive, to be worthy of survival.*

> As I have already urged, the practice of that which is ethically best—what we call goodness or virtue—involves a course of conduct which, in all respects, is opposed to that which leads to success in the cosmic struggle for existence. In place of ruthless self-assertion it demands self-restraint; in place of thrusting aside, or treading down, all competitors, it requires that the individual shall not merely respect, but shall help his fellows; its influence is directed, not so much to the survival of the fittest, as to the fitting of as many as possible to survive. It repudiates the gladiatorial theory of existence. . . . Laws and moral precepts are directed to the end of curbing the cosmic process and reminding the individual of his duty to the community, to the protection and influence of which he owes, if not existence itself, at least of something better than a brutal savage.[35]

Ethical Progress. Fanatical individualism, stoical injunctions to follow nature, and egoistic self-assertion are all attempts to dignify, to justify, and to misapply cosmic nature; i.e., they constitute a misapplication of the theory of evolution to society. Here is involved the fallacy of assuming that the struggle for existence in cosmic nature functions equally well in the ethical realm. Society achieves ethical progress by combating the cosmic process, not by emulating it. "Social progress means a checking of the cosmic process at every step and the substitution for it of another, which may be called the ethical process; the end of which is not the survival of those who may happen to be the fittest,

35. T. H. Huxley, "Evolution and Ethics" (1893), in *Selections from the Essays of Thomas Henry Huxley,* ed. Albury Castell (New York: Appleton-Century-Crofts, 1948), p. 108.

in respect of the whole of the conditions which obtain, but of those who are ethically the best."[36]

Man can elevate himself so that he will become a higher being, an ethical person who has exchanged savage instincts for the moral ones of civilized humanity. (He has similarly modified the instincts of a member of the wolf family so that the animal could serve as a faithful guardian of the sheep.) Human moral progress is social progress, a "gradual strengthening of the social bond,"[37] an ethical advancement detectable in the history of civilization. Society's ethical or political task is that of attending to "the struggle for the means of enjoyment"[38] by selecting as officials men of energy, industry, intellectual capability, resolute purpose, and with "as much sympathy as is necessary to make a man understand the feelings of his fellows."[39] Unless social laws are enacted to prevent fools, knaves, and incompetent persons from becoming rulers of society, then *administrative nihilism* ("the absence from society of a machinery for facilitating the descent of incapacity")[40] will occur.

COMMENTS ON HUXLEY'S ETHICAL THEORY. Huxley's principal and most valuable contribution is that of popularizing Darwinian evolutionary theory. However, it was a reciprocal effort, for Darwin borrowed the term "agnosticism" (professed ignorance as to God's existence) from Huxley, whose coinage it was. While Darwin believed in gradual adjustment within the evolutionary process, Huxley held that "transmutation may take place without transition,"[41] occurring as a sudden event of emergent evolution.

36. Ibid.
37. Huxley, "Prolegomena to Evolution and Ethics" (1894), in *Essays of Thomas Henry Huxley*, p. 113.
38. Ibid., p. 116.
39. Ibid.
40. Ibid.
41. Leonard Huxley, *Life and Letters of Thomas Henry Huxley* (1900), 1:173.

II

Ethical Pessimism and Existentialism: The Ethics of Philosophical Irrationalism

Three influential proponents of pessimism and existentialism, representing markedly different positions, are Arthur Schopenhauer (1788–1860), perhaps the foremost systematic pessimist; Søren Kierkegaard (1813–1855), an intensely religious exponent of existentialism credited as its ideational founder; and Jean-Paul Sartre (1905–), an inveterate contemporary propagator of atheistic existentialism.

There are those who would take exception to uniting pessimism with existentialism, and others who would challenge the criterion by which a philosopher is classified as an existentialist. Some scholars even regard Socrates and Jesus as existentialists, others limit existentialism to Kierkegaard and his intellectual successors, and still others would insist that Schopenhauer and Nietzsche unquestionably belong to the fold.

What characterizes existentialists? Walter Kaufmann's answer is "their perfervid individualism,"[1] while Sartre's is their belief that "existence precedes essence"; and Kierkegaard would probably cite their agreement with his dictum "Subjectivity is truth," in addition to the thesis that "existence precedes essence." These answers involve or overlap one another, hence connote more or less the same idea of the primacy of the individual subject. If one adds to this concept moral freedom, responsibility, together with the philosophy of irrationalism and its usual concomitant, pessimism, he will possess concepts constituting basic aspects of the philosophy of existentialism.

Arthur Schopenhauer: Philosophic Pessimism and the Ethics of Sympathy. According to Schopenhauer, ultimate reality, *will,* creates the external physical world order, *phenomenon,* or *idea.* Idea, the world as it appears in time and space, and connected by laws of cause and effect, is known by the intellect as representation. Though idea, the phenomenal world, is quite intelligible, the ultimately real world, whose essence is irrational will, is not. Hegel's philosophical outlook, based

1. Walter Kaufmann, *Existentialism from Dostoevsky to Sartre* (New York: Meridian, 1956), p. 11.

on the idea that *reason* is the ultimate ground of reality, leads to optimism, whereas the Schopenhauerian concept of the *will* as the ultimate ground for reality leads to philosophical pessimism.

For Schopenhauer, the irrational forces of will appear in man in the form of instinctual urges, impulses, desires, or strivings, while pleasure is merely their scant and temporary satisfaction, and is negative, the mere absence or quiescence of those desires that are the substance and genuine reality of life. Desires, irrational and aimless striving, produce life's miseries. Salvation from them is effected through the annihilation of the will, complete ascetic denial, Nirvana; or they are temporarily quieted by taking refuge in contemplation, by becoming lost in music, in art, or in the thought of Platonic ideals. Under these conditions of human misery, the only ethical course of action indicated is the expression of pity, a feeling of compassion or sympathy arising out of our kinship (as human beings in pain) to each other.

PHILOSOPHY OF PESSIMISM. As Schopenhauer viewed the human situation, he found life a continuous striving between willing (deep, driving desire) and its incomplete satisfaction. He regarded this willing, striving, desiring, this craving for satisfaction, as quite *painful,* and consequently evil. "Suffering is simply unfulfilled and crossed volition."[2] Inasmuch as life is a continuous and unrelenting state of desires craving satisfaction, pain is the essence of life, a positive or real aspect of human nature, while the moments of satisfaction, being fleeting, transitory, momentary, are negative aspects of human life. Thus pleasure is simply the elimination of pain, the alleviation of desire. Life, owing to its preponderance of pain, together with its all too brief passing moments of pleasure (when desire has been satisfied), is not worth living. Human wants and their satisfaction are unequally balanced, weighted overwhelmingly in favor of gnawing, unfulfilled desire; therefore, it would be preferable not to have been born. "The greatest crime of man is that he ever was born,"[3] wrote Schopenhauer, quoting Calderón, and elsewhere added, "Human life must be some kind of mistake."[4]

The physical manifestation of the will in all nature is its phenomenal appearance, its outward manifestation. This phenomenal physical manifestation of will Schopenhauer called the principle of individuation (*principium individuationis*); man with his sex organs is one example of this phenomenal manifestation. Physical sex is insatiable because the

2. Arthur Schopenhauer, *The World as Will and Idea,* trans. R. B. Haldane and J. Kemp (London: K. Paul, Trench, Trübner, 1896), bk. 4, chap. 65.

3. Ibid., bk. 4, chap. 63.

4. Arthur Schopenhauer, "The Vanity of Existence," in *Studies in Pessimism,* in *The Essays of Arthur Schopenhauer* (New York: Wiley, n.d.), p. 23.

sex drive (will) is insatiable; its constant recurrence, repetition, and compulsion are evidence of the fact. The will, moreover, is concerned solely for the race, never for the individual; the individual's suffering is for the benefit of the race. The will, active in the drive of self-preservation, forces an individual to continue his existence at all costs, regardless of how unreasonable, merely to accommodate the wishes of the drive, racial survival, without concern for the individual's preferences, which might at times include a predilection for extinction.

> The life of the great majority is only a constant struggle for existence itself, with the certainty of losing it at last. But what enables them to endure this wearisome battle is not so much the love of life as the fear of death, which yet stands in the background as inevitable, and may come upon them at any moment. Life itself is a sea, full of rocks and whirlpools, which a man avoids with the greatest care and solicitude, although he knows that even if he succeeds in getting through with all his efforts and skill, he yet by doing so comes nearer at every step to the greatest, the total, inevitable, and irremediable shipwreck, death.[5]

Human misery is intensified by self-consciousness and intelligence; as man becomes more aware of misery, the greater it becomes; and "the more intelligent he is, the more pain he has." These consequences vary with the strength or intensity of the drive within a particular person; the greater the intensity or need, the severer the suffering, owing to the profundity of the feeling of frustration. Inasmuch as "no satisfaction is lasting, rather it is merely the starting point of a new effort," therefore "there is no final end of striving, there is no measure and end of suffering."

The endless, vain pursuit continues throughout life, and even beyond it, because the will is indestructible. Accordingly, suicide is no solution, but merely a "clumsy experiment to make; for it involves the destruction of the very consciousness which puts the question and awaits the answer."[6] The answer might be a terrible mistake, not the mistake of experiencing annihilation, but that of discovering the life to come is as bad as, or even worse than, the present one.

The individual oscillates between two miserable human conditions, namely, need and boredom (or desire and ennui). Either he miserably strives in vain to find permanent satisfaction in life or else, having satisfied his needs, he is completely bored. "No attained object of desire can give lasting satisfaction, but merely a fleeting gratification; it is like the alms thrown to the beggar, that keeps him alive today that his misery may be prolonged till the morrow."[7]

5. Schopenhauer, *World as Will and Idea,* bk. 4, chap. 57.
6. Schopenhauer, "On Suicide," *Studies in Pessimism,* p. 31.
7. Schopenhauer, *World as Will and Idea,* bk. 3, chap. 38.

AN ETHICS OF SYMPATHY. Ultimately, there is but one will, not many, which permeates everywhere and penetrates everything; accordingly, the desire and sense of pain in another person is in us as well. His misery is ours and ours his; under these circumstances, the most that can be done is to be sympathetic and to pity each other. Misery or pain is grounded in egoistic drives; only sympathy is altruistically motivated. Schopenhauer speaks of "that natural compassion, which in every man is innate and indestructible, and which has been shown to be the sole source of non-egoistic conduct, this kind alone being of real worth."[8] Immorality stems from egoism and indifference, whereas morality is based upon the sympathetic feeling of another's hurt as one's own that prompts us to alleviate his painful condition. Pity, not condemnation, is the proper attitude to assume toward the sinner; for his sin is ours, the will in him is the same as that found in us, and his anguish is ours. We must be able to face the misery of the sinner and say to ourselves, "This thou art."

ETHICAL SALVATION. Sympathy does not solve the problem of misery, but merely abates and stems its rising tide; the solution of the problem must be found in the complete destruction of the will, which is identified with the state of unhappiness. As long as the will remains, misery does, too; its form may differ, but not its unpleasant content. There is no other way to find peace of soul except by complete denial, asceticism, self-mortification, repudiation of life and pleasure. Denial of the will to live, a denial which represents a state of combined holiness and blessedness, is achieved when one realizes through insight that the nature of one's finite existence is *nothingness,* Nirvana, the soul's state of supreme peace and reality.

Partial deliverance from the driving will can be found not only in the experience of sympathy, but also in intellectual states, by becoming lost in art, in music, in the contemplation of Platonic ideals, for in such a state a person has risen above the storms of desire, although, unfortunately, he must eventually descend to the raging tumult of will and desire below. Inasmuch as these intellectual states are only transitory, Nirvana, the permanent state of nothingness, the complete negation or denial of will, is man's sole salvation.

CRITIQUE OF THE ETHICAL PHILOSOPHY OF SCHOPENHAUER. A number of Schopenhauer's critics, especially the psychologists and psychiatrists, have attributed his pessimism to his neuroticism and unhappy life. It may be quite true that Schopenhauer's philosophy is the product of a miserable existence, but it would be fallacious to conclude from such assumptions that Schopenhauer's findings are necessarily false.

8. Arthur Schopenhauer, *The Basis of Morality* (London: Swan Sonnenschein, 1903), p. 264.

However, there is a justified criticism, namely, the one-sided consideration of facts adduced by Schopenhauer. Schopenhauer is guilty of focusing his attention on life's miseries and vicissitudes only, as if facts of happiness never truly existed, a fault committed by most existentialists. Life may have its seamy aspect, but it also contains its beautiful moments.

Analyzing three common objections to Schopenhauer's pessimism, Hospers listed them as follows: (1) The state of desire is not necessarily painful or even unpleasant. (2) The process of satisfying the desire may itself be pleasant. (3) People often *do* achieve their goals and experience great happiness in so doing.[9]

Perhaps Schopenhauer experienced his own desires as constantly distressing, but most persons find that desire is usually a pleasant experience, adding much color and enthusiasm to life as well as a form of motivation that renders life meaningful instead of listless. Not only is the experiential fact of desire normally attractive, but also the activity directed toward fulfillment may be in itself as enjoyable as the final outcome. For example, an artist who has an intense desire to create a painting will often find that both the successful result (the finished work of art) and the activity involved in its actualization are satisfying. To assert, as Schopenhauer did, that once a person's goal is achieved, he no longer experiences the happiness attending it while working on it or the expected happiness accompanying its completion *is false*. It is tragic if such joy eluded Schopenhauer because many people derive lasting satisfaction from a job well done, a family well reared, or a charitable deed well performed.

Nevertheless, one must grant Schopenhauer his due, for his philosophy exerted a strong influence on many distinguished thinkers, including, among others, Freud, Kierkegaard, Nietzsche, Schweitzer, and Eduard von Hartmann. Moreover, there is a positive side to Schopenhauer's contribution, especially his insight in perceiving the liberating, cathartic, and sublimating effect of music, art, and philosophy. On the other hand, even this contribution has been criticized by DeWitt H. Parker, who asserted that Schopenhauer "was wrong in thinking that art liberates by ridding us of desire; for it is rather by giving a new, imaginative form to desire that art frees us, not from desire, itself, but from its burdensomeness."[10]

Søren Kierkegaard: Qualitative Dialectical Ethics. The qualitative dialectic, an irreconcilable antithesis, permeates Kierkegaardian existentialism, and its import is made obvious by the title of one of his most famous books, *Either/Or*. Life itself, as well as its many varied aspects,

9. John Hospers, *Human Conduct: An Introduction to the Problems of Ethics* (New York: Harcourt, Brace & World, 1961), p. 69.

10. DeWitt H. Parker, *Schopenhauer Selections* (New York: Scribner, 1928), p. xxv.

is a *disjunctive conjunction,* an either/or choice, and no amount of logic, including the Hegelian dialectic, is capable of uniting it into a synthesis.

Like Schopenhauer before him, Kierkegaard too proposed a philosophy of irrationalism, but not one based on the concept of an irrational will; rather, it was based on a qualitative dialectical predicament wherein the nature of thought is regarded as lacking agreement with reality, resulting in the paradoxical nature of truth. Reason cannot capture, define, explain, or understand life, because "life must be lived forward, but understood backwards."[11] Reason cannot help in man's decisions in life except to inform him in retrospect as a "Monday-morning quarterback." The choice itself, a decision of free will, is beyond rational explanation; it is a leap of logic, a logical gap, a logical jerk or disruption, a breach of scientific continuity.

THE CHOICE AND THE TELEOLOGICAL SUSPENSION OF THE ETHICAL. Man's highest task is that of becoming subjective, and his most decisive act is found in choice itself. "Man is granted a choice. . . . Man not merely *can* choose . . . he *must* choose."[12] Inspired by this thought, Sartre later construed it to mean that man is condemned to freedom. The teleological suspension of the ethical is the suspension of the universal maxims of morality and their rationale for the leap of faith to the revelation of God. Kierkegaard used as an example God's command to Abraham that he kill his son Isaac. Abraham's rational mind regarded God's request for the sacrifice of his son as irrational, immoral, and murderous, but the teleological suspension of the ethical value and a leap into faith directed otherwise. Abraham consented to the sacrifice because God required this proof of his faith. "What ordinarily tempts a man is that which would keep him from doing his duty, but in this case the temptation itself is the ethical . . . which would keep him from doing God's will."[13]

Objectivity seeks rational explanations, whereas "subjectivity is the truth."[14] The truth is absurd. For example, Christian salvation is the absurd doctrine "that the eternal truth has come into being in time, that God has come into being,"[15] namely, Jesus Christ. In order to grasp this absurdity, it is necessary to suspend teleological thinking by the leap of faith—the "intensity of faith in inwardness." The definitions

11. Søren Kierkegaard, *The Journals* (New York: Harper, 1958), p. 23.
12. Søren Kierkegaard, "What We Learn from the Lilies of the Field and the Birds of the Air," in *The Gospel of Suffering* (Minneapolis, Minn.: Augsburg, 1948), p. 228.
13. Søren Kierkegaard, *Fear and Trembling* (Garden City, N.Y.: Doubleday, 1955), p. 70.
14. Søren Kierkegaard, *Concluding Unscientific Postscript* (Princeton, N.J.: Princeton University Press, 1941), p. 191.
15. Ibid., p. 188.

of truth and faith are equivalent. "When subjectivity, inwardness, is the truth, the truth becomes objectively a paradox."[16]

THE THREE STADIA, OR PHILOSOPHIES, OF LIFE. Kierkegaard referred to three stages along life's way, or three philosophical views of life, namely, (1) the aesthetic, (2) the ethical, and (3) the religious. These three are levels of individual existence, different life-conceptions; each is a *Weltanschauung,* a philosophy of life whereby a person seeks to find his own salvation on earth.

THE AESTHETIC STAGE: THE LIFE OF PLEASURE AND THE LIFE OF THE INTELLECT. The aestheticist lives for the moment, attempting to squeeze out of life whatever he can before it is terminated, before it is too late, but the irony of life is that what seems to the aestheticist to be pleasurable turns out to be disguised despair, because the pleasure that he pursues does not exist; it is merely imaginary, fanciful, ephemeral. Beauty fades, and boredom quickly follows in the wake of pleasure. The emptiness of pleasure makes for despair, and in despair one is driven to the ethical stage or mode of life. "The ethical self is supposed to be found immanently in the despair, so that the individual by persisting in his despair at last wins himself."[17] This, the moment of decision, characterizes the ethical stage, an existential experience of passion and inwardness making one aware "of the religious—and of the *leap.*"[18]

THE ETHICAL STAGE. In despair owing to the futility of the aesthetic way of life, the self by decision and commitment passes to another stage, the ethical, wherein it finds its authentic selfhood by choosing itself, by truly knowing the self in the Socratic sense. Choosing himself (knowing himself), man in this stage acts resolutely with complete commitment, inwardness, and passion; whereas the aestheticist, in a state of indecision, flounders through life. By choice, one chooses himself; that is, he makes his own and authentic personality.

THE RELIGIOUS STAGE. When an individual passes to the third stage of life, the religious, he commits himself to God, not to duty for duty's sake, but to obedience to God. Acknowledgment of sin awakens a person to a commitment to God, and in the moment of decision when a man commits himself to God, his life can be conclusively altered. Thus, the distinctive existential features of the three stages are, respectively: enjoyment-perdition; action-victory; and suffering.

Eventually, Kierkegaard reduced the three stages to two, the aesthetic and the ethical-religious (the ethical being incorporated into the religious), with only two choices remaining, that of pleasure and that of suffering. "The aesthetic hero is great for the fact that he *conquers,* the

16. Ibid., p. 183.
17. Ibid., p. 230.
18. Ibid., p. 231.

religious hero is great for the fact that he *suffers*."[19] The highest expression of subjectivity, its most intense and complete expression of inwardness, is suffering. "While the aesthetic existence is essentially enjoyment, ethical existence, essentially struggle and victory, religious existence is essentially suffering."[20] There is no greater intensity of inwardness than that experienced in suffering.

THE INDIVIDUAL. The most important category for understanding is the *subjective individual;* Kierkegaard's emphasis on this category is indicated by his request: "Had I to crave an inscription on my grave I would ask for none other than 'the individual.' "[21] Even his book, *Purity of Heart,* was dedicated to "that solitary individual." All things real are individual: persons are individuals, the history of civilization is that of individuals; morality refers to individuals, as does existence itself. Humanity does not exist, but this or that individual person does. The crowd is false, for by it we are seduced, we shift responsibility, we lose our identity, our individuality, our will. "In eternity, the individual, yes, you my listener, and I as individuals will each be asked solely about himself as an individual, and the individual details in his life."[22] In eternity, there is no counting, for there exists only one, an individual, not a crowd of people but an individual alone with his conscience and with God.

A person cannot be truthful in a crowd; the ethical individual stands alone. He, as a subjective individual, is true and real; "subjectivity is truth, subjectivity is reality."[23] Truth is inwardness, subjectivity, and so is faith, the "passion of inwardness." Reason is the opposite of faith; while reason attempts to be objective and seeks security in consistent explanations, faith is inwardness, subjectivity, and a state of risk. Seeking objective security through reason, but finding the objective world laden with paradoxes only—for essential truth is a paradox—the individual, finding himself in this state of existence, pained with anguish and sin, embraces faith, the passion of inwardness. The opposite of faith is sin. It is the lack of faith in man, his lack of confidence, that leads to sin.

CRITIQUE OF KIERKEGAARDIAN ETHICS. Brand Blanshard stated that from Kierkegaard "it is useless to look for clearly stated theses, still less for ordered arguments in support of them."[24] However, this criticism is applicable to virtually all existentialists. Blanshard added that

19. Søren Kierkegaard, *Stages on Life's Way* (Princeton: Princeton University Press, 1940), p. 411.

20. Kierkegaard, *Concluding Unscientific Postscript,* p. 256.

21. Kierkegaard, *Journals,* 1847 entry.

22. Søren Kierkegaard, *Purity of Heart Is to Will One Thing* (New York: Harper, 1938), p. 212.

23. Kierkegaard, *Concluding Unscientific Postscript,* p. 306.

24. Brand Blanshard, "Kierkegaard on Religious Knowledge," address delivered at the American Philosophical Association, New York, N.Y., 1969.

Kierkegaard's "contention that thought cannot deal with existence is put so obscurely that there is difficulty in extracting from it a meaning clear enough to refute. Furthermore, he seems never to have worked out what was involved for the normal exercise of reason by its breakdown at crucial points—for ethics by the suspension of its clearest rules, and for logic by the admission of contradictions to the status of higher truths."[25] Moreover, Kierkegaard rejected rational ethics without offering a constructive reformed moral theory to substitute in its place.

L. Harold DeWolf was equally severe in his criticisms, among which are the following: (1) the self-destructiveness of irrationalism; (2) the employment of paradox by Kierkegaard, which "threatens the very possibility of communication";[26] (3) the inability to maintain without the employment of reason "the internal meaning of a system of belief concerning existence";[27] (4) the fact that to assert that objects (e.g., God) are beyond reason requires reason as a necessary base to arrive at such a conclusion; (5) the necessity of using reason to distinguish the true from the false, including revelation; and (6) predication of the value of faith on an appeal to reason.

When Kierkegaard spoke of the "leap of faith" or the "teleological suspension of the ethical," he was advocating an abandonment of reason for faith; and this advocacy explains why the above staunch proponents of reason, Blanshard and DeWolf, are so vehement in their condemnations of Kierkegaard. What these men are contending is that irrationalism is a self-defeating philosophy falling under the ax of a reductio ad absurdum argument. Essentially, when a Kierkegaardian irrationalist asserts that reason cannot arrive at truth, the implication is that something other than reason can (some nonrational or irrational course, such as blind faith or revelation). But to substantiate such a claim requires the employment of reason, hence the tacit acceptance of it.

Noteworthy addenda to the foregoing criticisms of Kierkegaard are certain penetrating comments by Alasdair MacIntyre, who held that Kierkegaard left two important queries unanswered, the first being whether there are criterionless choices, and the second being whether it is by criterionless choices that one arrives at the criterion of valid beliefs.[28] Also unhappy about Kierkegaard's abuse of logic, MacIntyre contends that Kierkegaard was almost frivolous with the logic of contradiction, not having taken the time to distinguish between

25. Ibid.

26. L. Harold DeWolf, *The Religious Revolt against Reason* (New York: Harper & Row, 1949), p. 141.

27. Ibid., p. 142.

28. Alasdair MacIntyre, "Kierkegaard, Søren Aabye," in *The Encyclopedia of Philosophy,* ed. Paul Edwards (New York: Macmillan & Free Press, 1967), 4:340.

"paradox" and inconsistency, so that, in failing to make this distinction, Kierkegaard's entire philosophy based on *paradox* is "fatally unclear."

Jean-Paul Sartre: An Ethics of Irrational Freedom. Sartrean existentialism is a philosophy that may be defined as "existence precedes essence," or what is tantamount to the same idea, "subjectivity must be the starting point"; and man is defined as a "being in whom existence precedes essence."[29]

The fundamental significance of existentialism is more easily illustrated than defined. Consider, as an example, a paper-cutting machine; as is true of all material things, its *essence precedes existence,* whereas in the case of a human being, his *existence precedes essence.* A paper cutter is an object made by an engineer under a given set of specifications and for a particular use. The essence of the paper cutter has been determined before it has come into existence; hence its nature, essence, precedes its existence. Nonexistentialist philosophers believe that in like manner God, as a superior artisan, with the concept of man in mind, creates him; accordingly, man is the realization of a concept, the essential nature of which is in the mind of God. That is to say, theists hold to the belief that man's essence precedes existence, for, according to their belief, man possesses a human nature, a nature common to all men.

On the other hand, atheistic existentialism, the view which Sartre propounds, holds that man is a being whose *existence precedes essence,* because there is no God to give him any nature, to fashion him according to a design, conception, or essence. To assert that human reality, man, is a being whose existence precedes essence signifies that man simply happens to exist, happens to turn up, suddenly makes an appearance upon the scene; consequently, there is no previous mold into which man was poured to give him an essence that is definable. Only subsequent to his introduction into the world of existence, after he has made some choices by virtue of his freedom, then he will have made himself, chosen himself for the man he actually is. Inasmuch as there is no God to conceive of man, to think of what nature to assign him and to what use he is to be put, then man is only what he makes of himself, what he *wills* himself to be, what he creates of himself by willing himself into being, becoming. "In fact we are a freedom which chooses, but we do not choose to be free. We are condemned to freedom."[30] Accordingly, the fundamental moral law is: *Choose thyself!* The full weight and responsibility of what a particular individual is,

29. Jean-Paul Sartre, *Existentialism* (New York: Philosophical Library, 1947), pp. 15, 54. This book is the English translation of Sartre's *L'existentialisme est un humanisme.*

30. Jean-Paul Sartre, *Being and Nothingness* (New York: Philosophical Library, 1956), pp. 484–485.

and what he will be in the future, rests squarely upon his own shoulders alone. Man is no other than what he himself has made of himself.

BAD FAITH. If a man seeks to excuse himself for his heinous behavior, character, or nature by attempting to claim that he is not responsible for himself and his actions because they are due to deterministic causes, then he is a "coward," and if he excuses himself on the grounds that he had no choice in being born in the first place, then he is a "stinker." Nor may one lie to himself, deceive himself, for self-deception is *bad faith*. "Bad is a lie to oneself. . . . In bad faith it is from myself that I am hiding the truth."[31] Intellectual dishonesty, the rejection of thoughts from consciousness, the refusal to face disagreeable facts, are examples of bad faith. Such behavior removes an individual from his responsibilities by reducing a subject into an object, so that he does not accept himself as a free person with attendant responsibilities.

MAN AS THE CREATOR OF VALUES. An individual's choices have far-reaching consequences; he is responsible not only for himself but for others as well, because by his choices he chooses all men. By his choices he not only makes himself in the image of the man he thinks he ought to be, but an image that is valid for every other individual, an example for others to emulate. Others weigh heavily on one. "Hell is—other people."[32] In this respect Sartre is Kantian; a person's willing brings into existence the categorical imperative. For example, when a person chooses a monogamous marriage, he is in effect involving all mankind, by creating a certain image of what man ought to be, simply by his own choosing. "In choosing myself, I choose man."[33] In choosing myself, I am in effect building the universal to which everyone ought to adhere.

An individual more than makes himself, his life, and his situation; he makes his *values*. "Human reality is that by which value arrives in the world."[34] Prior to man's existence, life is nothing; it is man who gives it meaning; likewise, values obtain meaning only by man's choice. Otherwise, "value is beyond being."[35] By individual choice, personal and collective values are created. Values are constantly in the making, as man himself is continuously in the making. By *existential humanism* is meant precisely the "human" universe where the individual alone and forlorn decides by himself as a lawmaker.

ABANDONMENTS. There is no God to direct man; hence, man, whose nature is freedom, completely undetermined, must make his

31. Ibid., pp. 48–49.
32. Jean-Paul Sartre, *No Exit* (New York: Vintage, 1958), p. 47.
33. Sartre, *Existentialism,* p. 21.
34. Sartre, *Being and Nothingness,* p. 93.
35. Ibid.

own decisions, unbound by eternal law, and without excusing himself, but responsible for all that he does. Man is free, man is freedom . . . man is condemned to be free."[36] He must now lean on himself, not on God, for "God is an outdated hypothesis."[37] Caught in this abandoned state of existence, without being able to turn to God for assistance, man experiences anguish, forlornness, despair. Man's consciousness of the self as freedom, which strikes him as a state of nothingness, is dread, and inasmuch as freedom is inescapable, man is his own state of dread. The intensity of responsibility brings anxiety into our existence; anyone who claims not to be anxiety-stricken is merely hiding, disguising, or fleeing from it, and this is *bad faith.* Even when anguish is concealed, it is evident. Anguish is intensified by sense of forlornness, that state of having been abandoned by God. Since God does not exist, one must act on his own without relying on God. Facing life under these dreaded circumstances, ridden with anxiety, the individual becomes consciously aware of his absolute freedom; then nausea and despair result.

SARTREAN PESSIMISM: MAN, A USELESS PASSION. Sartre's system is fundamentally one of *pessimism,* reducing freedom (the nature of man) to absurdity, nausea, meaninglessness. In his works *Nausea* and *The Flies,* he not only characterizes man's nature as freedom, but also maintains that there is nothing rational about freedom of choice. "I am free: there is absolutely no more reason for living. . . . My past is dead. . . . Alone and free. But this freedom is like death."[38] Actually, freedom binds a man, and a man bound to choice is determined; he has no choice but to choose; he must choose; choice is a necessity; man becomes enslaved to freedom. "Hence, the absurdity of freedom."

Man is a tragedy, condemned to freedom, and his cruel destiny and real anguish lie in being forced without any reason for it to play a meaningless part in life, a painful crime whose end, death, is likewise meaningless. Man's freedom consists in existing for nothing, for no purpose whatever; yet despite all this, man being essentially freedom, condemned to freedom, has no choice but to choose, a senseless contradiction. This is man's situation; man *is* himself a situation, empty, a situation of emptiness, the emptiness of freedom. Man's fate, the nemesis of being cursed with choice, choices that are meaningless, an existence that is irrational, renders him a tragic man of anguish and nausea.

COMMENTARY ON THE ETHICAL THEORY OF SARTRE. As Manser has remarked, Sartre, like Locke and others before him, began with a

36. Sartre, *Existentialism,* p. 27.
37. Ibid., p. 26.
38. Jean-Paul Sartre, *Nausea* (Norfolk, Conn.: New Directions, 1959), p. 209.

tabula rasa (blank tablet), but in Sartre's case it is an ethical *tabula rasa.* At birth there is no moral quality in man, inasmuch as his moral being is a later acquisition.

> Undoubtedly some of his critics, and even Sartre himself, have assumed that the object of his ethical discussion was to start with a clean slate, an ethical *tabula rasa,* and hence have supposed that the failure to produce a set of rules marks the failure of the whole enterprise. In so far as Sartre has thought this, he has fallen into one of the traps he criticises other thinkers for falling into, that of regarding morality as a single set of rules.[39]

A more penetrating criticism is cited by Manser concerning Sartre's notion of human nature, which renders the production of morality impossible, "for to do such a thing would be to deny the facts on which his whole work is based."[40] To eliminate the belief that values are a structural component of the world, Sartre attacked man, disrobing him of a human nature, and identified him as a being who is both "not what he is and is what he is not," the result being that no single manner of moral behavior exists. In his desire to be radical, contends Manser, Sartre reduced

> moral action to the level of arbitrary decision. It is even doubtful if we would talk of 'decisions' here, for a decision can only be made in the context of a meaningful way of life. For Sartre it would appear that the meaning is subsequent to the decision, in which case it is impossible to know what is being decided. Similarly, if mortality results from a bare project, it is hard to see in what sense it can be called a morality. . . . The danger is that all we are given is a do-it-yourself kit, not a morality.[41]

Sartre left one without a formula for "deciding what [one] ought to do; it is difficult even to conceive what form such a decision would take."[42] Mary Warnock added another criticism: "We know from the novels, and indeed from everything that Sartre has written, that freedom is in his view the supreme value. But we must admit that it is not wholly clear to what a man is committed if he chooses freedom, or what his alternatives are."[43]

Warnock concluded that the ethical theory of Sartre leads to absurdity, terminating in extreme subjectivism and libertarianism, because of the expectation that a person will always elect to choose precisely

39. Anthony Manser, *Sartre: A Philosophic Study* (New York: Oxford University Press, 1966), p. 162.
40. Ibid., p. 164.
41. Ibid., pp. 164–165.
42. Mary Warnock, *Ethics Since 1900,* 2d ed. (London: Oxford University Press, 1966), p. 138.
43. Ibid.

what he feels. To "interiorise" ethics is one thing, "but without *some* element of objectivity, without *any* criterion for preferring one scheme of values to another, except the criterion of what looks most attractive to oneself, there cannot in fact be any morality at all, and moral theory must consist only in the assertion that there is no morality."[44]

One of the puzzling questions left unanswered by Sartre relates to the creation of values by man, for values lack objectivity. The question is: If each person creates his own particular, personal, and peculiar set of values on a purely subjective basis, then is it not strange that there exists so great a consensus about values? Most values are shared by great numbers of persons, yet if each created his own peculiar value, the outcome would be—no two values alike.

44. Mary Warnock, *Existentialist Ethics* (London: Macmillan, 1967), p. 56.

12

Phenomenological Value Theory: Moral Values as Real Objects of Consciousness

Phenomenology, a contemporary school of philosophy whose founding has been attributed to Edmund Husserl (1859–1938), is a philosophy of *essence,* a school of thought that seeks *ideal intelligible structure* in phenomena. It is a philosophy that is also defined as the *descriptive analysis of subjective processes* that is, a philosophical movement that attempts to obtain the form, structure, and essence of phenomena in complete abstraction, free from interpretation or evaluation. The major theorists of this school discussed in the present chapter are Max Ferdinand Scheler (1874–1928) and Nicolai Hartmann (1882–1950). These two men have been the most effective of the group in applying phenomenology to moral values.

Max Scheler: The Emotional Intuition and Apriorism of Value. Scheler adapted Blaise Pascal's dictum "the heart has its reasons that the mind knows not of" to his own ethical system. From Pascal's *ordre du coeur* (order of the heart) or *logique du coeur* (logic of the heart), Scheler concluded that the heart possesses, in a manner analogous to the intellect's understanding of logic, a realm of its own in which it knows moral values as the intellect apprehends logical ones. The world of values is a reality that one may judge without the aid of intelligence, i.e., nonrationally, independently of the intellect. Value judgments possess objectivity, universality, necessity, and intuitive content (structure).

THE A PRIORI INTUITION OF VALUES. According to phenomenological value theory, knowledge is not limited to scientific method or mere sense perception, but man can intuitively describe phenomena that transcend both sense and reason. By the method of phenomenology, the *given* of reality, those intelligible essential objects, can be intuited, an act which Scheler termed *essential insight.* Intelligible essential structures are intuited by an a priori act, the ability of a human being to ascertain immediately the given objective phenomena, the material content of moral values.

As a value realist, Scheler held to the existence of value facts in addition to scientific facts. While valuations may exist in the mind, concreteness, or materiality of value (*Wertmaterie*), exists as an ontologically real object, and notwithstanding its being outside of the mind, it nevertheless corresponds to the internal subjective content of the mind. Although one apprehends values by an *emotional intuition* of them (an immediate discernment), an intentional act of feeling, pure sentiment, nevertheless they are objective entities entirely different from subjective states of feeling. Values exist independently of man's subjective emotional state.

THE OBJECTIVE HIERARCHY OF MORAL VALUES. The realms of values reveal themselves to one in various hierarchal arrangements, in aristocratic order; and, although their hierarchal order is objective, they are immediately apprehended by an intuitive *value preferential sentiment,* rather than by reason. Of the various differences among values, two important types of differences are discernible: (1) a difference in *degree,* and (2) a difference in *mode,* or quality.

Degree: A Scale of Relative Worth of Values. Values are classified into an ascending order of rank, from lower to higher, on the basis of their *quantitative* differences, according to the following criteria: (*a*) *duration,* lasting values being preferable to those which are perishable and transient; (*b*) *extension and indivisibility,* the value's worth being greater, the larger the number of individuals sharing in a particular value without the necessity of dividing it up among them; (*c*) *foundational value,* i.e., a value that is the by-product of another having less worth than the one upon which it depends for its existence; and (*d*) *depth of satisfaction,* i.e., the more satisfying the value, the greater its worth. Values, as treated in the above discussion, do not differ in kind, but merely in degree.

Value Modalities. The second order of values is that of *modes of value.* Here values are classified into the following ascending hierarchal order on the basis of their *qualitative* distinctions: (*a*) *sensuous values,* or those which issue personal pleasure, i.e., are agreeable or disagreeable, pleasant or unpleasant; (*b*) *vital values,* or those important to human welfare, life, health, well-being, vitality, and strength; (*c*) *spiritual values,* including cultural and aesthetic values, such as those of science and philosophy, beauty, morality, truth, and justice; (*d*) *religious values,* sacred values, holy values, or those related to worship and reverence; those in this group are discerned by love and are grounded in God, an infinite personal spirit and the value of values.

ETHICAL RELATIVITY AND PERSPECTIVISM. While moral values are basically absolute, there is a sense in which they may be considered relative, that is, either relative to different societies practicing diverse ethics, or to the same society whose ethics at the present time differs markedly from what it was in previous generations. According to Scheler, values are eternal and immutable, consequently not susceptible to change or variation. The fact that different groups have different moral practices does not mean that values differ in the sense that they are merely relative to a given society, but rather that each society is simply viewing absolute values from its own divergent perspective, i.e., each is looking into a different window at the absolute, as Hegel would say. Thus, it is not moral values that are relative, but one's knowledge which is relative; not value relativism, but *value perspectivism* is the case. If one could view values from the vantage point of God, then he would see values in their true perspective and entirely, as absolute values.

LOVE AND SYMPATHY. Scheler held that love not only is the principal means of deriving ethical insight, but also establishes the quality and degree of a person's moral merit and character. Without love and sympathy, man would be devoid of the intuitive insight necessary for contacting moral reality. By acts of love and expressions of sympathy, one gets to know others directly as *concrete unities of action* (Scheler's definition of a person) or as personal wholes. The essence of another person is manifested to us in acts of love. Sympathy, the apex of human emotional existence, identifies, communicates, or establishes a community of sentiment between two or more persons, without the loss of personal identity.

Although neutral in moral value, sympathy transforms whatever is moral into a value, and is itself transformed into love when activated, love being the fundamental moral act. While love is a spontaneous act, sympathy is merely a reaction, a response. Love, entirely autonomous, is creative, realizing the loved object, bringing it into existence and augmenting its value.

Love of self and of others is the model for the love of God, the supreme object of love, the value of values, the love of loves, the source of all value. Hence, all values converge on God, the *summum bonum* (greatest good).

Love is theistic, for its direction and supreme object is God, the source of all value. Consequently, man's search for values as an ordered, coherent, systematic whole is a religious act, the same act by which God's existence is proved. The religious act (spiritual love) *intends* its object, a personal infinite God, the essential structure of the religious act. Thus, holy love proves the existence of God by immediate intuition as an actuality. The religious act establishes the objective reality of God; "for this great urge to love, to serve, to bend down, is God's own essence."[1]

MAN'S PLACE IN THE COSMOS. In the last phase of Scheler's life, he underwent a severe disruption in life and thought, repudiating earlier loftier values for an evolutionary pantheism based upon Darwinism,

1. Max Scheler, *Ressentiment* (New York: Free Press, 1961), p. 89.

Freudianism, and Bergsonism. These ideas included Bergson's concept that the world is a machine for the making of God—"man cooperates in the creation of God"[2]—thus assuming that God is unfinished, in the process of becoming, still in the making. From Darwin and Freud, Scheler developed the idea that the lower, the biological, aspects of man are responsible for the higher, the spiritual; the spiritual characteristics of man would be impotent without energy supplied to them from the lower instincts. Man's spiritual life is merely the sublimation of his animal organism.

Faced with pure nothingness, man seeks refuge in religion as a defense against nihilism. However, here he finds God not a personal being, but a *ground of being,* with whom man must cooperate in bringing God to full realization. Man's self-realization is, in effect, self-deification. Evolution is the historical process of an incomplete God moving progressively toward full actualization. God, the highest being, must rely upon man's cooperation for his determination and fulfillment.

EVALUATION OF SCHELER'S THEORY. Scheler's is a descriptive rather than a philosophical phenomenology. Consequently, in his description of phenomenological data, his attitude is that he need not defend his position because he is simply presenting facts of experience. Recently a leading phenomenologist, Marvin Farber, has referred to Scheler's theory as a "dogmatic defense of selected articles of faith."

Nicolai Hartmann: The Emotional A Priori Apprehension of Value. While Hartmann agreed with Scheler on some basic points, such as the method of phenomenology, value absolutism, and value essences as nonrational (in the sense that value essences must be intuited by a means other than man's reason), he did, nevertheless, disagree with him on other basic issues, such as theism and personalism. Hartmann repudiated Scheler's personalism together with his doctrine of collective persons, in favor of Aristotelian individualism, i.e., the idea that only individuals, not groups, are persons. Furthermore, Scheler's conception of God as the teleological principle of man's value striving is rejected by Hartmann, who claimed that man's autonomous being is absolute, and that his will is bound—yet not determined—not by God, but by moral law.

VALUES AS OBJECTIVE AND INTUITED. Defending Platonic idealism, namely the view that values are objective, i.e., belong to an absolute realm of eternal essences discerned a priori by man, Hartmann advanced the claim that value essences, comparable to those of mathematics and logic, do not emanate from reason, but are intuitively ascertained by direct a priori insight. "There is a pure valuational a priori which directly, intuitively, in accordance with feeling, penetrates our practical consciousness, our whole conception of life, and which

2. Max Scheler, *Man's Place in Nature* (Boston: Beacon Press, 1961), p. 93.

lends to everything which falls within the range of our vision the mark of value or anti-value."[3]

VALUE REALISM. When one speaks of moral knowledge, it must be regarded as distinct from rational knowledge, inasmuch as values are sui generis (real in their own right). "The a priori element of worth contained implicitly in living morality belongs therefore in fact . . . to the given phenomenon, to the situational complex, to the 'factum' of ethical reality."[4] Values have real content, including virtues. The apriorism of Hartmann allies his system with intuitionism, and his concept of a value as a *factum* makes him an *ethical realist*.

MORAL VALUES: AXIOLOGY OF MORALS. Values form a complex integrated whole, but, owing to man's imperfect knowledge, values as a systematic whole for man are fragmentary. A precondition to the actualization of higher values (moral) is the actualization of the lower values, that is, the nonmoral and the elementary moral ones. Consequently, contrary to Scheler's opinion, the lower values have a priority claim on the individual. The fundamental categorical ethical law is: "The lower categories are the stronger and more independent, while the weaker and more conditioned are the higher and more complex."[5]

A single absolute value scale cannot be established, but the relative worth of values can be arranged multidimensionally. In the gradation of values, a relative superiority of rank is indicated in the fact of choice, and values may be ranked according to content, force, and height. "The consciousness of their being higher is utterly decisive. Every morally selective consciousness of values is necessarily a consciousness of the scale of values."[6] By virtue of its own peculiar characteristic quality, one value may be distinguished from another by its height and strength factor; the higher the axiological quality of a value, the lower its strength and the greater its dependency upon the lower value.

The "law of inverse variation of strength and height" governs at this point: "To sin against a lower value is in general more grievious than to sin against a higher; but the fulfilment of a higher is morally more valuable than that of a lower."[7] To illustrate: Murder as a most deplorable act is low on the scale of heinous deeds, but its inverse, the respect for the life of another person (not to be confused with friendship, love, or trustworthiness), is not proportionately high on the moral value scale.

THE FOUR FUNDAMENTAL MORAL VALUES: THE GOOD, THE NOBLE, RICHNESS OF EXPERIENCE, PURITY. There are four fundamental moral values: (1) The *good*, both indefinable and partially irrational

3. Nicolai Hartmann, *Ethics* (New York: Macmillan, 1932), 1:177.
4. Ibid., p. 178.
5. Ibid., 2:53.
6. Ibid., p. 47.
7. Ibid., p. 53.

owing to its highly complex material, is close to the Leibnizian concept of perfection. All values are indefinable in the strictest sense of the word. The good is identical with the morally valuable, and is *the* fundamental moral value. "Goodness is neither the ideal Being or concept of values, nor simply their actual existence, but only the pursuit of them as ends in the real world."[8] Thus, it is found that goodness is defined as the pursuit of values as ends, and this in itself is valuable. (2) The *noble,* the lofty moral value opposed to prevalent attitudes, is exemplified by the individual who despises value compromises and devotes himself freely to that which is great (knightly virtue), self-reliant, and magnanimous. (3) *Richness of experience* is the search for rich, new, full experiences, and synthesizing them into a unity. The principle relating to fullness of life may be expressed as "the greatest unity of the greatest diversity."[9] (4) *Purity,* the basis for sincerity, frankness, and openness, is characteristic of the pure in heart. A law governs purity, namely, the law stating that once it is lost, it can never be recovered.

MORAL FREEDOM. Unless the world is subject to the laws of cause and effect, both within the personality and in the outer physical sphere, then morality is impossible. But natural laws of causation do not preclude personal freedom. Mechanistic laws cannot explain organic life; neither can the laws of psychological or physiological processes explain the moral life. Moral consciousness, with its sense of responsibility, self-determination, and feelings of guilt (inasmuch as they suggest that man may have chosen otherwise), implies human freedom. To deny the existence of man's moral consciousness, his sense of responsibility and guilt, by dismissing them as mere illusions, is not sufficient. Their nonexistence must be proved, and the burden of proof rests with the skeptic, who himself labors under a false illusion.

COMMENTS ON HARTMANN'S VALUE THEORY. Although Hartmann was not affiliated with the phenomenological movement, he was directly influenced by Scheler and Husserl, his value theory being decidedly phenomenological in character. Unlike Scheler, Hartmann found no need to introduce God or religion into his system. He had less influence than Scheler, even though his tome on ethics was widely admired for its clarity and simplicity and reflected his intellectual integrity. In contrast to Scheler's dogmatism, Hartmann occasionally took no stand, was always open-minded, and in most instances sought diligently to improve upon his own conclusions.

Werkmeister has criticized Hartmann's theory of moral value on the ground that "no matter how sympathetic we may be towards the idea of a primal value-feeling, the further contention that the values dis-

8. Ibid., p. 179.
9. Ibid., p. 207.

closed in that feeling are self-existent essences can find support only in blind trust."[10] The same objection could be made to Scheler's point of view, for neither Scheler nor Hartmann could adequately cope with this particular difficulty.

Furthermore, according to Werkmeister, Hartmann's recourse to the realm of Platonic essences is both unwarranted and unnecessary. Werkmeister has objected to Hartmann's view that artistic creations are based upon an apprehension of a preexisting value which is then actualized in his art object. "One might argue, however—and with good reason, I believe—that not values but persons are creative, and through the creative acts of persons values come into being which did not exist previously."[11] Werkmeister's personalistic inclination impelled him to emphasize such objections; Hartmann could reply that value essences materialize as facts in the human world through an individual's creative act, which would still allow for the subsistence of values as essences in the Platonic realm where values reside. This rebuttal would not, however, entirely dispose of the issue.

10. William Werkmeister, *Theories of Ethics* (Lincoln, Nebr.: Johnsen, 1961), p. 269.

11. Ibid., p. 273.

13

Philosophies of Nonviolence

The objective of this chapter is to examine ethical philosophies whose common denominator is *nonviolence*. Like the ethical theories previously discussed, philosophies of nonviolence also have a family tree, stemming back to an origin, in this case the ethical teachings of Jesus, particularly the ideas in his *Sermon on the Mount*. Jesus' statement, "He that lives by the sword shall die by the sword,"[1] sums up the central thought undergirding these philosophies, namely, the thesis that violence cannot permanently solve human problems, which require loftier forms of conduct for their solution.

Some great thinkers who have distinguished themselves most as philosophers of nonviolence have earned a second distinction as well: they have been living exemplars of their ideas, a singular feat in the speculative world of philosophy. Three such representatives have been selected for examination: Jesus (ca. 4 B.C.–A.D. ca. 29), Mohandas Karamchand Gandhi (1869–1948), and Albert Schweitzer (1875–1965), but there are many others, including, for example, Leo Tolstoy (1828–1910) and Martin Luther King, Jr. (1929–1968), to mention only two.

Jesus: Christian Ethics (An Ethics of Inwardness). The type of ethic espoused by Jesus of Nazareth, though not systematized or integrated, resembles most nearly that of the ethical intuitionists because of his insistence that morality is an inner experience, not an overt act but a state of being. Morality is not so much a question of doing good as being good.

PERSONS AS OF INFINITE INTRINSIC VALUE. The ethics of Jesus is grounded on respect for the infinite intrinsic value of each human personality. An individual is worth more than anything else within the universe or even the world in its entirety. The person is regarded as an eternal soul, priceless, with no object equivalent to him in value. "What will a man gain by winning the whole world, at the cost of his true self? Or what can he give that will buy that self back?"[2]

1. Matt. 26:52. Biblical quotations throughout this section, unless specified otherwise, are from *The New English Bible* (Oxford University Press; Cambridge University Press, 1970).
2. Matt. 16:26.

A single personality, possessing dignity or infinite worth, is equal to a hundred persons in moral value; for a value scale with but one person on one side of the scale would be able to balance the scale on the other, inasmuch as infinity balances infinity (or, 100 times infinity is still equal to infinity).[3] Furthermore, concern for a solitary individual takes precedence over concern for a hundred persons if that particular person happens to be one who is in need. This value principle was enunciated by Jesus in his parable of a hundred sheep, and was implied in the parable of the landowner hiring laborers in his vineyard.

BROTHERHOOD OF MAN. Jesus' concept of the fatherhood of God implies the brotherhood of man. As children of God, each person becomes infinitely precious in worth, each man being of equal value to any other. Jesus identified himself so completely with each human being regardless of his station in life that whatever harm the victim suffered was personally experienced through sympathetic induction by Jesus, as when he said, "I tell you this: anything you did for one of my brothers here, however humble, you did for me."[4] The most wretched specimens of humanity became one with him, despite the undesirable social status assigned to them by society. For Jesus, societal distinctions did not necessarily coincide with those of God, since society often construes as God's doctrines "the commandments of men."

His doctrine elevating all humanity to a status of supreme worth applied to social rejects as well as to women and children as a class who in his time were regarded as vastly inferior to men. For him, a child was a paradigm for adult behavior, free from complexes, authentically genuine in personality, exemplifying simplicity in behavior. "Unless you turn round and become like children, you will never enter the kingdom of Heaven."[5]

LOVE: THE SUPREME VIRTUE. In view of this attitude toward human beings and God, it is not surprising that for him the primary virtue is love—not love in the sense of sex, or tenderness, or even friendship, but *agapē,* i.e., a love resembling that with which God loves man. Accordingly, the commandment which Jesus regarded as of cardinal importance was to love God with every fiber of one's being (with heart, soul, strength, and mind), and to love one's fellow man as oneself. Such love may assume the aforementioned forms, but *agapē* is loftier love than those cited because of its capability of enabling man to perform the most noble of deeds; "there is no greater love than this, that a man should lay down his life for his friends."[6]

Love is the paramount virtue, not only in the ethical teachings of Jesus but in Pauline ethics as well. Eulogizing this supreme virtue, St. Paul wrote, "Love is kind and envies no one. Love is never boastful,

3. This illustration is the author's.
4. Matt. 25:40.
5. Matt. 18:3.
6. John 15:13.

nor conceited, nor rude; never selfish, not quick to take offence. Love keeps no score of wrongs; does not gloat over other men's sins, but delights in the truth. There is nothing love cannot face; there is no limit to its faith, its hope, and its endurance. . . . There are three things that last for ever: faith, hope and love; but the greatest of them all is love."[7] From this early Christian concept of love, St. Augustine and St. Thomas Aquinas developed their ethical systems.

THE CRITERION OF MORALITY: LOVE. For Jesus, love is the criterion of morality as well as of a person's moral standing; that is to say, love is the measure of his moral worth. Ordinary instances of love, as in giving love only to those loving you, are not sufficiently meritorious, inasmuch as criminals and those in disrepute are willing to return love as if returning favor for favor, but moral standards on an ethical level much higher than the criminal's code of behavior require man to love even his enemies. "If you love only those who love you, what reward can you expect? Surely the taxgatherers [persons regarded as racketeers] do as much as that. And if you greet only your brothers, what is there extraordinary about that? Even the heathen do as much."[8]

The Christian mandate is to love one another, love being significant evidence of discipleship. The love which Jesus enjoins us to practice encompasses not only persons of our own nationality and religious affiliation, but all mankind, including our enemies. His parable of the good Samaritan is an unequivocal enunciation of this point. Prior to the teaching of Jesus concerning the universal brotherhood of mankind, ethical indoctrination made allowance for only the limited or restricted love of coreligionists, brothers of the faith. Jesus taught that any human being, of whatever origin, class, or condition, has a claim, as a child of God, on one's love and compassion when in need of assistance.

The transition of man from his narcissistic animal nature acquired at birth to a state of moral excellence is effected through a process of spiritual regeneration, an experience of being "born again." Moral rebirth, a transvaluation of all values, is a vitally necessary moral transmigration. Mundane values are exchanged for celestial values.

Love acquired the meaning of charity, connoting almsgiving because the person giving love to another often did so at a time when the recipient was in dire need of sympathy and assistance. But charity, Jesus taught, must be given without a fanfare of trumpets, not ostentatiously or hypocritically, but in such secrecy that even the recipient is unaware of his benefactor—"Do not let your left hand know what your right is doing."[9] Furthermore, said Jesus, if you lend

7. I Cor. 13:4–7, 13.
8. Matt. 6:46–47.
9. Matt. 6:4.

money to those in need and wish to observe a high moral standard, you must not expect repayment.

Characteristics of the Ideal Moral Personality. The ideal character was described by Jesus in the Beatitudes, which list the traits of the blessed, consummately blissful, or truly happy person. His portrayal of the ideal personality is a transvaluation of prevailing values, a reversal of bourgeois ethical codes that were then (and still are) in existence, for he identified supernal felicity with those who are poor, sorrowful, gentle, merciful, pure of heart, peaceful, and imbued with a thirst for righteousness. Certain attitudes which make for happiness and moral character are stated in the beatitudes as follows:

How blest are those who know that they are poor;
the kingdom of Heaven is theirs.
How blest are the sorrowful;
they shall find consolation.
How blest are those of a gentle spirit;
they shall have the earth for their possession.
How blest are those who hunger and thirst to see right prevail,
they shall be satisfied.
How blest are those who show mercy;
mercy shall be shown to them.
How blest are those whose hearts are pure;
they shall see God.
How blest are the peacemakers;
God shall call them his sons.
How blest are those who have suffered persecution for the cause of right;
the Kingdom of Heaven is theirs.[10]

Revision of the Ten Commandments. Jesus revised the "Decalogue" and other Mosaic commandments, contending that these had served past generations well but that moral progress henceforth required supplementation or modification. Accordingly, he introduced doctrines which he believed would add higher steps to the moral ladder constructed by Moses. Whereas in the Deuteronomic law, Moses enjoined, "Thou shalt not kill," Jesus' emendation declared that "anyone who nurses anger against his brother" is in a comparable moral position to the one who murders, for evil actions emanate from an evil heart. Not overt sins committed, but motive, intent, will, and traits residing deep within the recesses of the personality are the roots of evil. "Wicked thoughts, murder, adultery, fornication, theft, perjury, slander —these all proceed from the heart; and these are the things that defile a man."[11] Evil is not an act, it is more—it is a state of being, a quality of character. Thus, the act of murder issues from an intent to abuse

10. Matt. 5:3–10.
11. Matt. 15:19.

others; it is the attitude of contempt for others that deserves the punishment of hell's fire.

Jesus' pronouncements about the ethics of sex similarly go beyond overt action and emphasize intent and attitude. Not merely is the adulterous act wrong, but the lustful heart or imagination prompting lascivious behavior is equally immoral, since "if a man looks on a woman with a lustful eye, he has already committed adultery with her in his heart."[12]

Although good men had been expected to keep their promises and intended to do so, Jesus forbade the making of any promises, saying that what is not made cannot be broken, and that, moreover, future events are in God's hands alone. He implied that only God can make and fulfill promises. As for man, let him not swear oaths, for an honest man does not need to do so, because, owing to his inner integrity, a simple *yes* or *no* suffices.

LEX TALIONIS (LAW OF RETALIATION) REVISED. Retaliation is repugnant to the ethical posture of Jesus; the law of retaliation must be scaled upward. Moses' code of "an eye for an eye, and a tooth for a tooth" permits violence to be repaid with violence, for that was the essence of his code of justice. But Jesus' revision is: "Resist not evil. If someone slaps you on the right cheek, turn and offer him your left."[13]

Gandhi interpreted this teaching of Jesus to mean that it is beneath the dignity of man to strike back when smitten. Violence may be the norm or mode of behavior in the animal kingdom, but it is inappropriate among human beings. The philosophers of nonviolence believe that violence has never resolved issues in any permanent manner, that the power of love as a genuine force is more effectual and enduring.

ANXIETY AS A MORAL ISSUE. Even anxiety becomes a moral issue for Jesus. God is more concerned for man than man is for himself, and, in view of the fact that God cares well for the lilies of the fields, which grow in splendor without anxiety or self-concern, it is immoral for man to mistrust God's providential care by being overly anxious about life's necessities. A life well lived according to Christian statutes will prove itself true—"By their fruits ye shall know them." Therefore, "set your mind on God's kingdom and his justice before everything else, and all the rest will come to you as well."[14]

Furthermore, said Jesus, no person should act as if he had to live through an entire lifetime of problems in a single day, borrowing future problems that should be dealt with gradually over an extended lifetime and concentrating on solving them all in a single moment. On the contrary, living one day at a time will enable us to cope with a lifetime of

12. Matt. 5:28.
13. Matt. 5:39.
14. Matt. 6:33.

problems. Each day has its own ration of troubles; we should deal with them singly and in sequence as they occur. "Do not be anxious about tomorrow; tomorrow will look after itself. Each day has troubles enough of its own."[15] Excessive worrying cannot add to anyone's life span, and may shorten it, whereas intelligent living can sometimes extend life.

CRITICAL JUDGMENT OF OTHERS. Censoriousness is self-defeating and worthy of severe condemnation. Whoever censures another person thereby condemns himself. "Pass no judgment, and you will not be judged. For as you judge others, so you will yourselves be judged, and whatever measure you deal out to others will be dealt back to you."[16] Disdain for other human beings is evidence of the psychological defense mechanism of projection; emotional condemnation of another indicates that the fault criticized lies within oneself as well, but to a greater degree. "Why do you look at the speck of sawdust in your brother's eye, with never a thought for the great plank in your own? Or how can you say to your brother, 'Let me take the speck out of your eye,' when all the time there is the plank in your own? You hypocrite! First take the plank out of your own eye, and then you will see clearly to take the speck out of your brother's."[17]

Jesus' injunctions were never negative but always positive, as typified by the Golden Rule: "Always treat others as you would like them to treat you."[18] Other great thinkers, such as Confucius, have presented the rule in its negative form; in its negative form, the rule is occasionally referred to as the Silver Rule. The rule finds its antecedent in negative and inchoate form in the Old Testament in the apocryphal book of Tobit 4:15, and in many of the living religions of the world, as well as in the writings of Plato, Aristotle, and Hillel (a Jewish leader approximately twenty years Jesus' senior). Its universality is thought by some to be an innate moral principle imbedded in the mind of man.

COMMENTS ON THE ETHICS OF JESUS. The ethics of Jesus is complex and subject to numerous difficulties of interpretation, as in his typical injunction: "Be ye therefore perfect, even as your Father which is in heaven."[19] Luke's version of the Gospel moderates this behest to read: "Be compassionate as your Father is compassionate."[20] The ethics of Jesus was not meant to be crystallized into the straitjacket of a system, and indeed it cannot be. It is chiefly composed of evaluations of random topics relevant to the situation confronting him at the moment. It lacks not only integration but also verbal proof of the moral judg-

15. Matt. 6:34.
16. Matt. 7:1–2.
17. Matt. 7:3–5.
18. Matt. 7:12.
19. Matt. 5:48; King James version.
20. Luke 6:36.

ments rendered, although Jesus does offer a pragmatic argument in support of his position. "If any man will do his will, he shall know of the doctrine."[21] The proof lies in the implementation of his moral ideas by himself and others during an exemplary life. "Christ did not argue about virtue, but commanded it,"[22] affirmed John Stuart Mill.

Furthermore, the Gospels provide one with only fragments of Jesus' moral philosophy, omitting much of what he said and did, as well as editing some of his remarks, but this does not diminish or cast doubt on his principal teaching, namely, *universal love*.

Some New Testament scholars contend that the ethics of Jesus is intended not as a code of everyday behavior, but only as an ideal code, or general guide, since the moral requirements are much too stringent for the individual to assimilate in his daily activities. Referring to the moral code of Jesus as an emergency ethic, Schweitzer commented that it could be pursued only by a few persons and only briefly prior to the end of the New Testament period, while its long-term application serves inspirational purposes.

Mohandas Gandhi: The Ethics of Nonviolence. Gandhi, who characterized his own life as "an experiment with truth," was influenced especially by Jesus, Thoreau, Tolstoy, and the Hindu scriptures, and more specifically by Jesus' Sermon on the Mount, Tolstoy's *The Kingdom of God Is within You* (1894), the Hindu *Bhagavad Gita,* and Henry David Thoreau's *Civil Disobedience* (1849). On a lesser scale, Ruskin also had an influence on Gandhi's views.

The idea responsible for Gandhi's profound and lasting conversion, *ahimsa,* is the doctrine of *nonviolence,* the preservation and nondestruction of life; and coupled to it, *satyagraha,* truth-force or soul-force, which was translated into practice as *passive resistance.*

THE DOCTRINE OF *Ahimsa* (NONVIOLENCE). In his autobiography, Gandhi concisely stated the doctrine of *ahimsa:*

> *Ahimsa* is a comprehensive principle. We are helpless mortals caught in the conflagration of *himsa.* The saying that life lives on life has a deep meaning in it. Man cannot for a moment live without consciously or unconsciously committing outward *himsa.* The very fact of his living—eating, drinking and moving about—necessarily involves some *himsa,* destruction of life, be it ever so minute. A votary of *ahimsa* therefore remains true to his faith if the spring of all his actions is compassion, if he shuns to the best of his ability the destruction of the tiniest creature, tries to save it, and thus incessantly strives to be free from the deadly coil of *himsa.* He will be constantly growing in

21. John 7:17.
22. John Stuart Mill, "Comment on Plato's *Gorgias,*" in *Mill's Ethical Writings* (New York: Collier, 1965), p. 77.

> self-restraint and compassion, but he can never become entirely free from outward *himsa*.[23]

Ahimsa has many ramifications: for example, each adherent must endeavor to end hostilities between belligerent warring nations, must seek unity among all living beings, must be humble, and must practice *ahimsa* in all walks of life. To him, the "individual is the one supreme consideration,"[24] whereas the state, unweaned from violence, is a "soulless machine."

Although *ahimsa* literally means nonkilling, its Gandhian application is based on the doctrine of nonviolence with the broadest interpretation and widest ramifications possible, since it requires each adherent to refrain from offending others and advocates repression of any uncharitable thoughts, even those directed against one's so-called enemy. It not only prohibits retaliation by the victim of violence (just as Jesus taught) but also forbids even the feeling of resentment against another person or the desire for revenge.

Ahimsa, then, is the expression of love for all mankind, including one's adversaries. To refrain from avenging an aggressor's attack requires greater courage than returning blow for blow. To continue to love your enemy when he strikes you again and again, to return love for violence, will eventually cause him to yield, for a human being in a normal state of mind is constitutionally incapable of continually striking one who does him good, and ultimately must relinquish his aggressive attitude in order to avoid self-condemnation as the lowest being in creation.

The exercise of perfect love is man's duty; to this end, a man must feel completely dispossessed, or even become "nonpossessed," of his body if the necessity arises; that is to say, he must be willing to die for the sake of human service. A person's joy must be derived not from inflicting pain on others, but from voluntary acceptance of his own cross, bearing pain willingly. Truth has value because it is an inner resource of persons willing to die for it; a man's freedom is never lost except through personal weakness; and liberation from fear belongs to those who can defy death.

THE DOCTRINE OF *Satyagraha* (TRUTH-FORCE OR SOUL-FORCE). *Satyagraha,* a term coined from *sadagraha* (truth-firmness), was at first applied to the tenet of *passive resistance* and eventually was used to designate the entire struggle of Gandhi and his people for freedom in India. Its background stems from a variety of sources, including Jesus' Sermon on the Mount, the *karmayoga* (selfless, dutiful service)

23. M. K. Gandhi, *The Story of My Experiments with Truth* (Washington, D.C.: Public Affairs Press, 1948), pp. 427–428.
24. M. K. Gandhi, *Young India* (November 13, 1924).

of the *Bhagavad Gita,* Thoreau's principle of civil disobedience, and Ruskin. Gandhi's doctrine was not identical with Thoreau's notion of "civil disobedience," for Gandhi felt that civil disobedience (civil resistance, or passive resistance) could connote violence and hatred, as it sometimes did. Furthermore, civil disobedience was commonly regarded as a weapon of last resort in the hands of weak persons and, consequently, he objected to use of the term unless it was given a specific meaning consistent with his point of view.

Satyagraha (literally, "clinging to truth") refers to a life dedicated to God. Men devoted to this doctrine conduct themselves in accordance with the principles of nonviolence, truth, fearlessness, continence, appetite control, poverty or nonpossession, religious equality, opposition to untouchability, bread-labor, and restriction of purchases to local goods. Gandhi explained that the term's "root meaning is holding on to truth, hence, *truth-force*. I have also called it Love-force or Soul-force."[25] Loyalty to this doctrine impels adherents to resist such evils as injustice, exploitation, cruelty, and oppression. Strength or power to resist evils is rallied from inner resources (truth or its equivalent, God) of the individual, who succeeds in this effort through loving-service to others, or nonviolence. *Satyagraha* is the soul-force used as a weapon to overcome evil. Effective use of the soul-force requires: self-discipline, enabling one to live a simple life of self-control; the ability to suffer without hatred or fear; a life of disinterested (yet whole-hearted) service to others; and understanding of the unity that exists among all living things. The rationale of the theory of nonviolence states that one can appeal directly to the conscience and reason of an antagonist by subjecting oneself to suffering, which will convert him. More efficacious than weapons of violence is the human appeal to the conscience and heart. At best, violence cannot be permanently effective because, instead of overcoming evil, it merely represses it temporarily and generates more intense opposition, whereas nonviolent techniques obliterate evil permanently through conversion to friendship.

To be sure, the nonviolent fighter is a courageous soul because *satyagraha* requires inner strength, fortitude, self-discipline, determined devotion, selflessness, a smiling countenance, and a heart devoid of hatred. There is a great difference between the person who is merely a passive resister and the nonviolent resister. The former resort to passive resistance only as an expedient measure, ready to replace it as soon as possible with violent means.

SATYAGRAHA AS A SOCIAL ETHIC. Nonviolence, or *satyagraha,* assumes a variety of forms, among them being *noncooperation, fasting,* and *civil disobedience.* It is not the person who commits evil, but his

25. M. K. Gandhi, *Non-Violent Resistance* (New York: Schocken, 1961), p. 6.

deed that is the object of noncooperation, for hatred of any person is eschewed. Fasting should be motivated by the highest devotion to duty and the love of one's opponent, its object being self-purification and a salutary influence on one's adversary. Fasting should be used only as a measure of last resort by one who is fully convinced of the justice of his cause. *Civil disobedience* consists of nonviolent mass resistance for political purposes, such as actions or protests against futile, immoral, or harmful laws. It is practiced with courtesy, gentleness, and love, without attempts to embarrass an opponent. Examples of civil disobedience include resignations from government positions, repudiations of titles of honor, boycotting of courts of justice, and refusals to pay taxes.

Violence aims at victory through defeat. Nonviolence aims at victory without defeat, through truth and self-purification. Gandhi was convinced that truth has a lasting potent force in it, whereas violence achieves no permanent results. The force of violence is merely physical; the force of truth is spiritual.

EVALUATION OF GANDHI'S VIEWS. Lofty as Gandhi's moral ideas were, they were not justified by consequences, such as the deaths of one million persons during civil disturbances following his nonviolent campaigns of civil disobedience. Nevertheless, the alternative of violent resistance could have resulted in even greater disasters. Like Jesus, Gandhi lived by his moral ideals, even to his death in 1948, when he forgave and defended the assassin who inflicted the wounds which proved to be fatal. The long-term pragmatic test of Gandhi's doctrines is not yet finished. Bertrand Russell wrote: "A world full of happiness is not beyond human power to create. . . . The real obstacles lie in the heart of man, and the cure for these is a firm hope informed and fortified by thought."[26]

Albert Schweitzer: Reverence for Life. Schweitzer called his ethical philosophy *reverence for life* because of its central doctrine of *nonviolence,* which can be traced as far back as the ethics of Jesus. For some of his basic concepts, he was indebted to the works of Schopenhauer and Nietzsche. His philosophy reflects Schopenhauer's emphasis upon the drive for *self-preservation* and Nietzsche's insistence upon the importance of *life-affirmation* instincts. "In the world the infinite will-to-live reveals itself to us as will-to-create, and this is full of dark and painful riddles for us; in ourselves it is revealed as will-to-love, which will through us remove the dilemma of the will-to-live."[27] Schweitzer recalled that even in early childhood he had learned to respect the fundamental ethical injunction of Mosaic law, "Thou shalt not kill,"

26. Bertrand Russell, *Roads to Freedom,* 4th ed. (London: Allen & Unwin, 1966), p. 111.
27. Albert Schweitzer, *Out of My Life and Thought* (New York: New American Library, 1953), p. 182.

and that he had been taught by his mother a silent prayer akin to the principle of reverence for life: "O, heavenly Father, protect and bless all things that have breath; guard them from all evil, and let them sleep in peace."[28]

REVERENCE FOR LIFE. Accordingly, the respect for every living thing ran deep in the spirit of Schweitzer, and it encompassed *every* living thing, even bacteria. He argued that to draw a line arbitrarily between higher and lower forms of life might relegate human beings to the latter category owing to their primitive state.

> To undertake to lay down universally valid distinction of value between different kinds of life will end in judging them by the greater or lesser distance at which they seem to stand from us human beings—as we ourselves judge. But that is a purely subjective criterion. Who among us knows what significance any other kind of life has in itself, and as a part of the universe?
>
> Following on such a distinction there comes next the view that there can be life which is worthless, injury to which or destruction of which does not matter. Then in the category of worthless life we come to include, according to circumstances, different kinds of insects, or primitive peoples.[29]

Reverence for life means to aid and enhance life, not to harm or destroy it.

The principle of reverence for life repudiates the wanton destruction of life.

> Standing, as he does, with the whole body of living creatures under the law of this dilemma in the will-to-live, man comes again and again into the position of being able to preserve his own life and life generally only at the cost of other life. If he has been touched by the ethic of Reverence for Life, he injures and destroys life only under a necessity which he cannot avoid.[30]

Animal life is to be destroyed only when necessary, and its promiscuous destruction is evil. It is evil for a dual reason: first, it is wrong to take life because it is precious in itself, and second, it is reprehensible owing to the deterioration that it causes in the spirit of the one who kills.

Murder damages the murderer as well as his victim, whereas kindness has the opposite effect. "All ordinary violence produces its own limitations, for it calls forth an answering violence which sooner or later becomes its equal or its superior. But kindness . . . produces no strained relations which prejudice its working; strained relations which already exist it relaxes. Mistrust and misunderstanding it puts to

28. Albert Schweitzer, *Memoirs of Childhood and Youth* (New York: Macmillan, 1963), p. 47.
29. Schweitzer, *My Life and Thought,* p. 180.
30. Ibid., p. 181.

flight, and it strengthens itself by calling forth answering kindness."[31]

The criterion of morality is reverence for life, interpreted by Schweitzer to mean: "It is good to maintain and to encourage life; it is bad to destroy life or to obstruct it."[32] Paraphrasing the Golden Rule, Schweitzer considered ethics to consist in "my experiencing the compulsion to show to all will-to-live the same reverence as I do to my own."[33] Accordingly, ethics is life-affirmation, which requires one not merely to continue his existence but also to enjoy life with optimistic enthusiasm.

In this respect, the philosophy of reverence for life is a world-affirmation *Weltanschauung* (world-view, or philosophy of life), a wholesome love of things alive, and a wholesome thirst for living. The attempt to assist living creatures and keep them alive has two desirable consequences, namely, it protects a life and it also regenerates the spirit of the person who incurs sacrifices in order to save life. Whoever augments the life of others, be they human or nonhuman, raises his own spiritual being to its highest value. "Through Reverence for Life I raise my existence to its highest value and offer it to the world."[34] Thus, reverence for life is an ethics of self-perfection.

GOOD DEFINED. Universal protection of life is the definition of good, and a truly ethical man is he who senses a deep compulsion to assist life, or at least to recoil from injuring anything that lives. "Life as such is sacred to him. He tears no leaf from a tree, plucks no flower, and takes care to crush no insect."[35] If the masses disagree or ridicule one for so behaving, then it is wise to remember that the masses do not exemplify moral right. "To the man who is truly ethical all life is sacred, including that which from the human point of view seems lower in the scale."[36] If you assume that you have a right to kill merely because it does not bother your conscience, then remember that "the good conscience is an invention of the devil,"[37] whereas the highest court of appeal is reverence for life.

RAMIFICATIONS OF THE REVERENCE FOR LIFE PHILOSOPHY. An ethics of reverence for life expresses itself through many facets. It manifests itself in love, including "fellowship in suffering, in joy, and in effort." It is evident in "devotion to life inspired by reverence for life"; and it is unmistakably visible in mercy, in sacrifice, in sympathy, in forgiveness—not ordinary forgiveness which is merely a "sweetened

31. Schweitzer, *Memoirs of Childhood and Youth,* pp. 123–124.
32. Albert Schweitzer, *The Philosophy of Civilization* (New York: Macmillan, 1951), p. 309.
33. Ibid.
34. Albert Schweitzer, *The Light within Us* (New York: Philosophical Library, 1959), p. 47.
35. Schweitzer, *Philosophy of Civilization,* p. 310.
36. Schweitzer, *My Life and Thought,* p. 181.
37. Schweitzer, *Philosophy of Civilization,* p. 318.

triumph of self-devotion," but forgiveness with no intent to humiliate the recipient.

Reverence for life is a philosophy of self-realization, a "spiritual self-realization which springs from reverence for one's own life."[38] It is potent, and like other sources of genuine power, it makes no noise. "It is not from kindness to others that I am gentle, peaceable, forbearing, and friendly, but because by such behavior I prove my own profoundest self-realization to be true."[39]

One who sacrifices his own life for others does not lose his life thereby but finds it, for he thus achieves life's true value. The ethical value in the philosophy of reverence for life rests upon the claim that it humanizes, making the individual a humane being, and, further, that it spiritualizes him, making him a spiritual being. Since a person who holds all life sacred experiences a spiritual regeneration within himself, reverence for life is an inner philosophy.

SOCIAL ETHICS AND A PHILOSOPHICAL WORLD VIEW. According to Schweitzer's view of man in society, civilization is facing its end, its suicide, unless it finds an effective solution to its dilemma. The solution is a proper *Weltanschauung* consisting of reverence for life, a good theory of the universe, and an optimistic philosophy. Philosophers should not be the *philosopher kings* Plato recommended, but should guide the rulers as did Kant and Hegel, who ruled many who had never even heard of these two philosophers, but came subsequently under the influence of their philosophies. The ruling philosophy of the present age must be one that is optimistic and ethical, making man's purpose the development of his real personality, a personality which holds life to be of intrinsic value, respecting it with reverence and sanctity, alleviating human ills and engaging in humanitarian endeavor. In this way ethics becomes the inner perfection of our personalities. The goal of society and of the world is ethical; the world's failure stems from its lack of ethical development and its lack of optimistic hope. Consequently, the civilized society is that state which is the outcome or product of reverence for life.

> My life carries its own meaning in itself. This meaning lies in my living out the highest idea which shows itself in my will-to-live, the idea of reverence for life. With that for a starting-point I give value to my own life and to all the will-to-live which surrounds me, I persevere in activity, and I produce values.[40]

This is not only the starting point but also the climax of Schweitzer's ethical philosophy. How interesting to find that he held that man produces values as well as being the supreme value!

38. Ibid., p. 315.
39. Ibid.
40. Ibid., p. 79.

Concluding Comments. The extremes to which Schweitzer carried his principle of reverence for life is more than reason will allow. Reverence for human life is an attitude that is rationally tenable, but reverence for the life of an anopheles mosquito strains credulity. (In fairness to Schweitzer, however, it should be noted that he does justify the destruction of the mosquito, though not the indiscriminate destruction of animals.) Even in the matter of reverence for human life, it is not life per se that is respected, but the human personality; there is reverence not for the living cell that happens to be part of a human being (body cells are constantly being destroyed) but for the entire personality of the individual whose life should be protected.

14

Ethical Subjectivism and Relativity: Ethics as Opinion

Subjectivism is the theory that truth is solely a matter of opinion, a subjective state of the individual, lacking any basis in objectivity. Ethical subjectivism reduces moral truth to subjective states, such as feeling, sentiment, personal (subjective) opinion, and personal or social approval (based either on the feeling of an individual or on collective feeling, the consensus of feeling of society).

Ethical subjectivism is usually found in one of two forms: (*a*) *social,* wherein the opinion of the group is the decisive factor, and (*b*) *personal,* wherein the individual's own opinion is the sole determinant of right and wrong. In each case, however, not reason but subjective states, such as feelings, are the criteria of morality, since, if there were a rational or scientific basis for moral decisions, subjectivity would yield to objectivity.

The ethical subjectivists discussed in this chapter are David Hume (1711–1776), a social subjectivist who identifies moral values with the feelings of the group—he would say that *X is good* means *We like X,* or means *We have a feeling generally in favor of it;* William Graham Sumner (1840–1910), another social subjectivist; and Edward Westermarck (1862–1939), a personal subjectivist who would say that *X is right* means *I like X,* or means *I personally have certain feelings in favor of it.* On the extreme side of subjectivism are the emotivists, for whom *X is right* means *I am simply emoting.*

SOCIAL SUBJECTIVISM: ETHICS AS SOCIAL OPINION

The first subjectivist chosen for examination, David Hume, regarded social approbation as the criterion of moral right, an approbation that ultimately stems from social sentiment. The second social subjectivist, William Graham Sumner, made no distinction between ethical theory and moral practices in a society.

David Hume: Ethics as Social Approbation. The ethical theory of Hume is set forth mainly in his *Treatise on Human Nature* (1740) and *An Enquiry concerning the Principles of Morals* (1751). His moral philosophy developed in opposition to the philosophical trend in his time in favor of egoistic utilitarianism. In reaction to this philosophy, Hume attributed ethical motivation to *sympathy,* or feelings, especially *fellow feeling,* the ability to experience another's good and ill as if it were one's own. He asserted that, in dealing with the complicated relationships of life, the problems of politics and social ethics, men depend primarily on subjective feelings, but these feelings become complex, and they must be supplemented by *reason,* which clarifies and evaluates their circumstances and needs in society. The philosopher therefore seeks universal principles of behavior which are based on social praise or blame—principles such as benevolence, which receives high social acceptance owing to its social utility and sympathetic quality, and *utility* or *agreeableness,* which give worth to the widely admired virtues of humaneness, friendship, integrity, justice, and veracity. Nevertheless, a skeptic in ethics as well as in metaphysics and the philosophy of science, Hume regarded moral values as subjective values reducible to sentiment or feeling, not reason or logic.

MORAL VALUE GROUNDED IN SENTIMENT. Whatever is valued must either be useful or possess a quality "agreeable" to persons; otherwise, it lacks merit. Since celibacy, fasting, penance, mortification, and the like serve no useful purpose and awaken no sentiment in the individual, they are devoid of personal value and social worth; accordingly, they are pseudovirtues belonging rather to a catalogue of vices.

The only indisputable sentiment is the regard for others, *benevolence,* which engenders much social good, resulting in great service and use to mankind.

> The notion of morals implies some sentiment common to all mankind, which recommends the same object of general approbation, and makes every man, or most men, agree in the same opinion or decision concerning it. It also implies some sentiment, so universal and comprehensive as to extend to all mankind, and render the actions and conduct . . . an object of applause or censure, according as they agree or disagree with that rule of right which is established.[1]

Morality, then, is reduced to sentiment, not reason but feeling, and as such, morality is indisputable. Reasons can be debated pro and con, but when a person experiences a sentiment, all that he can say is that he likes it or does not like it, just as he might say that he likes or dislikes the color yellow. To argue with anyone about his liking for yellow would be futile and meaningless, for such a preference falls outside the realm of reason. The case is similar in regard to moral values: the moral idea or standard to which we respond is termed good, and that which is repugnant to us is called bad.

1. David Hume, *An Essay concerning the Principles of Morals* (1777), (LaSalle, Ill.: Open Court, 1953), p. 110.

However, it is not the sentiments of a particular individual, but those held in common by one's society that are valid ground for establishing an ethical code which receives moral sanction. Personal likes or dislikes are not good or evil; only those shared by the group may be so designated.

THE ROLE OF REASON. While it is true that moral distinctions are derived not from reason but from moral sentiment, reason does play an active role in judging the utility of such sentiments, in evaluating them and resolving conflicts among them. For example, *justice* is one of the valued sentiments of society, but the numerous disputes about justice that occur are settled by means of rational deliberation. Nevertheless, reason without sentiment is incapable of sanctioning our actions or making some of them right and others wrong. Unaided reason can never tell us that ingratitude is bad; only through the sentiment of blame do we recognize this evil quality. Utility also does not enable us to determine that certain forms of behavior are moral and others immoral, because utility refers only to a means to an end, and if the end lacks any sentiment for us, then both the means and the end will be morally neutral.

THE SENTIMENT OF BENEVOLENCE. Only sentiment can be morally significant. Thus, the sentiment of benevolence, a feeling for the happiness of mankind, is good and virtuous, whereas contrary feelings are evil and vicious. Our own sentiments of approval and disapproval decide for us what is morally good and what is morally bad. Proof of this theory is easily seen when we compare nature's destructive actions with those men commit: a tree which falls upon and destroys its parent tree is not considered immoral, but a human being who harms his own parent in the same way offends our moral sentiments and is therefore condemned. It is our sentiment which makes the action of the tree morally neutral but the identical action of the human being involved in the same activity morally evil.

If Hume's theory is true, then morality becomes a question of taste, of inner feeling which distinguishes good from evil, approving the one and condemning the other. Taste, by which we discern pleasure or pain, motivates our actions and energizes our volitions.

SOCIAL APPROBATION AS THE CRITERION OF MORAL VALUE. A consensus of sentiment, feelings shared in common with one's own society, that is to say social approbation, is the criterion of moral value, designating those patterns of behavior prized by the human community. These commonly shared sentiments, the affections of humanity, are the foundation of morals, the basis upon which moral praise or censure is established. There is a kind of universality in sentiments, for what one person cherishes is cherished by the group, since "the humanity of one man is the humanity of every one."[2]

2. Ibid., p. 111.

Selfish sentiments are not shared by the group in common, and consequently provide no basis for establishing a common ethic. Immorality is fundamentally individual rather than social, stemming from those selfish sentiments of a solitary individual which are exposed by his tyrannical, insolent, or barbarous behavior, selfish sentiments which evoke expressions of repugnance and disapproval by others. "Whatever conduct gains my approbation, by touching my humanity, procures also the applause of all mankind, by affecting the same principle in them; but what serves my avarice or ambition pleases these passions in me alone, and affects not the avarice and ambition of the rest of mankind."[3] Thus, it is the sentiments which touch humanity that are approved as morally good, not what an individual alone prizes for his selfish ends. It is not personal opinion which determines right conduct, but the approval of the group that sanctions those things which benefit man as a member of humanity, not those things which benefit man as a self-centered being. Consequently, social approbation (group opinion and approval) is the criterion of moral value.

PERSONAL AND SOCIAL VALUES. Moral values become social values. Personal morality is defined as that "quality of mind, which is *useful* or *agreeable* to the *person himself* or to *others,* communicates a pleasure to the spectator, engages his esteem, and is admitted under the honourable denomination of virtue or merit."[4] Note the social values of moral virtues; veracity, justice, fidelity, honor, and loyalty are each esteemed for their value in promoting the interest and happiness of the individual in which each virtue is found. Moral value is ascribed to each virtue, owing to the warm sentiments it elicits from us, sentiments of warm approval. Virtue, like aesthetic taste, is undebatable, whereas the specific actions of an individual are debatable. If we ignore or extinguish these warm sentiments which virtues inspire in us, then virtue and vice become indistinguishable, and moral value ceases to exist.

THE DISINTERESTED SPECTATOR AS THE CRITERION OF THE RIGHT ACT. Hume reiterated that morality is based upon sentiment, and he defined virtue as "whatever mental action or quality gives to a spectator the pleasing sentiment of approbation."[5] To ascertain whether a contemplated action will be moral or immoral in a given situation, it is necessary to disassociate oneself (as it were) temporarily from the group, and, like an innocent bystander, to ascertain the sentiments of the group. What each society approves is moral, and what it censures is immoral. Public opinion shapes the moral climate and places its seal of approval upon specific actions of individuals.

Acting as if he were a disinterested observer, a spectator interpreting

3. Ibid., p. 112.
4. Ibid., p. 116.
5. Ibid., p. 129.

public sentiment, the individual can readily distinguish the virtuous from the vicious act, the good act from the evil act, the right act from the wrong act, and then he may proceed to act accordingly. Moral behavior varies with the sentiments prevailing in different societies; more specifically, the morality of an action depends upon the judgment of the group as to whether or not the action comports to a given approved sentiment of the society. The same sentiment may be put into practice in one society in one way and in another society in another—for example, monogamy may be approved in one society, polygamy in another. It is the task of reason, or judgment, to determine which practice will be approved as the best means to implement a socially accepted virtue or moral sentiment. For Hume, as for other ethical subjectivists, overt acts chosen by reason are in themselves morally neutral, and it is only the subjective feeling of the group, a matter of mere opinion, that possesses moral value.

William Graham Sumner: Ethics as Mores. Sumner, the second social subjectivist to be discussed in this chapter, held that in every society, its ethical theories and moral practices are inseparable traditions. He rejected sharp distinctions between ethical standards and moral behavior, noting that historians and even scientists are subject to prejudices and biases, moral beliefs and habits, absorbed from their society as they arrive at their conclusions. All members of a society unconsciously adopt many of its traditional customs (or folkways) and moral doctrines (or mores).

MORES DEFINED. Sumner defined mores as "the popular usages and traditions, when they include a judgment that they are conducive to societal welfare, and when they exert a coercion of the individual to conform to them, although they are not coordinated by any authority."[6] In order to appreciate the meaning of mores, it is necessary to understand the significance of folkways, inasmuch as mores are basically folkways elevated to a higher plane.

FOLKWAYS DEFINED. Folkways are defined as "habits of the individual and customs of the society which arise from efforts to satisfy needs."[7] They gain traditional authority by being intertwined with primitive notions of luck, such as demonism and goblinism. Possessing authority, they hold regulative powers for succeeding generations by assuming a character of their own which acts as a social force. How or whence they arise, is unknown, but they grow by "internal life energy," and are subject to limited modification by men's efforts. Their nature is neither organic nor material, yet they control individual and social behavior until they perish or become transformed. Their

6. William G. Sumner, *Folkways* (New York: New American Library, 1960), p. v.
7. Ibid., p. v.

character is chiefly social; therefore, they are classified with interpersonal relations, institutions, and conventions.

RELATIONSHIP BETWEEN FOLKWAYS AND MORES. Folkways become mores on reaching a high level of sophistication involving doctrines of truth, right, and social welfare in a particular society. The mores are potent ethical values which bring about new social ideas, forms, and institutions, such as those of religion and law, thus shaping the character of the society. "Mores are the folkways, including the philosophical and ethical generalizations as to societal welfare which are suggested by them, and inherent in them, as they grow."[8]

Folkways and mores are intertwined with philosophy, but it is questionable where the priority lies. Does philosophy primarily determine mores, or is it the other way round? It may be that philosophy regulates folkways, but does not create them. Sumner defined *mores* as "the ways of doing things which are current in a society to satisfy human needs and desires, together with the faiths, notions, codes, and standards of well living which inhere in those ways, having a genetic connection with them."[9] In any given period, a society will be seen to have these specific traits, the mores, controlling and pervading the ways, thoughts, and life of that society by means of abstract principles motivating and guiding group action. The mores function on an unconscious level, independently of the will of any individual person, and, in fact, conscious reflection only disrupts their even flow or progress. Mores are a dominating force directing historical events as well as molding the life of a particular society.

THE MORAL CRITERION. The folkways and mores constitute the criteria of morality, and determine which acts are right and which are wrong. They are decisive influences because their de facto role and respect for them have become traditional. Whatever is traditional is accepted as right. Thus, the traditional forces, the mores, decide morality both in theory and in action. Tradition guarantees right, for whatever is, is right; the opposite idea or action, being contrary to tradition, is wrong, immoral, and taboo.

Inasmuch as the accepted standards for morally good and right behavior are a part of the mores themselves, these standards are accepted without question, so that their moral validity remains unchallenged. The values of one society are often considered evil by another society with different mores (ethnocentrism), but not by its own individuals. In each society, however, the good mores are widely regarded as modes of living well adapted to the social situation, while the bad mores are rejected as unsuitable or conflicting proposals. Mores develop because in general they contribute to the well-being of a society. They do not imperil social stability but enhance it. The

8. Ibid., pp. 42–43.
9. Ibid., p. 66.

few rebels who reject certain mores of the community may be subjected to witch hunts or persecution, for the society prizes its mores, which never seem immoral to people in their own era. Later, when mores have changed, the society may come to view the old mores and persecutions as having been evil and stupid, but the prevailing mores of the time are imbedded in the people from birth onward, and thus the ethical standards, prejudices, moral customs, and mores of living seldom encounter critical analysis, being accepted without question.

PERSONAL SUBJECTIVISM: ETHICS AS PERSONAL OPINION

Unlike Sumner and Hume, Edward Westermarck advocated an ethical philosophy of personal subjectivism (as contrasted to social subjectivism) which makes personal opinion the sole criterion of morality. Moral right is relative to the individual who holds such an opinion.

Edward Westermarck: Ethical Relativity. Westermarck's views appeared originally in his two-volume *The Origin and Development of the Moral Ideas* (1912), and were later elaborated more explicitly (as a rebuttal against his critics) in his *Ethical Relativity* (1932). It was his fundamental thesis that "moral consciousness is ultimately based on emotions, that the moral judgment lacks objective validity, that the moral values are not absolute but relative to the emotions they express."[10] Thus, the subjectivism advocated by Westermarck relegates morality to the feelings of the individual involved.

Initially, Westermarck hit upon the idea of *ethical relativity* as a possible explanation when he noticed that his discussions with other people concerning morality regularly terminated in disagreement. Why is it that conclusions regarding moral issues differ so radically? Why is there general agreement in some cases? Why do we have any moral ideas whatever? Does a disagreement originate in defective knowledge, or does it stem from moral ideas originating in sentiment rather than knowledge? Westermarck in his earlier work concluded that "moral judgments are ultimately based on emotions, the moral concepts being generalizations of emotional tendencies. . . . The emotional origin of moral judgments consistently leads to a denial of the objective validity ascribed to them both by common sense and by normative theories of ethics."[11]

Intellectual considerations, however, do affect the moral emotions, for knowledge can change the character and influence of such emotions. People disagree about moral judgments because they have different information and ideas associated with emotions; for example,

10. Edward Westermarck, *Ethical Relativity* (Paterson, N.J.: Littlefield, Adams, 1960), p. xvi.
11. Ibid., p. xvii.

one person may feel highly indignant when a lie is being told, but another who knows that it was necessary in order to save the life of an innocent man will tolerate or even applaud the falsehood.

MORAL JUDGMENTS EMOTIONALLY GROUNDED. Ethical subjectivism, or *ethical relativity,* as Westermarck termed his system of ethics, was the logical outcome of his conclusion that the objective validity of moral judgments cannot be proved because there are no moral truths and ultimately the predicates of all moral judgments are based upon emotions. Objective validity cannot be derived from emotion; that is to say, one cannot ascribe truth or falsity to any emotion, except to say that it may be true or false that we are at a particular moment experiencing a certain emotion. Consequently, there are no moral truths or objective moral standards.

TWO MORAL EMOTIONS: APPROVAL AND DISAPPROVAL. If there is no objective standard of morality, and only a subjective one remains, then precisely what is the nature of this ethical relativity? Westermarck described it as a subjective state of feeling, emotion, state of mind, or what he termed *moral emotions,* that is, "specific emotions that have led to the formation of the concepts of right and wrong, good and bad, and all other moral concepts."[12] Basically, there are two moral emotions: moral approval and moral disapproval.

Moral judgments and moral concepts can eventually be traced to their origins in emotions of a *retributive* type, a state of mind either friendly or hostile. Of these retributive emotions, two divergent ones can be found: *resentment* (a hostile attitude of mind) and *retributive kindly emotion* (a friendly attitude of mind). Anger, revenge, and moral disapproval are of the resentment type, while gratitude and moral approval are of the kindly type of retributive emotion. However, only moral approval and moral disapproval are properly said to be moral emotions, whereas the others, though retributive emotions, are classified as nonmoral concomitants of moral emotions. Westermarck supplied a schema classifying the emotions in question:[13]

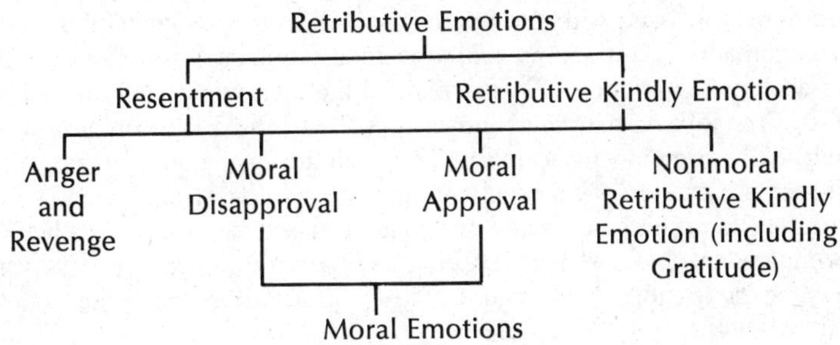

12. Ibid., p. 62.

13. Edward Westermarck, *The Origin and Development of the Moral Ideas* (New York: Macmillan, 1912), 1:1.

Inasmuch as moral approval (or disapproval) is an emotion, morality is relative, relative to emotion, and therefore is a subjective state of mind. To assert that "*X* is right" means "I have a personal feeling of approval toward it," and to say that it is wrong means that "I am indignant toward it." In either case, not social approval but personal approval is the basis for moral judgment, even though feelings of moral approval and disapproval are shared with others in the society. Westermarck concluded his treatise *Ethical Relativity* by restating the fundamental premise of personal subjectivism: "that the moral consciousness is ultimately based on emotions, that the moral judgment lacks objective validity, that the moral values are not absolute but relative to the emotions they express."[14]

CRITICISM OF ETHICAL SUBJECTIVISM

Ethical subjectivism is susceptible to four major criticisms discussed in the following paragraphs. These criticisms pose a dilemma for philosophers in this school of ethics, for they have thus far been unable to rebut the criticisms satisfactorily.

An Argumentum ad Absurdum Refutation of Ethical Relativism. If ethical subjectivism were true, it would produce extreme ramifications unacceptable to rational persons. The subjectivistic ethical thesis implies moral approval of such evils as the use of galley slaves in the Roman Empire, Hitler's holocaust when he was supported by the German people, and other tragic miscarriages of justice and morality attested to in the annals of history. Rational men agree that wholesale crimes against humanity are wrong even though they may have been tolerated or approved at the time of their occurrence. Psychologists know that perversity or abnormal behavior can occur on a mass level, involving all or nearly all members of a society. Personal opinions cannot always be trusted as a basis for moral choices which offend reason or other enduring attributes of human nature.

Ethical Subjectivism Self-Contradictory. In Plato's *Theaetetus,* Socrates took issue with the relativism of Protagoras, contending that Protagoras had placed himself in a position requiring him to agree with his objectivist opponent. Plato explained the dilemma as follows: "The best of the joke is, that he acknowledges the truth of their opinion who believes his opinion to be false; for in admitting that the opinions of all men are true, in effect he grants that the opinion of his opponents is true."[15] To argue consistently for relativism is not only impossible; it terminates in objectivism. According to relativism, moreover, a person may be both moral and immoral when performing the same act at

14. Westermarck, *Ethical Relativity,* p. 289.
15. Plato *Theaetatus,* in *The Dialogues of Plato* (New York: Scribner, 1895), 3:373.

about the same time; for example, a surgeon willing to perform an abortion would be considered highly moral in a community favoring it, but highly immoral in a neighboring community opposed to the procedure.

Ethics Reduced to Statistical Count. A relativistic ethic based on shifting popular opinion, reflected in the adage "When in Rome do as the Romans do," make ethics dependent upon mere head-counting, or statistical enumeration. The moral person is identified as one who accedes to whatever opinions and attitudes happen to be espoused by the multitude. If the crowds favor war, then war is moral and the conscientious objector is immoral. Relativistic ethics is ruthless, makes no allowance for individualism, and misleads the masses, who do not think for themselves. It is therefore antagonistic to ideals of self-direction, independent thinking, and the appeal to the reason or logic of individual human beings.

Relativism an Inconsistent Ethic. Still more difficult to accept is the view of social subjectivists that all reformers are invariably immoral. A reformer must of necessity deviate from popular moral opinion, for it is that very opinion which he seeks to reform. Yet, all the while that he evaluates and endeavors to improve current mores, he is labeled immoral by ethical subjectivists. Eventually, if he succeeds in reforming public opinion, he regains the reputation of high morality. Lack of success makes the reformer an immoral outcast. Since most reformers never achieve their moral purposes, they are condemned as immoral by ethical subjectivism throughout their lifetimes, whereas, on the contrary, evildoers could be logically defended as moral if approved by mass opinion. Only defeat and death destroyed Hitler's moral reputation in German society.

A decisive objection, comparable to Plato's, was proposed by G. E. Moore, who noted that, if subjectivism were true, it would be impossible for two persons to contradict each other on moral issues.[16] If one defended the morality of extortion, but the other preferred philanthropy, both persons would be morally and equally right, since each was sincerely expressing his personal opinion. If subjective opinion determined morality, any opinion would be morally right as an expression of the individual's preferences.

16. See G. E. Moore, *Ethics* (London: Oxford University Press, 1912), pp. 100–105.

15

Metaethics: The Analysis of Ethical Predicates

Contemporary British philosophy has centered its attention upon *linguistic analysis,* or investigation of ethical terms as interpreted by the "plain man" (the so-called man on the street, or layman), instead of dealing with the specific problems and theories of ethics which were major concerns of the classical philosophers. British philosophers have broken with past philosophy and have gone beyond the traditional boundaries of ethical theory to emphasize analysis of ethical vocabulary—not in the traditional sense of normative definitions, but from the point of view of the actual uses of ethical terms. The new approach to ethics, based on linguistic analysis, is known as *metaethics.*

Ethics and Metaethics. The term metaethics was coined in 1949 by A. J. Ayer in an article, "On the Analysis of Moral Judgments," written to defend his philosophy of moral skepticism against the charge that it was a weakening influence upon the moral values and standards of people. Ayer contended that all ethical theories (regardless of the school in question, such as intuitionism, naturalism, or emotivism) do not belong technically in ethics but in *metaethics*. His contention would restrict ethics to the activity of moral reform, relegating ethical ideas to the status of verbal statements subject to linguistic analysis. In this text, however, the term *ethics* will be used to denote moral theories; the term *morals* will denote ethical practices; and the term *metaethics* will refer to those schools of moral philosophy which offer no ethical code, no ethical conclusions, no principles of ethics, but rather a "non-philosophical" philosophy (a nonevaluative philosophy), which rejects ethical theory in the traditional sense and restricts itself to the analysis of ethical statements commonly used in diverse ethical theories.

Analytic Philosophy and Linguistic Analysis. In contemporary British philosophy, ethics (in its traditional sense) is rapidly becoming a vanishing philosophical discipline and, as indicated above, is giving way to metaethics, under the enormous influence of *analytic philosophy,* whose chief tool is *linguistic analysis*. The analytic school of philosophers has been accused of "trivializing" the subject, refusing to commit themselves to any philosophical opinions on ethics, and being content merely to analyze the logic of moral discourse. Concerning this school, "critics have found it narrow and inhuman."[1] M. Warnock of Oxford University believes that "the most boring days are over"[2] and that the deterioration of ethics to a discussion of "grading fruit"[3] or "choosing fictitious games equipment" is now coming to a close, and that a new era of British ethics is about to break upon the scene, one with genuine ethical conclusions and more interesting concepts than the old worn-out ones of 'the right' and 'the good.'

Although there is a tendency among philosophers to use the term *logical positivism* to include analytic philosophy, the linguistic philosophers repudiate logical positivism as Philistine, especially its *verifiability principle,* and prefer to disassociate themselves from positivism. One of the analytic philosophers, Antony Flew, regards logical positivism as a betrayal of philosophy, as indicated by its slogan: "Philosophical questions are not problems to be solved but (pseudoproblems or) puzzles to be (dis)solved."[4] On the other hand, the philosophers of linguistic analysis have been severely criticized by logical positivists as *verbosophers,* who are "selling their truthright for a mess of verbiage."[5]

Despite these distinctions and reciprocal criticisms, this chapter will discuss both of these schools of philosophy in sequence. At times it is most difficult to distinguish between them, for men such as Charles L. Stevenson could easily fit into a middle category; he is often quoted sympathetically by the analytic philosophers, but he is usually classified with the emotivists. Furthermore, both groups have a common philosophical ancestry in Wittgenstein. At the present time emotivism (or value skepticism) is a rapidly vanishing philosophy, since virtually all the contemporary theorists repudiate the emotive theory of ethics. Nevertheless, owing to their historical role, the emotivists merit our attention. This chapter is accordingly divided into two sections: *Value Skepticism,* on the emotive theory, and *Linguistic Analysis,* on the use of ethical language.

Distinction between Logical Positivism and Linguistic Analysis. The logical positivists (the principal school from which the emotivists emerged) express disdain for metaphysics, including moral values, whereas the school of linguistic analysis is neutral in regard to meta-

1. H. J. Paton, "Fifty Years of Philosophy," *Contemporary British Philosophy,* ed. J. B. Baille et al. (London: George Allen & Unwin, 1956).
2. See M. Warnock, *Ethics Since 1900* (London: Oxford University Press, 1960), pp. 204–207.
3. Warnock is here referring to J. O. Urmson, "On Grading." Urmson compared ethical evaluations with grading *apples.*
4. Antony Flew, *Logic and Language,* 2d series (Oxford: Basil Blackwell Mott, 1953), p. 5.
5. Ibid.

physics and moral values, and considers its chief task to be the analysis of ethical terms and their general use by the "plain man." The linguistic analysts have been referred to as the school of nonphilosophical philosophy, owing to their nonevaluative position, which differs in this respect from that of the logical positivists. The latter propound the emotive theory of ethics (evaluating ethics as the evincing of emotions) and regard ethical statements as invalid judgments, on the ground that valid judgments refer to facts, while emotional ejaculations are not judgments at all, not even judgments about emotions. The two schools are alike in declining to propose any normative ethic, but do so for different reasons: the logical positivists deny the existence of ethical norms; the linguistic analysts prefer to ignore the entire contentious matter of norms and concentrate on the task of analyzing language and tracing the implications for ethical theory.

The logical positivists rest their philosophy upon the *verification principle* (which states that meaningful propositions are verified by sense observation solely), but proponents of analytic philosophy tend to reject this principle as metaphysical and adhere to their dictum "Don't look for the meaning, look for the use." These divergent views correspond to the basic differences between the early and later theories of Wittgenstein. The logical positivists follow the earlier Wittgensteinian philosophy, which found meaning solely in the "propositions of natural science," while the analytic philosophers adhere to his later theories, which held that one should ignore scientific verification of meaning and should "look for the use" of words because "the meaning is the use." In fact, as far back as 1935, the British philosopher W. H. F. Barnes had characterized value judgments as mere "exclamations of approval." He concluded that moral disputes cannot be resolved by rational dialogue, for "all attempts to persuade others of the truth of value judgment are thus really attempts to make others approve the things we approve."[6]

VALUE SKEPTICISM: THE EMOTIVE THEORY OF ETHICS

The following adherents of the emotive theory of ethics will be discussed in this section: C. K. Ogden, I. A. Richards, Bertrand Russell, A. J. Ayer, and Charles L. Stevenson.

C. K. Ogden and I. A. Richards: The Emotive Function of Language. Ogden and Richards, in their book *The Meaning of Meaning* (which appeared as early as 1923, and since then has been published in numerous new editions) presented an *emotive theory of ethics* derived from the standpoint of literary criticism, yet with a decided

6. W. H. F. Barnes, "A Suggestion about Value," *Analysis* 1 (1934), p. 46.

philosophical emphasis. Richards, however, in other works of his, such as *Principles of Literary Criticism* (1924), advocated an ethical naturalism or hedonism which reduces good to pleasure and condemns evil as "self-thwarting" or as "conducive to stultifying conflicts."[7] Whatever thwarts impulses is evil; whatever satisfies them has value.

DUAL FUNCTION OF LANGUAGE. The emotive theory of ethics was derived from the discovery of a dual function of language: symbolic and emotive. The symbolic function describes matters of fact by means of cognitive statements (as in the sciences), whereas the emotive function does not make cognitive statements but expresses emotions. Less sophisticated language, or primitive language, was "almost purely emotive."[8]

This latter function of language, the emotive, is commonly found in ethics, religion, and poetry—those disciplines concerned with emotional expression rather than scientific description of facts. In descriptive statements, symbols refer to factual entities and have cognitive value; emotive statements are verbal signs of attitude, mood, interest, purpose, and desire. Symbolic language, with its objective or common meanings, has factual content, and consequently its statements may be judged true or false as vehicles of reference. The assertion that the Eiffel Tower is 900 feet high is a statement which is theoretically verifiable because the symbols communicate a reference to fact.

EMOTIVE VALUE OF TERMS. Emotive terms lack an objective referent; such terms, being devoid of factual content, are not statements of which true and false may be predicated. Actually, they are not even statements, but terms that elicit emotions and moods or solicit attitudes. "If we say 'Hurrah!' or 'Poetry is a spirit' or 'Man is a worm,' we may not be making statements, not even false statements; we are most probably using words merely to evoke certain attitudes."[9] Emotive terms, despite their ambiguity, do have a function, that of evoking emotions or stimulating attitudes. Ogden and Richards agreed with Bentham's assertion in his *Theory of Fictions* that "the word *right* is the name of a fictitious entity; one of those objects the existence of which is feigned for the purpose of discourse—by a fiction so necessary that without it human discourse could not be carried on. . . . Though fictitious, the language cannot be termed deceptious."[10] Although emotive statements are neither right nor wrong, they have emotive efficiency—emotive value.

7. Ivor Armstrong Richards, *Science and Poetry* (London: Kegan Paul, Trench, Trubner, 1935), p. 42.

8. C. K. Ogden, *Practical Criticism* (New York: Harcourt, Brace, 1930), p. 353.

9. C. K. Ogden and I. A. Richards, *The Meaning of Meaning* (New York: Harcourt, Brace, 1946), pp. 149, 151.

10. C. K. Ogden, *Bentham's Theory of Fictions* (New York: Littlefield, Adams, 1959), p. 118.

VALUE NIHILISM. Moral statements do not exist; they are mistaken forms of "emotive suasions." The term *good* is unanalyzable owing to its lack of symbolic meaning, and its significance lies in its emotive value; expressions such as "You are good" give us greater satisfaction than expressions such as "You are satisfying our impulses." Ogden and Richards rejected G. E. Moore's doctrine of the indefinability of good:

> 'Good' is alleged to stand for a unique, unanalysable concept. This concept, it is said, is the subject-matter of Ethics. This peculiar use of the word 'good' is, we suggest, a purely emotive use. When so used the word stands for nothing whatever, and has no symbolic function. Thus when we so use it in the sentence, '*This* is good', we merely refer to *this,* and the addition of 'is good' makes no difference whatever to our reference. When, on the other hand, we say, '*This* is red', the addition of 'is red' to 'this' does symbolize an extension of our reference, namely, to some other red thing. But 'is good' has no comparable *symbolic* function; it serves only as an emotive sign expressing our attitude to *this,* and perhaps evoking similar attitudes in other persons, or inciting them to actions of one kind or another. . . . The indefinable 'good'. . . we suggest to be a purely emotive sign. The 'something more' or 'something else' which, it is alleged, is not covered by any definition of 'good' is the emotional aura of the word.[11]

Richards, in complete accord with logical positivists, relegated all metaphysical assertions to the emotive realm, dismissing them as an *imbroglio,* utterances merely inciting attitudes, and held that such questions are raised merely as "requests for emotive satisfaction."[12]

CRITIQUE OF THE ETHICAL THEORY OF OGDEN AND RICHARDS. Claiming that there are only two kinds of terms, the informative and the emotive, Ogden and Richards sought to prove that only the informative (or symbolic) terms have meaning, while the emotive terms merely express feelings. They did not realize that both types of terms have meaning, though not the same kind of meaning. It appears that they have become victimized by their own language. Osborne, criticizing Ogden and Richards, commented, "Certain philosophers have been systematically trained to mistake the grammar of language for the grammar of Reality."[13]

The emotive use of language would have no effect upon emotion were it not for the fact that emotive terms convey meaning as well as

11. Ogden and Richards, *Meaning of Meaning,* p. 125.

12. I. A. Richards, *Principles of Literary Criticism* (New York: Harcourt, Brace, 1926), p. 84.

13. H. Osborne, *Foundations of the Philosophy of Value* (Cambridge: Cambridge University Press, 1933), p. 84.

command feeling. Moreover, the meaning conveyed is quite specific, for the emotion elicited is one of a certain nature, not just any incoherent reaction; i.e., certain emotive terms elicit one distinct emotion, whereas other emotive words evoke a different emotional expression. It is not an orator's emotive term per se but rather its meaning for the audience that influences emotions.

Finally, many terms can serve both informative and emotive functions. Symbolic terms often elicit emotion as well as conveying information, and strongly emotive terms may also be informative. Ogden and Richards have committed what may be called the fallacy of the singular function of terms by assuming that when words are being used to elicit emotions, that is their sole function and significance.

Bertrand Russell: Ethics of Skepticism and Desire. Russell's point of view in ethics reflected the influence of subjectivism, naturalism, and, particularly, emotivism based on *ethical skepticism,* a concomitant of his *scientism. Scientism* is the theory that "the methods of science alone give valid knowledge, or that knowledge beyond the scope of science is invalid"[14]—thus critically limiting the scope of knowledge. Scientism takes on the overtones of a religion, with its adherents placing their faith in, and commitment to, it alone.

SCIENTISM AND MORAL VALUES. Scientism precludes normative ethics and all values, inasmuch as values cannot be subjected to the techniques of science; it is impossible, for example, to place a value into a test tube or under a microscope, or measure its height and weight. Consequently, moral values fall outside the scientific realm, and, ipso facto, outside human knowledge, a limitation which Russell emphasized:

> There remains, however, a vast field, traditionally included in philosophy, where scientific methods are inadequate. This field includes ultimate questions of value; science alone, for example, cannot prove that it is bad to enjoy the infliction of cruelty. Whatever can be known, can be known by means of science; but things which are legitimately matters of feeling lie outside its province.[15]

Inasmuch as ethics cannot be dealt with on a scientific plane, it is devoid of cognitive meaning, and accordingly, is neither true nor false.

VALUE SKEPTICISM. Russell's emotive theory of ethics is found in a variety of sources; his most recent view was discussed concisely in his *Religion and Science* (1935), which described his ethical position as "quite different" from the one he had advocated thirty years previously. With the view of those philosophers who assert the "insufficiency of

14. William S. Sahakian and Mabel Lewis Sahakian, *Realms of Philosophy* (Cambridge, Mass.: Schenkman, 1965), p. 481.

15. Bertrand Russell, *A History of Western Philosophy* (New York: Simon and Schuster, 1945), p. 834.

science" because it is silent on *values,* he concurred, "but when it is inferred that ethics contains truths which cannot be proved or disproved by science, I disagree";[16] and he added that his ethical theory is not the "dictum of science," but his own personal opinion.

Russell's ethical skepticism was clearly stated in the same work (in the final paragraph of his chapter "Science and Ethics"): "I conclude that, while it is true that science cannot decide questions of value, that is because they cannot be intellectually decided at all, and lie outside the realm of truth and falsehood. Whatever knowledge is attainable, must be attained by scientific methods; and what science cannot discover, mankind cannot know." The question might be asked: If ethical ideas do not come from knowledge which only science can give, what, then, is their origin? In reply, Russell could only refer to mystical religion and philosophy as the sources of ethical values.

Russell pointed out that traditional ethics dealt with two types of subject matter: rules of conduct and intrinsic good. The former are essential to achievement of the latter. After an intrinsic good has been defined with approval, then the ethical rules are applied to create as much of this good as possible. Once ultimate good has been ascertained, the rest (the framing of ethical rules) remains for science to establish; only the proposition affirming the nature of good, such as "Pleasure is good," lies outside of the sphere of science.

"But in a question as to whether this or that is the ultimate Good, there is no evidence either way; each disputant can only appeal to his own emotions, and employ such rhetorical devices as shall rouse similar emotions in others."[17] In this statement, Russell's emotivism becomes apparent. Unlike ethical questions, scientific issues are resolved by appeal to evidence being adduced on both sides of the issue that is debated, and each issue is settled intellectually or scientifically by persuading others to accept one's own position on the basis of available facts.

However, to alter another person's opinion on moral matters requires an appeal to his emotions, not to his intellect.[18] Values "lie outside the domain of science, as the defenders of religion emphatically assert. I think that in this they are right, but I draw the further conclusion, which they do not draw, that questions as to 'values' lie wholly outside the domain of knowledge. That is to say, when we assert that this or that has 'value,' we are giving expression to our own emotions, not to a fact which would still be true if our personal feelings were dif-

16. Bertrand Russell, *Religion and Science* (London: Oxford University Press, 1935), p. 223.
17. Ibid., p. 229.
18. See Bertrand Russell, *Philosophy* (New York: W. W. Norton, 1927), p. 226; and "Reply to Criticisms" in *The Philosophy of Bertrand Russell,* ed. Paul A. Schilpp (Evanston, Ill.: Northwestern University Press, 1944), pp. 722–724.

ferent."[19] Language has a twofold function: (1) descriptive and emotive; (2) communicative and expressive. The emotive function is used in influencing moral behavior.[20]

Ethical Subjectivity. Russell regarded ethics as an attempt to escape from subjectivity. Good is desire, but desire is subjective; yet moralists seek to universalize good, to render it objective, to prove that one's own desires are "more worthy of respect" than those held by another person. Each individual seeks allies for his own point of view, until his personal desires become the collective desires of the group, i.e., those sanctioned and adopted by his society. The attempt of an individual to make his desires appear objective is really an attempt to impersonalize them by claiming that they can be enjoyed in common and will serve the welfare of mankind, not merely that of the single individual in question. Good desires are merely shared desires. "Ethics is an attempt to give universal, and not merely personal, importance to certain of our desires."[21]

Such views justify the classification of Russell as an *ethical subjectivist,* as he himself admitted, but his *ethical emotivism* again seemed to have won his foremost allegiance when he declared, "Every attempt to persuade people that something is good (or bad) in itself, and not merely in its effects, depends upon the art of rousing feelings, not upon an appeal to evidence. In every case the preacher's skill consists in creating in others emotions similar to his own."[22] At the same time, he reiterated his *ethical skepticism,* denying the validity of all moral judgments, not even permitting them the status of a statement. "When a man says 'this is good in itself,' he *seems* to be making a statement, just as much as if he said 'this is square' or 'this is sweet.' I think that what the man really means is: 'I wish everybody to desire this,' or rather 'Would that everybody desired this.' If what he says is interpreted as a statement, it is merely an affirmation of his own personal wish; if, on the other hand, it is interpreted in a general way, it states nothing, but merely desires something."[23] Ethical valuations are simply expressions of wishes, not assertions, for they affirm nothing; consequently, they neither possess truth nor falsehood. "An ethical judgment, according to me, expresses a desire, but only inferentially implies that I feel this desire."[24]

Russell was fully aware of the fact that the implications of this philosophical position are quite radical. Sins and virtues become indistinguishable. Morality and evil cannot be proved. "Punishment

19. Ibid., pp. 230–231.
20. See Bertrand Russell, *Human Knowledge: Its Scope and Limits* (New York: Simon and Schuster, 1948), p. 59.
21. Ibid., p. 232.
22. Ibid., p. 235.
23. Ibid., pp. 235–236.
24. Ibid.

cannot be justified on the ground that the criminal is 'wicked,' but only on the ground that he has behaved in a way which others wish to discourage."[25] Morality is solely a matter of influencing another's desires. Desires produce morality by achieving wide acceptance, but in the final analysis, all values, despite the part played by desire, are neither true nor false, because they are unknowable.

RUSSELL'S INCONSISTENCIES. Not completely satisfied with his own ethical theory, Russell discussed some objections severely critical of it. The basic premise of the emotive theory of values is that judgments of moral value do not exist, but he was not quite satisfied with the idea that value statements are only emotive expressions, and in fact referred to them as if they were genuine value judgments, as, for example, in his *Marriage and Morals.* Provoked by persons who ignore or refuse to acknowledge the immorality of antisocial behavior, he expressed disdain for their attitude in *What I Believe,* and he castigated clergymen who "condone cruelty and condemn innocent pleasure," for "they can only do harm as guardians of the morals of the young."[26] Ironically, however, he later asserted that one "cannot prove that it is bad to enjoy . . . the infliction of cruelty."[27] This inconsistency was compounded by his statement that "pleasure in the spectacle of cruelty horrifies me, and I am not ashamed of the fact that it does."[28] In his philosophy, he defended high moral value judgments of this kind: "The good life is one inspired by love and guided by knowledge."[29]

Russell was aware of these inconsistencies: "I am accused of inconsistency, perhaps justly, because although I hold ultimate ethical valuations to be subjective, I nevertheless allow myself emphatic opinions on ethical questions. If there is an inconsistency, it is one that I cannot get rid of without insincerity."[30] He felt himself to be passionately loyal to moral standards, as if they were objective entities worthy of allegiance, yet he considered them to be grounded in subjective feelings and opinions. Defending his *right* to express himself on moral issues, he asserted, "I am not prepared to forego my right to feel and express ethical passions; no amount of logic, even though it be my own, will persuade me that I ought to do so."[31] What a remarkable statement for the coauthor of *Principia Mathematica,* that majestic treatise on logic, to make! Not only does his statement reject

25. Ibid., p. 239.
26. Bertrand Russell, *What I Believe* (New York: E. P. Dutton, 1925), p. 47.
27. Bertrand Russell, *A History of Western Philosophy* (New York: Simon and Schuster, 1946), p. 834.
28. Russell, *Philosophy of Bertrand Russell,* p. 720.
29. Bertrand Russell, *Philosophy* (New York: W. W. Norton, 1927), p. 235.
30. Russell, *Philosophy of Bertrand Russell,* p. 720.
31. Ibid.

emotivism, but it runs counter to the principles of logical positivism. Either the statement is incorrect or the principles of positivism are false.

Complications do not terminate at this point, for he added, "I am no more prepared to give up all this than I am to give up the multiplication table. . . . Suppose, for example, that someone were to advocate the introduction of bull-fighting in this country. In opposing the proposal, I should *feel,* not only that I was expressing my desires, but that my desires in the matter are *right.*"[32]

CRITICISM OF SUBJECTIVITY IN ETHICS. According to Russell, confusion and inconsistency are rooted in the subjective nature of moral valuations. Ethical subjectivism is inherently self-contradictory because it is impossible to defend subjectivism without being absolutist or at least objectivist, for when the subjectivist asserts that his moral views are right or the best available, he is claiming that this is the case irrespective of anyone else's opinion. His own opinion is the correct or best one, worthy of being defended against the contrary views of others. But C. E. M. Joad pointed out that subjectivity in morality would render all opinions of equal value, the "child's as good as the adult's, the idiots as the sage's, the savage's as the civilized man's."[33] Joad held that ethical subjectivity would destroy any possible logical basis for moral behavior:

> There is, then, on this view, no logical basis for fellow feeling or for sympathetic emotion. Hence, when I extend sympathy to somebody who is in trouble, I might just as well, so far as the logic of the matter goes, extend congratulation. Why, then, it may be asked, do many people concur in feeling sympathy on hearing of X's misfortune, instead of rejoicing at it.[34]

A. J. Ayer: Emotivism. Alfred Jules Ayer (1910–), an Oxford University professor and outspoken adherent of logical positivism, offered a view of ethics based upon the presuppositions of the *verifiability principle* of logical positivism. His theory eliminating the concept of metaphysical entities (including moral values), terminates in *value skepticism.*

The logical positivists (or, as they are occasionally referred to, the *neopositivists*) state in their principle of verification that "a proposition is said to be verifiable in the strong sense of the term, if and only if its truth could be conclusively established in experience . . . it is verifiable, in the weak sense, if it is possible for experience to render it probable."[35] To be literally meaningful, statements must be either

32. Ibid., pp. 720, 724.
33. C. E. M. Joad, *Decadence* (London: Faber and Faber, 1948), p. 151.
34. Ibid., p. 150.
35. A. J. Ayer, *Language, Truth and Logic,* 2d ed. (New York: Dover, 1946), p. 9.

empirically verifiable in the above sense or analytically verifiable in the a priori sense. An observation-statement resulting from an experience with sense-content is one which is actually or directly verified by the senses; or it can be indirectly verifiable if it entails verifiable statements. Statements falling outside the scope of this verifiability principle, such as metaphysical values (including moral values), are not literally meaningful statements; consequently, they are neither true nor false. Ethical sentences are emotionally significant, not literally meaningful.

In a subsequent modification of his position,[36] although he still held to the view that "ethical statements are not really statements at all, that they are not descriptive of anything, that they cannot be either true or false,"[37] Ayer admitted a sense in which it is in error, namely, that owing to the way in which the English language is used, it is proper to refer to ethical utterances as statements, rather than ejaculations. He conceded that "to say, as I once did, that these moral judgments are merely expressive of certain feelings, feelings of approval or disapproval, is an oversimplification."[38] Ayer's real preference, however, was to exclude the use of ethical judgments as meaningful statements, yet not to go so far as his earlier view of ethical values as mere expressions of feelings, evincings, and ejaculations, but to regard them as "patterns of behavior," and to include moral judgments as elements in these patterns.

THE EMOTIVE THEORY OF ETHICS. Ayer defined emotivism as the doctrine "that moral judgments are emotive rather than descriptive, that they are persuasive expressions of attitudes and not statements of fact, and consequently that they cannot be either true or false, or at least that it would make for clarity if the categories of truth and falsehood were not applied to them."[39] There is no truth or falsehood even in negative statements, such as "Nothing is good or bad," and "It does not matter what a person does," for such assertions are only tacit expressions of moral attitude.

According to Ayer, traditional ethical theories fall into four classes: (1) propositions expressing definitions of ethical terms, i.e., judgments dealing with the legitimacy of definitions; (2) those propositions which describe moral experience, its phenomena and causes; (3) sentences which are exhortations summoning us to duty or virtue; and (4) propositions which are actual ethical judgments. Of the four

36. The earlier position was offered in his very influential book, *Language, Truth and Logic,* which first appeared in 1936 and was revised in 1946. The later position appeared in *Horizon* (1949) and *Philosophical Essays* (1954).

37. A. J. Ayer, "On the Analysis of Moral Judgment," in *Horizon* 20 (1949) and *Philosophical Essays* (London: Macmillan, 1954), p. 231.

38. Ibid., p. 238.

39. Ibid., p. 246.

classes, only the first genuinely constitutes ethical philosophy; the second class is allocated to the sciences—e.g., sociology and psychology. The third class cannot even be said to be propositions at all, but rather mere ejaculations designed to induce others to act or to follow a given pattern of behavior. The fourth category, actual ethical judgments, are unclassified, owing to their failure to qualify as definitions, descriptions, or exhortations, but they are unquestionably foreign to ethical philosophy, since moral philosophy makes no ethical pronouncements, but restricts itself to the analyses of terms used in ethics; this task belongs to the province of metaethics.

Ayer assigned himself the metaethical task of "reducing the whole sphere of ethical terms to non-ethical"[40] ones, if possible. Both the subjectivists who regard ethics as feelings of approval, or matters of opinion, and the utilitarians who define ethics in terms of goodness and happiness, contend that they have succeeded. But Ayer repudiated the conclusions of both of these schools of thought because they appeal to the social sciences to provide descriptive ethical symbols, and they are definable in factual terms; in Ayer's view, normative ethical symbols, intuitively discerned, are simply unverifiable value statements.

Ayer held that normative ethical statements are unanalyzable, that they are pseudoconcepts simulating genuine propositions or judgments, and he asserted that the mere "presence of an ethical symbol in a proposition adds nothing to its factual content."[41] He cited an example to clarify this point:

> Thus to say to someone, "You acted wrongly in stealing that money," I am not stating anything more than if I had simply said, "You stole that money." In adding that this action is wrong I am not making any further statement about it. I am simply evincing my moral disapproval of it. It is as if I had said, "You stole that money," in a peculiar tone of horror, or written it with the addition of some special exclamation marks. The tone, or the exclamation marks, adds nothing to the literal meaning of the sentence. It merely serves to show that the expression of it is attended by certain feelings in the speaker.[42]

A general rule of morality, such as "Stealing money is wrong," is factually meaningless; consequently, it is not a proposition of which truth or falsity can be predicated. It is comparable to the exclamatory utterance, "Stealing money!!!" wherein the exclamation marks convey a feeling of moral disapproval; but, as a statement, it is neither true nor false. For another to disagree with me on such a matter merely signifies that he does not share my feelings about it, but he cannot contradict me on any valid basis since our quarrel has to do with feel-

40. Ayer, *Language, Truth and Logic,* p. 104.
41. Ibid., p. 107.
42. Ibid.

ings, not with genuine true or false judgments. My assertion that a given pattern of behavior is wrong does not constitute a factual statement, nor even, as the subjectivists contend, a statement about my own state of mind, but simply expresses certain moral sentiments, not genuine propositions or judgments to which the predicates truth or falsity may be applied.

VALUE SKEPTICISM. All ethical norms discussed above result in *value skepticism,* the view that moral values are unknowable, or, still better, *value nihilism,* the theory that moral principles do not exist. Ethical judgments are reduced to emotive expressions, calculated to arouse feeling, stimulate behavior of a certain type, or command action of a given type. The tone of the command lends emphasis, designed to provoke action, but is significantly meaningless as a proposition. Thus, in the case of the moral command "Tell the truth," no ethical judgment has been rendered, for I have been simply "evincing my feelings."

Ayer's reason for our inability to arrive at a criterion for validating ethical judgments is that they lack objective validity, not that they possess absolute validity independent of sense experience. Ethical statements are not even assertions of feeling, but merely expressions of feeling, ejaculations expressed in a specific tone of voice or with gestures designed to excite feeling. "Ethical judgments have no validity."[43] According to this theory, all dispute about questions of value ceases, since dispute must be over factual matters, not those pertaining to value. Even to assert that one's own ethical theory is superior to an opponent's is to render a value judgment, hence to contradict this system; all such judgments fall outside the limits of proper argument. Ayer concluded that "we find that ethical philosophy consists simply in saying that ethical concepts are pseudo-concepts and therefore unanalysable . . . and consequently indefinable."[44]

AYER'S REVISED EMOTIVISM. As indicated earlier, Ayer moderated his stand by conceding that there is a sense in which ethical utterances are statements, and that to regard them as ejaculations is unconventional, but he still refused to accept ethical judgments as genuine judgments or propositions. However, he did admit that to regard moral judgments merely as expressions of behavior is oversimplifying the matter and that it would be preferable to assert that "what may be described as moral attitudes consist in certain patterns of behaviour, and that the expression of a moral judgement is an element in the pattern. The moral judgement expresses the attitude in the sense that it contributes to defining it."[45] Finding the reasons why persons respond in a given manner to a set of facts is the task of the social scientist; the philosopher's (at least Ayer's) concern is "to analyse the use of ethical

43. Ibid., p. 110.
44. Ibid., p. 112.
45. Ayer, *Philosophical Essays,* p. 238.

terms," not the scientific explanation of moral attitudes. "To analyse moral judgements is not itself to moralize."[46]

In a sense moral judgments are directives, persuasive expressions of attitude, not statements of fact; they are emotive expressions rather than descriptive statements. The ethicist's task in the light of this theory is not to moralize, but to engage in the metaethical activity of analyzing moral judgments, a nonmoral activity. It is interesting to note that Ayer, who does not permit value judgments, does allow himself the liberty of one pertaining to truth. He concluded his "On the Analysis of Moral Judgements" with the value judgment: "What I have tried to show is not that the theory I am defending is expedient, but that it is true."[47]

Criticism of Emotivism. Brand Blanshard[48] severely criticized emotivism, presenting the following salient points predicated on emotive premises: (1) nothing is actually "better or worse than anything else"; (2) the only goodness in enjoyment is our attitude toward it, and it therefore disappears with the lapse of attention; (3) there is no way to explain the value of an experience when it no longer presently exists; (4) "emotivism dislocates values from the place where they belong";[49] (5) pain and death, or their infliction on another, is neither evil nor wrong; (6) moral attitudes are arbitrary; (7) two persons can neither agree nor disagree on the validity or worth of an ethical belief; (8) it is impossible to achieve moral progress; (10) no one can give relevant arguments for or against ethical judgments; (11) there is no "objective court of appeal" for settling ethical disputes; and (12) emotivism fails to provide an accurate account or explanation of moral ideas.

According to C. I. Lewis, emotivism is

> one of the strangest aberrations ever to visit the mind of man. The denial to value-apprehensions in general of the character of truth or falsity and of knowledge, would imply both moral and practical cynicism. It would invalidate all action; because action is pointless unless there can be some measure of assurance of a valuable result which it may realize. And this negation, if it be carried out consistently, likewise invalidates all knowledge; both because believing is itself an active attitude which should have no point if it were not better to be right than wrong in what one believes, and because knowledge in general is for the sake of action.[50]

46. Ibid., p. 247.
47. Ibid., p. 249.
48. Brand Blanshard, *Reason and Goodness* (London: George Allen & Unwin, 1961), chap. 8.
49. Ibid., p. 213.
50. C. I. Lewis, *An Analysis of Knowledge and Valuation* (LaSalle, Ill.: Open Court, 1946), p. 366.

In a similar vein, S. L. Hart ascribed emotivism's anaesthetic indifference about man's valuations to "mental derangement and moral callousness."[51]

Emotivism, especially Ayer's version of it, has evoked considerable opposition in philosophical circles. The British philosopher Joad wrote an entire critique on logical positivism in which he repudiated emotivism:

> If the word "moral" stands for nothing, then we cannot understand how ethical judgments came to be formulated and to be differentiated from aesthetic judgments. If it stands for something, something that is both specific and unique, then Ayer's theory fails wholly to explain how and why it came to do so, since it denies the presence in the universe of any factor which is at once objective and unique to which the judgments could refer and to which the feeling which the judgment expresses could serve as a response.[52]

Joad contended that a person will cease to believe that stealing is wrong if he is persuaded that the statement "Stealing is wrong" is merely an expression of horror devoid of moral connotation. Martin D'Arcy, Luther J. Binkley, and other philosophers have criticized emotivism for its unsalutary effects, arguing that "if the theory is widely accepted it will prove damaging to society."[53] Binkley, agreeing with Joad, commented that "what the emotivists say ethical judgments mean is not what people do in fact mean by them."[54]

G. E. Moore[55] pointed out that to deny the validity of judgments of moral value begs the question, "Why do men argue over ethical propositions?" Wheelright agreed with Moore's point of view:

> Now just as two physicists cannot discuss their proper subject unless they postulate the existence of *some* kind of real physical world, about the specific nature of which they can then proceed to inquire; so too no ethical discussion is possible without postulating that there are goods and bads, rights and wrongs, in human affairs, and that it is the business of ethics to discover these if possible and raise questions about them.[56]

51. Samuel L. Hart, *Treatise on Values* (New York: Philosophical Library, 1949), p. 63.
52. C. E. M. Joad, *A Critique of Logical Positivism* (London: Victor Gollancz, 1950), p. 132.
53. Luther J. Binkley, *Contemporary Ethical Theories* (New York: Philosophical Library, 1961), p. 78.
54. Ibid., p. 79.
55. G. E. Moore, "The Nature of Moral Philosophy," in *Philosophical Studies* (Paterson, N.J.: Littlefield, Adams, 1959), pp. 310–339.
56. Philip Wheelright, *A Critical Introduction to Ethics,* 3d ed. (New York: Odyssey Press, 1959), p. 299.

Skeptical views in epistemology suffer from self-contradiction, for the skeptic who argues that no knowledge is possible begs the question, "How did he obtain that valuable piece of knowledge?" The value skeptic is caught in a similar predicament; if values do not exist, he cannot ascribe any value to his own ethical views, nor can he claim that his own position is as true as or better than existing ones, since this would be an appeal to a value judgment. How ironic that the value skeptic who denies all values, tacitly appeals to values for support of his own theory! Since the emotivists seek to persuade others that all views are false except their own, which states that there is no truth or value, then their own system is also void of truth nor can any value be ascribed to it. As C. I. Lewis asserted, "Those who deny the character of cognition and the possibility of truth to value-apprehensions must find themselves, ultimately, in the position of Epimenides the Cretan who said that all Cretans are liars. Either their thesis must be false or it is not worth believing or discussing."[57]

The most impressive criticism confronting Ayer and all other logical positivists today attacks the verification principle as the logically defective foundation of the entire philosophy. The principle is condemned as one that destroys itself when it rejects all principles owing to their metaphysical character. If principles must be repudiated because they are metaphysical in nature, then the verification principle also must be rejected, and with its demise all emotivist theories, together with the entire philosophy of logical positivism, collapse.

The philosophy that dismisses all metaphysics as nonexistent turns out to be metaphysical in nature and must therefore reject itself. Among eminent philosophers who have confronted the logical positivists with this dilemma is the Cantabrigian philosopher John Wisdom, who referred to the verification principle as a "generalization of a very large class of metaphysical theories."[58]

Charles L. Stevenson: The Noncognitive Theory of Ethics. Metaethical doctrines, which have dominated the British philosophical scene, have also become familiar in American philosophical circles, in considerable measure because of the work of Charles L. Stevenson (1908–), an American philosopher trained at Harvard and Cambridge universities.

Ethical Judgments, Attitudes, and Emotive Meaning. Stevenson is indebted to Ogden and Richards for ethical ideas and to Hume for an empirical approach to ethics. It is Stevenson's view that ethical judgments do not merely express attitudes but actually mold and alter

57. Lewis, *Analysis of Knowledge and Valuation,* p. 373.

58. John Wisdom, "Metaphysics and Verification," in *Mind* 47 (1938), p. 452; and in his *Philosophy and Psycho-Analysis* (Oxford: Basil Blackwell, 1953), p. 51.

them. They lack scientific support and nonnatural qualities, but they can be recognized because of their distinctive features, namely, (1) emotive meanings, and (2) disagreements in attitude. When a person witnesses and evaluates an action, he experiences a feeling about it—its emotive meaning. He adopts an attitude toward it, one of approval or disapproval, which may depend upon the facts of the situation. People who agree on the facts may differ in their attitudes toward them. Ethical debates reflect disagreements *in* attitude, i.e., in a specific psychological attitude, just as love and hate are specific psychological attitudes. "Normative ethics is more than a science. . . . Ethical issues involve personal and social decisions about what is to be approved, and . . . these decisions, though they vitally depend upon knowledge, do not themselves constitute knowledge."[59] This conclusion resembles Hume's, namely, that morals are a matter of social approval or censure. The essential employment of ethical judgments is "not to indicate facts, but to *create an influence,*"[60] i.e., to influence the *attitudes* of another. The termination of ethical disputes coincides with attitudinal agreement.

ATTITUDE AND THE APPROVAL THEORY OF VALUE JUDGMENTS. According to Stevenson, a special meaning inheres in ethical terms, just as an emotive meaning is basic to the concept of *good*. His approval theory of moral values differs sharply from that of his predecessors in that he allows for genuine conflict in moral judgments, not simply dismissing them as mere "ejaculations" or "evincings," as Ayer did. Considered in their proper context, ethical statements contain both emotive and descriptive meaning. Although moral conflicts can entail disagreements in belief, they are primarily and distinctively disagreements in attitude. It is because people differ in their attitude toward them that ethical judgments possess cognitive value, ethical discussions become significant, and the meaning of the ethical judgments is to be found in the *attitudes* of individuals. Ethical disputes center, not in beliefs, but in emotions and feelings. "Ethical statements are used to influence people, . . . they change or intensify people's attitudes, rather than describe what these attitudes already are. The influence is mediated not by some occult property which the ethical terms mean, but simply by their *emotive* meaning, which fits them for use in suggestion."[61] Moral exhortations should be understood as pleas for an alteration in attitude, but they must not be regarded as moral obligations or moral principles, only as matters of approval. To censure an act is to assume an attitude

59. Charles L. Stevenson, *Ethics and Language* (New Haven: Yale University Press, 1944), preface.
60. Charles L. Stevenson, "The Emotive Meaning of Ethical Terms," *Logical Positivism*, ed. A. J. Ayer (New York: Free Press, 1959), p. 269.
61. Charles L. Stevenson, *Facts and Values: Studies in Ethical Analysis* (New Haven: Yale University Press, 1964), p. 138.

of condemnation toward it, and to approve of it is to ascribe moral status or value to it.

Those who seek changes in a person's attitudes are engaged in a moral endeavor, and their statements must be regarded not as descriptive (otherwise, they would fall within the province of psychology), but as imperatives calling for attitudinal changes. The line which demarcates the moralist from the scientist (psychologist) is the latter's concern for cause-and-effect relations which *describe* behavior or attitudes, whereas the former seeks to *influence* behavior by effecting a desired change in attitude. "The resolution of an ethical argument requires a resolution of disagreement in attitude, and so requires that the attitudes of one party or the other (or both) be changed or redirected."[62]

Normative ethics, then, seeks to resolve not disagreements of belief, but disagreements in attitude. Beliefs, however, do play an important role in ethical controversies, owing to their intimate relationship with attitudes.

> When a man is making an evaluative decision he is trying to resolve a conflict in his attitudes. For his beliefs serve as intermediaries between his attitudes, and by uniting them in new ways may alter their combined strength. The resolution of his conflict, then, will intimately depend upon his beliefs, which themselves will be of great variety.[63]

A disagreement in belief can be resolved by an analysis of methods, while a disagreement in ethics is resolved by a change in attitude; it is in attitude that significant ethical statements are to be found.

PERSUASIVE DEFINITIONS. Stevenson has cited the following working models of ethical sentences and imperatives:

(1) "This is wrong" means *I disapprove of this; do so as well.*
(2) "He ought to do this" means *I disapprove of his leaving this undone; do so as well.*
(3) "This is good" means *I approve of this; do so as well.*[64]

In each of the above cases, the speaker seeks to change the attitude of the person addressed to coincide with his own. The speaker's intent is not to describe or justify his feeling or belief, but to bring about an alteration in attitude. "Both imperative and ethical sentences are used more for encouraging, altering, or redirecting people's aims and conduct than for simply describing them."[65] If a person is incapable of using rational methods to change another's belief in order to effect a

62. Stevenson, *Ethics and Language*, p. 139.

63. Charles L. Stevenson, "The Emotive Conception of Ethics and Its Cognitive Implication," in *Bulletin of the Eastern Division of the American Philosophical Association* (1949), p. 7.

64. Stevenson, *Ethics and Language*, p. 21.

65. Ibid.

change of attitude, then such nonrational techniques may be employed, especially those referred to by Stevenson as *persuasive* techniques. "It depends on the sheer, direct emotional impact of words—on emotive meaning, rhetorical cadence, apt metaphor, stentorian, stimulating, or pleading tones of voice, dramatic gestures, care in establishing *rapport* with the hearer or audience, and so on."[66] To assert that persuasion is a nonrational method is not to imply that it is an irrational one; yet, by the same token, it is not a rational one either. Persuasive methods transcend the rational in the sense that they are not concerned with belief as are rational methods, but with attitudes. Their chief device is the employment of emotive language.

Persuasion also extends to definition; a *persuasive definition* is one "which gives a new conceptual meaning to a familiar word without substantially changing its emotive meaning, and which is used with the conscious or unconscious purpose of changing, by this means, the direction of people's interests."[67] Regarding persuasion or attitudes, validity is meaningless, for neither of these can be referred to as valid or invalid. Persuasive definitions must employ familiar terms which are both descriptive and rich in emotive value, because their purpose is to alter the descriptive meaning of sentences. In a persuasive definition, both descriptive and emotive meaning are *wedded,* so that the terms will have their maximum effectiveness in redirecting attitudes. "To choose a definition is to plead a cause, so long as the word defined is strongly emotive."[68] Attitudes are altered not only by ethical judgments, but by definitions as well. "Disagreement in attitude may be debated over the dictionary."[69] This does not mean that all definitions of emotive terms are of the persuasive variety, though the majority of them are.

THE DUAL PURPOSE OF LANGUAGE. "Broadly speaking, there are two different *purposes* which lead us to use language. On the one hand we use words (as in science), to record, clarify, and communicate *beliefs.* On the other hand we use words to give vent to our feelings (interjections), or to create moods (poetry), or to incite people to actions or attitudes (oratory)."[70] The decision as to whether the words used are of the first (descriptive) or the second (dynamic) type depends on the intention or purpose of the person involved. Statements of fact, such as scientific statements, illustrate the descriptive use, while the dynamic use is prevalent in exclamations. "When a person cuts himself and says 'Damn,' his purpose is not ordinarily to record, clarify, or

66. Ibid., p. 139.
67. Charles L. Stevenson, "Persuasive Definitions," *Mind* 47 (1938), p. 331.
68. Stevenson, *Ethics and Language,* p. 210.
69. Ibid.
70. Stevenson, "Emotive Meaning of Ethical Terms," p. 21.

communicate any belief,"[71] yet the word has value when used dynamically as employed here.

Intimately related to the dynamic use of words is the emotive meaning of them, their ability to create an immediate *aura of feeling,* to produce affective responses. Terms with emotive significance are well suited for particular types of dynamic use. Owing to their emotive meaning, moral judgments have a "quasi-imperative force" which proves effective in influencing attitudes in others. An accurate description of these attitudes falls within the province of the psychologist, who is concerned with the most effective way of causing change in attitude; the moralist attempts to effect attitudinal changes.

The study of *methods* of ethics falls within the scope of the ethicist, who, in addition to seeking attitudinal changes, seeks a clarification of the meaning of moral terms and proof of ethical judgments. Stevenson concluded his article "The Emotive Conception of Ethics and Its Cognitive Implications" by stating his central thesis: "The emotive conception of ethics, so far from depriving ethics from its thoughtful, reflective elements, in fact preserves them in all their variety."[72]

EVALUATION OF STEVENSON'S NONCOGNITIVISM. There is little doubt that Stevenson is right in claiming that debates revolving around moral issues are intended to alter attitudes, for this is an important intention of most if not all ethical arguments. Moreover, the same thing may be said regarding the resolution of conflict as the objective of deliberations in moral philosophy; nevertheless, the attempt to restrict the data of moral experience to noncognitivism fails to take into account important facts of moral experience. Many of the arguments used to criticize Ayer's theory are pertinent in respect to Stevenson's theory as well. Brandt has referred to Stevenson's noncognitivism as

> complicated and not very plausible. It assumes that somehow we know that the *basic* use of ethical terms in some sense is expressive and directive of attitudes, and that the property-referring use is secondary. It is difficult to imagine on what facts an emotive theorist might base such speculations. Sometimes the emotivist disdains any facts and makes it a matter of *definition,* saying that unless the expressive and attitude-moving features of an ethical term are fundamental on a given occasion, then the utterance does not qualify as an ethical or normative utterance on that occasion. There is no reason, however, why a critic of the emotive theory should be compelled to concede that the emotive theory is true by definition. What we want to know is the meaning and function of terms like "desirable" or "obligation" in contexts where their use is intuitively identifiable as a serious assertion. Whether, on such occasions, they are primarily

71. Ibid.

72. Charles L. Stevenson, "The Emotive Conception of Ethics and Its Cognitive Implications," *Philosophical Review* 59 (1950), p. 304.

> property-referring or primarily expressive and attitude-moving is a matter for observation to decide, not a matter of definition.[73]

He has noted further that people seek to change the attitudes of others for reasons other than those normally designated as moral. The noncognitivist who contends that ethical arguments have only the aim of changing attitudes is mistaken, for many arguments that are effective in altering a person's attitude need not be ethically relevant—consider, for example, a legislator who is influenced to change his vote in order that his daughter will be accepted by a particular university or in order that his alma mater will not suffer bankruptcy.

Brandt commented on Stevenson's concept of "disagreement in attitude" as follows:

> My conclusion is that Mr. Stevenson proves no more than that some, perhaps only a few, of the important analyses suffer from being unable to count as logically relevant, factual points we should all regard in practice as ethically relevant. And this means his argument falls very short indeed of showing that there is good reason for thinking a purely cognitive analysis cannot be carried through.[74]

Inasmuch as factual statements do not bear logically on peculiarly ethical disagreement, then such statements are merely "causal ancestors" of ethical attitudes. A person may disapprove of socialized medicine on the ground that it may jeopardize his professional standing, and such disapproval would be interpreted on the basis of emotive theory as ethically relevant. Yet, this change of attitude is not of the order that Stevenson has identified as ethical. Hence, one should distinguish between ethically relevant and irrelevant attitudes.

Even if Stevenson were right in contending that moral issues are means of resolving attitudinal conflicts, it would be severely debatable that they are such and no more. Attitudes, in and of themselves, may be of utmost moral value, as in the ethics of Jesus. Some attitudes are decidedly ethical, others are morally neutral. Moral attitudes of an individual have a salutary influence both on his personality and on his behavior, and thereby affect others either for good or ill. John Dewey objected to the theory that ethical standards are purely attitudinal:

> Our hope or expectation is that if "we can get an opponent to agree with us about the empirical facts of the case he will adopt the same moral attitude toward them as we do"—though once more it is not evident why the attitude is called "moral" rather

73. Richard B. Brandt, *Ethical Theory* (Englewood Cliffs, N.J.: Prentice-Hall, 1959), p. 214.

74. Richard B. Brandt, "The Emotive Theory of Ethics," *Philosophical Review* 59 (1950), p. 312.

than "magical," "belligerent," or any one of thousands of adjectives that might be selected at random.[75]

Dewey argued that the involuntary emotional reactions of an individual cannot be regarded as moral per se any more than can tears, smiles, or other organic behavior not ordinarily interpreted as expressions of value. Some cries are ejaculatory, while others are purposeful and serve as a means of communication.

Stevenson's assertion that the statement "*x* is wrong" is tantamount to saying that "I disapprove of this; do so as well" is questionable, inasmuch as most people would assume it to mean that "I disapprove of *x* because of a sense of obligation, and my feeling of obligation impels me to share my enlightened view with you." The sense of obligation is apparently one of the hard facts of daily experience which is grounded empirically in the same way as any other experience.

Stevenson assumed that because *good* refers to an attitude, it is devoid of objective connotation; but attitudes, though subjective in nature, may be evaluated on an objective basis, just as psychologists evaluate attitudes for their objective value from the standpoint of mental health or social-psychological connotations. Similarly, attitudes possessing moral quality may be assessed for their ethical values.

LINGUISTIC ANALYSIS: THE USE OF ETHICAL LANGUAGE

Emotivism had a rapid rise, but it was not sustained and currently has given way to *linguistic analysis*. Retreat from emotivism is attributable to numerous reasons, among them (according to Blanshard) being the denial of moral value judgments, extremism in the rejection of argument, and the confusion resulting from exaggerated claims about the significance of emotion. Linguistic ethicists believe that they have improved upon the views of the emotivists by accepting moral value judgments, though both groups concede that metaethical assertions are normatively neutral. The analysts agree with existentialists that, as expressions of moral commitments, ethical principles lack a rational basis, because value judgments are merely expressions of choice.

British philosophy, dominated by G. E. Moore and L. Wittgenstein, passed through at least three phases, typified by the following slogans, respectively: (1) "The meaning of a statement is the method of its verification"; (2) "Don't ask for the meaning, ask for the use"; and (3) "Every statement has its own logic."[76] These slogans, especially the third and, to a considerable extent, the second, caught the imagination

75. John Dewey, *Theory of Valuation* (Chicago: University of Chicago Press, 1939), p. 8.

76. J. O. Urmson, *Philosophical Analysis: Its Development between the Two World Wars* (Oxford: Clarendon Press, 1956), p. 179.

of the linguistic analysts. Shortly after the Second World War the Oxonian philosopher J. O. Urmson developed his grading theory, which gave the linguistic analysis movement considerable momentum.

J. O. Urmson: Ethical Evaluation as Grading. The term *grading* is derived from the British commercial growers' practice of sorting apples according to quality standards established by the Ministry of Agriculture. Urmson drew a striking parallel between grading apples and grading ethical values. (He analyzed only the value term *good,* however, excluding other value terms, such as right, wrong, and cognate words, because they have a different function and cannot be regarded as "grading labels.") His fundamental thesis attempted to prove that, logically, there is no difference between grading apples (things) as good and grading persons as good, except that in the latter case the grading is a moral evaluation and as such may be of greater importance.

Urmson analyzed the grading use of language and held that value grading (judging things as good or bad morally) falls under the subhead of grading in general. Adjectives used in grading (such as good, bad, first-rate) are referred to as *grading labels.* Grading (evaluating) is an activity or process either for classifying objects according to their respective order of merit, called *mental grading,* or for ordering (arranging) things in groups, called *physical grading.* Grading an apple as extra fancy is mental grading, while dropping it into a box with others of the same quality is physical grading. Grading labels indicate the order of merit; e.g., "good" is a grading label. The *ad hoc* labels have the advantage of avoiding controversial issues; for example, marking a student's paper with a Greek delta is less upsetting to him than grading it as "stupid and worthless." Professional (commercial) grading labels possess emotional appeal, as in grading a mediocre product "good," better ones "very good," and still better ones "excellent." Amateur sportsmen and hobbyists often use grading labels to classify their groups or to evaluate their skills in competition.

GRADING IN VARIOUS SCHOOLS OF ETHICS. The various schools of ethical theories emphasize different aspects of grading. Naturalists describe certain moral qualities in terms of natural consequences and then select grading labels which best describe these qualities; intuitionists refer to their own type of intuitively sensed moral characteristics and label them accordingly; emotivists label ethical values on the basis of the emotional responses associated with them. Thus, in grading apples, the naturalists would grade them as "good" if the taste were *good* enough to give us a pleasant physical response; the intuitionist would apply the label "good" to an indefinable nonnatural quality which he senses in or attributes to the apples; and the emotivist would apply the label "good" to the emotional response felt on tasting the apples.

Urmson concluded that, although each theory has a point in its favor, yet each is in error, that none is adequate, that no one theory can be explained in terms of another. "To describe is to describe, to grade is to grade, and to express one's feelings is to express one's feelings, and . . . none of these is reducible to either of the others; nor can any of them be reduced to, defined in terms of, anything else."[77]

GRADING CRITERIA. Misunderstandings and disagreements about the moral values involved in grading labels are due primarily to divergent views of *grading criteria.* The various ethical theories about the meaning or proper application of *good* can be regarded as theories of "how we arrive at criteria of goodness." Reformers, those who desire to modify behavior patterns or standards, are thereby repudiating accepted grading criteria, hence must seek other criteria that might be accepted for grading. The following reasons explain why there are disagreements about moral grading:

1. "We accept roughly or exactly the same criteria of goodness (or of being first class, etc.) but haven't yet examined them all."[78] Much discussion occurs over partial evidence, and the question can be settled by considering "other agreed material."
2. "We accept the same criteria but it is a marginal case."[79] Disputes arising from this situation will probably not be resolved.
3. "We have no agreement, or very little, on criteria."[80] Questions involving this point cannot be settled, because they cannot even be discussed.
4. "We may have important disagreements on criteria and . . . the reformer may know it. He may then openly reveal himself as not asking the question whether a thing is good or not by accepted standards, but as advocating new standards, new criteria."[81] In this matter, debates on moral issues are not dealt with in the usual way, and entail the problem of criteria under point (2).

The reformer debates moral values on the basis of his new criteria, treating them as if his values were the accepted standards. This is an effective technique in the efforts of the reformer to obtain acceptance of his new proposed criteria.

Urmson contended that, if we agree with the foregoing explanations for disagreements about moral values, we will thereby reduce the entire problem to a simple rule: "Grading words can only be *used* successfully for communication where criteria are accepted."[82] But, if we do not

77. J. O. Urmson, "On Grading," in *Mind* 59 (1950), pp. 145–159. Also in *Approaches to Ethics,* ed. W. T. Jones et al., 2d ed. (New York: McGraw-Hill, 1969); and in Antony Flew, ed., *Logic and Language,* 2d series (Oxford: Basil Blackwell, 1959), p. 171. Page references in the following discussion are from Flew's edition.

78. Ibid., p. 181.

79. Ibid.

80. Ibid.

81. Ibid., p. 186.

82. Ibid., p. 182.

agree with these explanations, confusion will be the only outcome; unless criteria for grading are adopted, grading words will merely be discussed, instead of being used. Urmson's system is fundamentally noncognitive because the evaluation of "*x* as good" is not the same thing as making a judgment, but is an act of choice. In this matter of prime importance, Urmson failed to supply us with a grading criterion—a test for resolving moral issues; consequently, he missed the central issue of ethics.

R. M. Hare: Ethics as Universal Prescriptivism. Hare, substituting for Stevenson's "emotive meaning" the term "evaluative meaning," viewed ethics as the *prescriptive* use of language, not its *descriptive* use. Prescriptive language is designed to guide human conduct, and such is the function of ethical principles. Terms such as "good" and "ought" are used evaluatively. A person who employs "I ought to do *x*" as a value judgment is at the same time asserting the command or demand, "Let me do *x*." Behind the first person imperative, there is "quasi-imperative" pertaining to everyone.

Universal prescriptivism is the designation Hare has chosen for his ethical theory. In his *Language of Morals* (1952), he defined ethics as "the logical study of the language of morals,"[83] and in a sequel to it, *Freedom and Reason* (1963), he asserted the function of ethics to be "that of helping us to think better about moral questions by exposing the logical structure of the language in which this thought is expressed."[84] He regarded the latter work as a progress report covering his ideas since the publication of the former. The premises of *The Language of Morals* are that moral judgments are prescriptive judgments, and that they are differentiated from other judgments by being *universalizable.* The rationale of moral judgments is not their imperative character, but their universalizability, which is their ground, or reason. Because man is a free agent, he raises prescriptive questions; moral judgments are guides to conduct.

To classify moral language we must first place it under the genus *prescriptive language,* distinguishing prescriptive from other kinds of language. The next step is to differentiate moral language from other types of prescriptive language; this step carries out the basic plan of Hare's earlier book. Note that not all prescriptive language is moral language, as is the case with certain imperative sentences which fall under the prescriptive use of language, but not necessarily its moral use; only those sentences used in a certain type of value judgment are moral language.

MORAL JUDGMENTS AS PRESCRIPTIVE. Prescriptive language con-

83. R. M. Hare, *The Language of Morals* (London: Oxford University Press, 1952), preface.

84. R. M. Hare, *Freedom and Reason* (London: Oxford University Press, 1963), p. v.

sists of two types: (*a*) *imperatives* and (*b*) *value judgments,* the former being subdivided into *singular* and *universal,* and the latter being subdivided into *nonmoral* and *moral,* as shown in Hare's diagram as follows:[85]

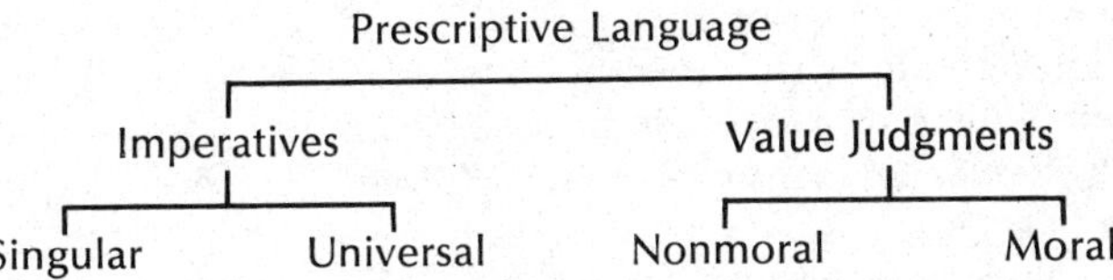

The basic theory of *The Language of Morals* is called "universal prescriptivism," a synthesis which combines the theory that moral judgments are capable of being universalized (in a sense comparable to scientific descriptive generalizations) with the view that moral judgments are prescriptive, i.e., conduct-guiding. Thus, moral judgments are universalizable and prescriptive. Moreover, they are rational. It is "because moral judgements are universalizable that we can speak of moral thought as rational (to universalize is to give the reason)."[86] Yet, moral choice is an act of will, i.e., a nonrational decision. Morality entails freedom.

The fundamental task of ethics is to establish the mutual consistency of moral judgments as both universalizable and prescriptive, so that jointly they become capable of "establishing the rationality of morals." Ethical naturalism is correct in ascribing descriptive meaning to moral terms, but wrong in thinking that it is the only meaning. If they lacked descriptive meaning, then morals could not be universalized into ethical principles, for there would be no particulars to universalize. Consequently, when rendering moral judgments, one does so by virtue of certain nonmoral qualities. Hare's universal prescriptivism retains some of the ideas of descriptivism, both its nonnatural as well as natural aspects, and unites it with his prescriptive, conduct-guiding statements.

METHOD OF UNIVERSAL PRESCRIPTIVISM. To obtain a moral principle, it is necessary to obtain a descriptive word, universalize it, and give it prescriptive meaning. Consider the word *good* as merely a descriptive word which identifies a person with certain characteristic moral qualities, then universalize it by saying that anyone who is exactly like the man we described as good is also good—i.e., all men with these qualities described are good. Add prescriptive meaning to this universalized descriptive statement (all men with these qualities are good) and you will obtain a synthetic moral principle, namely:

85. Hare, *Language of Morals,* p. 3.
86. Hare, *Freedom and Reason,* p. 5.

The good man's behavior is commended (prescribed) for imitation. "A man who wholeheartedly accepts such a rule is likely to *live,* not merely talk, differently from one who does not. Our descriptive meaning-rule has thus turned into a synthetic moral principle."[87]

MORALITY AND FREEDOM. Morality entails freedom; accordingly, decisions are of paramount importance. "I shall argue that it is because we are free agents that we need to ask prescriptive questions, and that the prescriptivity of moral judgements explains both why there should be thought to be a problem about moral freedom, and how to approach its solution."[88]

MODIFICATION OF ETHICAL STANDARDS. Social standards of morality are not inflexible, owing to the fact that the descriptive meaning of a given word changes. Standards of human excellence change in the real world; whereas in the past a good man could be a wife-beater, today it would be otherwise. Consequently, the designation "good man" changes according to changing standards. When "good man" is used to identify changing moral standards, one must allow for its logical character by making its prescriptive meaning primary, and its descriptive meaning secondary. But all value terms are not necessarily treated in this manner, for some moral words have descriptive meaning as their primary function, and the prescriptive meaning is only secondary.

P. H. Nowell-Smith: The Concepts of Moral Discourse. The point of view of the British analytic philosopher P. H. Nowell-Smith (1914–) was set forth in his book *Ethics* (1954), which had a foreword by A. J. Ayer, stating: "There is a distinction, which is not always sufficiently marked, between the activity of a moralist, who sets out to elaborate a moral code, or to encourage its observance, and that of a moral philosopher, whose concern is not primarily to make moral judgments but to analyse their nature."[89] (Note that the present text refers to the *moralist* as a moral reformer, who applies ethics in practice, as distinguished from the moral philosopher or *ethicist,* who makes judgments of moral value and offers grounds for their support. In this sense ethics is the theory of morals, whereas morals is the practice of ethics.)

THE PROVINCE OF ETHICS. Regarding ethics as a practical science, whose objective is to furnish answers to such questions as "What shall I do?" Nowell-Smith contended that answers cannot be found to deal with this type of question, except perhaps to paint pictures of different kinds of life and inquire as to which type one truly prefers, just as Plato did. The kind of life a person prefers depends upon his psychology. Although the psychology of a man will determine what type of life he considers satisfactory, nevertheless, decisions and imperatives are not logically inferred from his psychological makeup. The only

87. Ibid., p. 23.
88. Ibid., p. 6.
89. P. H. Nowell-Smith, *Ethics* (Baltimore: Penguin, 1954), foreword.

generalization one can make is that there are similarities in the psychology of different individuals. There can be general agreement that certain types of conduct or experience are unsatisfactory or dissatisfactory, but practical advice to make them acceptable is useless. When it is difficult to decide what is satisfactory in life, one would be presumptuous and vain to attempt an answer without sufficient knowledge of both the psychology of the individual in question and the specific case under consideration.

THE JANUS-PRINCIPLE. Nowell-Smith admitted that his purpose has not been that of ascertaining the satisfactory life, the life worth living, but the "less ambitious one of showing how the concepts that we use in practical discourse, in deciding, choosing, advising, appraising, praising, and blaming, and selecting and rejecting moral rules are related to each other. The questions 'What shall I do?' and 'What moral principles should I adopt?' must be answered by each man for himself; that at least is part of the connotation of the word 'moral.' "[90]

Unlike the other representatives of metaethics, Nowell-Smith offered no single or easy solution to the ethical problem. He repudiated the one-factor theories of his predecessors who attempted to explain ethical language as mere ejaculation, or only as grading, or only as imperatives, or any other single function, for there are ethical terms which have a dual or multiple function. "Since I shall make frequent use of the principle that a given word can not only do two or more jobs at once but also is often, in the absence of counter-evidence or express withdrawal, presumed to be doing two or more jobs at once, I shall give it the special name 'Janus-principle.' "[91]

A-, D-, AND G-WORDS (APTNESS-PROPERTIES, DESCRIPTIVE-PROPERTIES, AND GERUNDIVE-PROPERTIES). In addition to words that fall under the Janus-principle, there are some words which elicit a certain reaction or particular emotion as well as performing other characteristic functions. Such words are called *A-words* (short for aptness-words), "because they are words that indicate that an object has certain properties which are *apt* to arouse a certain emotion or range of emotions."[92] For example, the A-words *sublime* and *terrify* merely express the speaker's emotion. Consequently, A-words, with a logic peculiar to themselves, differ from *D-words* (descriptive words, such as red, hard, brittle) and *G-words* (gerundive words, such as praiseworthy, laudable, damnable). Such adjectives (A-words, e.g., sublime; D-words, e.g., red; and G-words, e.g., damnable) represent different kinds of properties: *aptness-properties, descriptive-properties,* and *gerundive-properties.*

THE LOGICAL PECULIARITY OF A-, D-, AND G-WORDS. Although all three types of words are adjectives, following the same rules of gram-

90. Ibid., p. 320.
91. Ibid., p. 100.
92. Ibid., p. 72.

mar, each has a *logical oddness* of its own. "I shall say that a question is 'logically odd' if there appears to be no further room for it in its context because it has already been answered. This is not to say that the question is necessarily senseless, but that we should be puzzled to know what it meant and should have to give it some unusual interpretation."[93] It is a logical oddity to inquire of a man who says that he is having a nice smoke, "Do you enjoy it?" In ethics, the philosopher's responsibility is to eliminate logical oddities existing among sentences and arguments. "The task of the moral philosopher is to map the mutual relationships of moral words, sentences, and arguments; and this is a task, not of showing how one statement entails or contradicts another, but of showing that in a certain context it would be logically odd to assert one thing and deny another or to ask a particular question."[94] Logical oddities often result from seeming inconsistencies and self-contradictions, such as my saying that a book is instructive, but adding that I was not instructed by it. Although odd, it is still logically possible, since I may have received my instructions from a different book. It would be a logical oddity to ask a man, "I know you thought it to be the best automobile, but why did you choose it?" or to say: "This is the ethical act for me to do, but I shall do another."

Stephen Toulmin: The Place of Reason in Ethics. Stephen Toulmin's ethical theory, expounded in his *Examination of the Place of Reason in Ethics* (1950), developed from his attempt to discover good reasons in defense of judgments of moral value. His ideas were inspired by Francis Bacon's ethical discourse *Of the Coulers of Good and Evill* (*Of The Colors of Good and Evil*) which appeared in revised form as Book VI of the *Advancement of Learning*. Toulmin's theory is a continuation of Bacon's, but extended in range. Whereas Bacon limited himself to those more common arguments, Toulmin sought "what it is that gives these arguments such value and scope as they possess,"[95] a task which entailed a lengthy consideration of the "nature of reasoning" and of the "foundations of logic."

REASON'S ROLE IN ETHICS. In his treatise on ethics, Toulmin stated his objective as that of ascertaining the place and function of reason in ethics. "Reasoning must be designed to influence behaviour if it is to be called 'ethical.' "[96] Cognitively, to assert that something is right is to claim valid reasons for so doing. The practices that are worthy of adoption are those which truly reduce conflicts of interest. Believing that ethical judgments are debatable, Toulmin rejected theories that held otherwise.

93. Ibid., p. 83.
94. Ibid.
95. Stephen Edelston Toulmin, *An Examination of the Place of Reason in Ethics* (London: Cambridge University Press, 1950), p. vi.
96. Ibid., p. 131.

He declined to accept the ethical theories of his predecessors, because they offer nothing to the "plain man" in his "everyday problems but confusion." Consequently, Toulmin abandoned existing ethical theories, though not without noting some genuinely ethical features in them. Each ethical theory, he said, possessed a common weakness, and "none of them gave any adequate account of the nature of ethical reasoning." These theories inquired as to the meaning of *good*—its objectivity, subjectivity, or emotive nature—when they should have asked, "What is a good reason for a particular ethical conclusion?" Ethical judgments utilize reason by altering a person's feeling and behavior. The justification of moral principles is predicated on the discovery of those principles which if implemented, would result in the least amount of suffering. To reconcile conflicting interests of men and harmonize their desires is the function of morality.

THE FUNCTION OF ETHICAL STATEMENTS. Toulmin's novel approach to ethics impelled him to examine the function and role of ethical judgments in life. It was his purpose to ascertain the *function* of ethical statements as we find them in ordinary everyday use, instead of attempting to formulate a particular code or ethical theory or to defend an existent one. He concluded that the proper function of ethics is that of correlating "our feelings and behaviour in such a way as to make the fulfillment of everyone's aims and desires as far as possible compatible."[97]

From Toulmin's point of view, ethical theories of the past terminated in failure because they were one-sided. The question they raised, "How are we to tell good ethical arguments from bad ones?" was left unanswered by three major ethical schools of thought, because they assumed that since an idea is true at times, it is therefore essential to ethical judgments. The first school, the *objective doctrinists,* assumed that value is an objective property (nonnatural property) which factually informed individuals would necessarily agree on; the second school, the *subjective doctrinists,* assumed that it is inevitable for persons to advocate differing standards of value; and the third school, the *emotivists,* or *imperative doctrinists,* assumed that moral judgments are purely hortatory in nature. Each of the three schools of ethical thought has misrepresented ethical concepts as we know them; their failure is attributable to their *ad hoc* modifications which overemphasized the following factors: in the first, *nonnatural properties;* in the second, *attitudes;* and in the third, *interplay of feelings.* "But this is like trying to overcome a mistake in natural history by saying 'Of course a ram is not an ordinary bull,' instead of admitting that it is not a bull at all and starting afresh."[98] Toulmin asserted that these theories are oversimplified, claiming too much, ignoring the logic involved, and treating

97. Ibid., p. 137.
98. Ibid., p. 62.

the matter of ethical theory as if "playing a private game." The error of these theorists is the assumption that, by adopting their views, we shall find answers to our ethical questions; but in fact, we are simply taken in by so doing, and end where we began. The three views are merely disguised comparisons.

It is time to begin anew unbiased, said Toulmin, not by restricting reason to mathematics and science as did Ayer and Wittgenstein, but by obtaining good reasons for moral action.

> If it is not nonsensical to talk of 'good and bad reasons' and of 'valid and invalid inferences', even over a mere word-game, how much less can it be so over the arguments we use in more important fields—in mathematics, in science, in ethics, in aesthetics, in expressing our reactions to things, in explaining our motives, in giving commands, and in our thousand-and-one other ways of using speech![99]

Everything, even every sentence, has its own logical criteria, found by examination of its own individual and peculiar uses.

FUNCTION OF ETHICS. The logic of each discipline determines its function; while the function of scientific judgments is that of altering one's expectations, the function of ethical judgments is that of altering the feelings and behavior of a person. Toulmin, defining the function of ethics as the correlation of "our feelings and behavior in such a way as to make the fulfilment of everyone's aims and desires as far as possible compatible,"[100] included as a characteristic function of ethics the process of harmonizing the desires and actions of each individual member to coincide with those of the community. Thus, the concept of duty is social, involving each individual in the social code, since some rules of behavior are necessary in every community. Comparable to standard codes of practice in the field of engineering are the established codes of moral conduct in any community; there are reasons for the choice and approval of existing moral codes, institutions, and laws, and they provide reliable guides for making appropriate choices. "Ethics is concerned with the harmonious satisfaction of desires and interests."[101]

THE MORALIST AND THE MORAL IDEAL. Yet, according to Toulmin, the unqualified acceptance of existing institutions is inadvisable, inasmuch as they must evolve, develop, and change in response to changing conditions. "There is, therefore, always a place in society for the 'moralist', the man who criticises the current morality and institutions, and advocates practices nearer to an ideal."[102] In every society, *the moral ideal must be one which eliminates misery and frustration* in the

99. Ibid., p. 83.
100. Ibid., p. 137.
101. Ibid., p. 223.
102. Ibid.

light of that society's best resources and knowledge. To ascertain precisely how this satisfaction and fulfillment can be accomplished is the responsibility of scientific experts, whose principal task is to make practicable what *ought to be* or what *could be*. The moralist makes these possibilities his policy, and thus, "what *can* be done becomes what *ought* to be done."

Good Reasons or the Criterion of Right. For Toulmin the *function* of ethics leads logically to a *critique* of ethical judgment, but it is necessary that the distinction between the two be preserved, a matter neglected by other ethical theorists, but a vital necessity if we are not to lose sight of the central problem. It is false to assume that producing good reasons for a given practice is equivalent to proving that the practice in question is right.

> Of course, "This practice would involve the least conflict of interests attainable under the circumstances" does not *mean* the same as "This would be the right practice"; nor does "This way of life would be more harmoniously satisfying" *mean* the same as "This would be better." But in each case, the first statement is *a good reason* for the second: the "ethically neutral" fact is *a good reason* for the "gerundive" moral judgment. If the adoption of the practice would genuinely reduce conflicts of interest, it is a practice *worthy of adoption,* and if the way of life would genuinely lead to deeper and more consistent happiness, it is one *worthy of pursuit*. And this seems so natural and intelligible, when one bears in mind the function of ethical judgments, that, if anyone asks me why they are "good reasons," I can only reply by asking in return, "What better kinds of reason could you want?"[103]

The rules which reason discerns in ethics are temporary, neither absolute nor final, always developing, incomplete, and eventually must be superseded by more satisfactory ones.

Critical Comments on Linguistic Analysis. The preceding discussion of linguistic analysis has revealed a number of departures currently taking place in philosophy. The linguistic ethicists in their ardent search for a *good* reason in ethics have inadvertently been driven to the activity of redefining "a good reason," according to Richard Brandt, Kai Nielsen, and others, and have maintained a normative neutrality in ethics or at least in reference to metaethical statements.

The Failure to Break with Emotivism. Less generous in his appraisal of the linguistic moralists, Blanshard attacked them on the ground that they had sought to break with emotivism, but had failed to break with it cleanly. In his view they had only made a futile attempt to resolve ethical issues which deteriorated into a mere discussion about language, and their erroneous notion that ethical theory is simply the

103. Ibid., p. 224.

study of the language of morals tended to reduce the subject to trivia and render it tiresomely misleading. With their combined efforts, they were unable to offer suitable meanings for ethical concepts such as 'good,' 'right', and 'ought', nor could they find any means of validating moral judgment, or even of identifying what moral judgments express. Exhausted of patience, Blanshard could hardly contain his disdain for this mode of thinking: "Meta-ethics has no ethical implications and may be discussed in a logical vacuum, antiseptic to moral commitments."[104] It seems, however, that one reason for the failure of these philosophers stems from their inability to sever the umbilical cord tying them to Wittgenstein's pronouncement "It is impossible for there to be propositions of ethics."[105] How easily Wittgenstein led so able a group of thinkers astray!

CRITICISM OF TOULMIN'S THEORY. Toulmin's efforts, though his discussions were more extensive than those of the other linguistic moralists, appear to have achieved no more than a tenuous union linking emotivism with utilitarianism, nor did he escape the difficulties inherent in the latter philosophy. Moreover, in explaining moral data by adducing factual accounts of how a person reasons, he was using a method more common among behavioral scientists than philosophers. Thus, he attributed the rightness of an action to its utilitarian values, merely adding that there must be some valid reason for so doing. It must be admitted that there are persons who will agree that a given action is worthy of approval and yet may have conflicting reasons, or even no reasons, for this judgment. It is possible for one to consider love and loyalty as worthy to be approved, without being able to offer suitable or valid reasons for loving or being loyal.

Hare (whose theories among the language moralists have been the most influential) objected to Toulmin's position on the ground that he vainly attempted to infer conclusions of moral value from premises that were purely factual.[106]

IRRATIONALISM IN LINGUISTIC ANALYSIS. An irrationalism appears to be prevalent in the thought of the British linguistic moralists which resembles that of the continental existentialists, for both groups regard a moral decision not as a product of reason but as an irrational or nonrational moral choice, an act of will accountable to itself solely. This view is held by the linguistic analysts as well as by the emotivists; the latter reduce moral judgments to interjections or ejaculations, while the former regard moral value judgments as imperatives, i.e., as acts of

104. Blanshard, *Reason and Goodness,* p. 263.

105. Ludwig Wittgenstein, *Tractatus Logico-Philosophicus* (New York: Humanities Press, 1961), p. 145 (Proposition 6.42).

106. R. M. Hare, "Book Review of Toulmin's *The Place of Reason in Ethics,*" in *Philosophical Quarterly* 1 (1951), p. 374.

choice, and in this sense may allow a minor role for rationality, as Toulmin has done.

CRITICAL COMMENTS ON HARE'S MORAL PHILOSOPHY. Critics of Hare's view of moral judgments as nonrational guides to conduct reprimand him for exaggerating the arbitrariness of reasoning in moral judgments. Kai Nielsen has commented, "To say 'Nothing that we discover about the nature of moral judgments entails that it is wrong to put all Jews in gas-chambers' is, it will be argued, a *reductio* of such a position."[107] Hare would reject this application of his philosophy and insist that his only intention was to establish the impossibility of deducing normative statements from nonnormative ones.

Binkley has summarized other objections to Hare's point of view:

> (1) that he has made too absolute a distinction between telling someone to do something and getting one to do it, (2) that he has too closely identified ethical principles with commands, (3) that his overstressing of the similarity of ethical principles to commands is based on an oversimplified analysis of the types of sentence which can be uttered in communication situations, and (4) that ought statements do not entail imperatives.[108]

CRITICISM OF URMSON'S ETHICAL POSITION. Urmson's statement comparing the grading of apples with the grading of people is obviously an illustration of the fallacy of false analogy. When the goodness of persons is reduced to the status of physical goodness like the goodness found in apples, then physicians should become our moralists, for they would be in the best position to determine how good a man is, just as a merchant assesses good apples. Qualities that make an apple good are certainly not those that identify human goodness. Good (as Urmson applied the term to apples) is used in the instrumental sense to characterize a good (but not necessarily moral) mechanic, but not in the intrinsic sense of a morally good person. Urmson would object to this criticism by asserting that the criteria used in each situation are different, just as they would be in evaluating a good mechanic (let us say) and comparing him with a good teacher. "Criteria are different in each different situation."[109] He claimed that this predicament arises from the "absurd situation that 'good' was a homonym with as many punning meanings as the situations it applied to."[110] Nevertheless, such a rebuttal does not extricate Urmson from the fallacy of false analogy,

107. Kai Nielsen, "Ethics, History of" in Paul Edwards, ed., *The Encyclopedia of Philosophy* (New York: Macmillan & Free Press, 1967), 3:110.

108. Luther J. Binkley, *Contemporary Ethical Theories* (New York: Philosophical Library, 1961), p. 152.

109. Urmson, "On Grading," p. 176.

110. Ibid.

for he is merely asserting that no two situations are analogous (an assertion which would therefore negate the analogy that he would like to draw).

CONCLUDING COMMENT REGARDING THE LOGIC AND CRITERION OF MORAL VALUES. In conclusion, it should be kept in mind that the issues confronting the emotivists and linguistic analysts are not identical. The question dealt with by the emotivists, such as Stevenson, relates to the logical nature of moral value judgments, whereas the problem explored by the linguistic analysts, such as Urmson, relates to the criterion of rights.

Index of Names

Index of Subjects

74 75 76 77 10 9 8 7 6 5 4 3 2 1